Cobra! *The* Attack Helicopter

Cobra! *The* Attack Helicopter

Fifty Years of Sharks Teeth and Fangs

Mike Verier

Pen & Sword
AVIATION

First published in Great Britain in 2014 by
Pen & Sword Aviation
an imprint of
Pen & Sword Books Ltd
47 Church Street
Barnsley
South Yorkshire
S70 2AS

ISBN 978 1 78159 338 7

Typeset in Ehrhardt by
Mac Style, Bridlington, East Yorkshire
Printed in India by Replika Press Pvt Ltd

Pen & Sword Books Ltd incorporates the imprints of Pen & Sword Archaeology,
Atlas, Aviation, Battleground, Discovery, Family History, History, Maritime,
Military, Naval, Politics, Railways, Select, Transport, True Crime, and Fiction,
Frontline Books, Leo Cooper, Praetorian Press, Seaforth Publishing and Wharncliffe.

For a complete list of Pen & Sword titles please contact
PEN & SWORD BOOKS LIMITED
47 Church Street, Barnsley, South Yorkshire, S70 2AS, England
E-mail: enquiries@pen-and-sword.co.uk
Website: www.pen-and-sword.co.uk

Contents

Acknowledgements

This book is as much about the people associated with the Cobra as the aircraft itself. In over thirty years writing about the 'Snake' it has been a true privilege to have been associated with the 'skid' community, soldiers, Marines or civilians, *et al*.

The 'Snake' is regarded with the same reverence that the Spitfire or Mustang is; it can bite the unwary, but in all those years I have only ever encountered enthusiasm for it. In taking this long view I have been particularly struck by the similarity of feeling and experience expressed by the men and women who fly the Cobra, whether they be from the Vietnam era or currently serving in Afghanistan.

Equally so the engineers who created the Cobra, those who operate Cobras as 'warbirds' and a growing army of folk who just plain love the thing – all of them have contributed to this book and deserve acknowledgement. I hope that they will forgive that space precludes the several pages a full list would require.

There are however some specific names without which this present volume would not exist. Over many years the good folk at Bell Helicopter have endured with unfailing support and patience visits and obscure questions from an itinerant Brit author. The list runs from senior management to the paint shop, and goes all the way back to Charlie Siebel (arguably the father of the Cobra). Most recently it has included Tom Dolney, Bob Leder and Hank Perry who (despite me stalking him over many years and several changes of job) has helped this author on many occasions. Particular tribute too for the late Jim Gooch who opened the first door those many years ago and even trusted me with his Jaguar that I might arrive at Bell in proper style!

Personal contributions and insights from pilots will be evident and include Dan Dugan at NASA and Roger Woolard of the US Customs Service, both of whose stories are consequently recounted here in full for the first time. Buck Simmons' account of the first USMC Cobra operations has added hugely to the story. Floyd Werner, Army pilot and 'Cobraphile' gave freely of his archive, and photographer Greg Davies kindly allowed me access to his superb images. In this context I am again indebted to Mike Brady and the incredible team at the Army Aviation Heritage Foundation who allowed me not only to fly with them, but also to polish (there are some who would say 'stroke') their stunning restored G Model.

Many of the unique historic photographs reproduced for the first time in this book are entirely thanks to the tireless efforts of one man. Ray Wilhite has doggedly searched and digitised archive material over many years, uncovering in the process previously lost photos this author has sought for decades. Similarly gratitude to Ray Ball and his Israeli colleagues for that part of the narrative and photos.

Specially commissioned for this book, technical artist Mark Rolfe has created some stunning profiles. His meticulous work amply illustrating the incredible range and diversity of colour schemes worn by the Snake over the years.

On the military side my undying thanks to the Commanding Officer of MCAS New River and his Public Affairs team, ably led by Lieutenant Kristen Dalton, for both the photo-opportunities and the singular privilege of attending Warrior Night and meeting so many of the Cobra veterans I had previously only written about. Thanks also to Colonel Harry Hewson USMC at NAVAIR for the extremely detailed briefing on the Zulu.

In the days before t'interweb, authors had to write letters. A quarter-century ago one such enquiry from an unknown budding Brit author made its way laboriously down the chain of command until it was finally dropped in the lap of an unsuspecting young Cobra pilot in a crew-room at MCAS Camp Pendleton.

The pilot in question was Peyton DeHart. He took the trouble to respond in detail to this strange request, beginning a friendship that is now in its third decade. Also responsible for introductions to many of those noted above and still flying Cobras as a member of the SkySoldiers demonstration team, it is no exaggeration to credit his infectious enthusiasm with being the inspiration and the rock on which three Cobra books have been founded.

Thank you all. I hope the following will serve as an adequate reflection of the enthusiasm and affection you have all shown for a truly great aircraft.

I have tried to tell the story of the world's first Attack helicopter and the people associated with it in proper historic context. In so doing, I hope that in its own small way it also stands as a tribute to the memory of those who didn't make it back to the crew room.

Mike Verier
Derbyshire

Introduction

A short magazine article on the AH-1 Cobra written almost exactly thirty years ago was to take me on a journey I could hardly have imagined at the time. Even then the Snake had been in service for sixteen years and was clearly a remarkable aircraft. Some five years later I was privileged to meet and interview many of the Bell engineers who had hand-built the Cobra prototype in great secrecy during the summer of 1966.

The Cold War was still with us then so I also talked to US Army crews who were holding the line on the East German border and Marines who had defended freedom in Grenada. I also had my first flight in a Snake.

At the time Bell had just delivered the first 'Whisky' Model and, aside from the eventual adoption of a four-blade rotor as an upgrade, it looked as if Cobra development had reached its zenith. The book that resulted concluded with a summary of the latest developments entitled (fortuitously as it turned out) *'Epilogue... or just another chapter?'*

A quarter century later I still cannot write the final chapter. The 'interim' Cobra could well serve for sixty years or more and continues to do what it has always done best, protect and support the troops on the ground. As you read these words, somewhere in the world a Cobra is defending its charges – be they known as 'grunts', 'squaddies', 'TIC' or just the 'PBI', the soldiers on the ground all know the sound of a Cobra overhead means they can depend on support at close quarters – something that still can't be done as well from 30,000ft and 350kts.

Snakes have flown over every continent, from the Arctic to the desert, from tropical jungle to European plains, dense urban environments to desolate mountain regions, on land and at sea. Quite apart from its original combat role the Cobra has mastered Forward Air Control, rescued downed pilots, furthered aviation technology, fought forest fires, arrested drug smugglers, deterred pirates, hauled logs and entered the 'Warbird' circuit having acquired 'Classic' status. Along the way the Snake set the standard for all subsequent attack helicopters and has outlived a surprising number of potential replacements. Whenever a new role arises the Cobra sheds its skin and emerges newer and stronger. Its reliability is legend and the range and breadth of its achievements just continues to grow.

Originally the Cobra was conceived as a daytime Infantry support platform with rifle-calibre guns and unguided rockets good for engagements at maybe 1000 metres. The Tube-launched, Optically-tracked, Wire-guided missile system (TOW) era saw it evolve into a tank-killer that could reach out to targets over 3 kilometres away. The AGM-114 Hellfire doubled its reach again and new technology gave it command of the night.

The hordes of WarPac armour that Cold War doctrine envisaged as the primary threat may have receded into history, but the world remains a troubled place and today the Snakes are busier and more capable than ever. 'Whisky' Models have amassed more combat hours than any previous Cobra variant, and the awesome 'Zulu' Cobra, at something like twice the weight and power of the first 'G's, can detect and deal with almost any threat, including air-to-air, with laser-guided precision, at well beyond visual range or in total darkness.

Notwithstanding the awesome array of long-range weaponry and technology it can deploy, the trusty Snake continues to provide truly close support on a daily basis where it matters; as they say in the Marine Corps *'Semper Fi'*.

Chapter One

Bugles and Guidons
… the cavalry's coming

To understand the need for the Cobra requires some backtracking. Post Second World War the US Army began to appraise its doctrine and tactics in the nuclear age. The Army fully expected to be fighting a tank war in Europe and was not focussed on 'bush' wars or insurgencies which it (wrongly) assumed would involve relatively poorly armed forces it could easily deal with (or leave to the US Marine Corps). This process was rudely interrupted by the Korean War which revealed obvious shortcomings regarding the mobility of troops, the vulnerability of their supply lines, and the inability of conventional air power to support them once isolated.

The catastrophic defeat of the French at Dien Bien Phu by General Giap's Viet Minh in 1954 drove the Korean lessons home and added urgency. Probably unappreciated at the time was that it also set in train events that would lead to the Vietnam War less than a decade later.

The Korean conflict had also, almost unnoticed, seen the first widespread use of helicopters, albeit primarily for what we would now call CASEVAC (CASualty EVACuation). Although helicopters of the time were underpowered and fragile, the Army could see their potential for moving troops around the battlefield. So could a manufacturer whose iconic Model 47 (immortalised in the book and motion picture 'M*A*S*H') had saved so many lives in Korea – Bell Helicopter.

Bell subsequently won a US Army contest for an improved Utility/Medical Evacuation helicopter in 1955, their Model 204 first flying as the YH-40 on 20 October 1956. The Army, in line with their practice of using the names of American Indian tribes, had called it 'Iroquois' and designated it HU-1 (Helicopter, Utility, first in series). It was thus instantly and forever destined to be known as 'Huey' notwithstanding the official name and being re-designated UH-1 before production started.

The Huey was a turning point in helicopter development. Its lightweight turbine engine produced a power-to-weight ratio that at last gave the helicopter a useful payload. It also featured Bell's two-blade rotor and stabilising bar which had proved so successful on the Model 47, bestowing in the process an aural signature so distinctive that even today it remains the sound most associated with helicopters.

Its design also featured a troop cabin with easy access on both sides, halving the time it took for troops to leave the aircraft and therefore the time the aircraft was on the ground and vulnerable on a DZ (Drop Zone).

With each machine capable of lifting an infantry squad, the Army set to work using their new Hueys to re-write their tactics. Developed in the vast training areas around Fort Rucker,

Where it all began. Bell's YH-40 with its light-weight turbine engine finally made the helicopter a useful battlefield vehicle that could lift a respectable payload. First flown in 1956 its descendants continue in production and service more than half a century later. (*Bell via Mike Verier*)

Alabama, the new Army would henceforth be 'Air Mobile' (as distinct from the two Divisions of 'Airborne' paratroopers).

The Air Mobile doctrine relied on tactical mobility; troops could be moved around the battlefield with a speed and flexibility not possible for mechanised formations, let alone foot soldiers. As it turned out the new tactics closely resembled those of light cavalry (essentially mounted infantry), considerable study being made of the Duke of Wellington's tactics at Waterloo where highly mobile cavalry and artillery had been decisive.

Indeed it proved possible to heavily plagiarise the Army's last manual for horse soldiers – dating from the 1890s and last published in 1936 – when writing the tactics book for the Airmobile Divisions.

The mode of transport may have changed, but, as with Britain's Royal Flying Corps before it, US Army Aviation found it had cavalry lineage.

The thrust of the new doctrine was principally concerned with moving infantry. Arming helicopters was not considered in any detail at the time as it reduced lift capacity and any support required would, it was assumed, come from the US Air Force whose responsibility it now was.

There were those who could see the flaw in this supposition. The 1947 National Security Act that separated the US Army and Air Force left the Army (unlike the US Marine Corps) without organic support aircraft; unfortunately any such support would have to come from the 'blue suits' who were looking to the sky not the ground.

The Army would need to ask an Air Force that by the mid 1950s was focussed on Strategic Air Command's big bombers and supersonic jets rather than the somewhat less glamorous business of what was then known as 'ground attack'.

Chapter Two

Fools and Horses

Trials at Rucker and the birth of AirMobile

As far back as 1942, a 25lb practice bomb had been hefted over the side of a Sikorsky XR-4 at Wright Field proving that the helicopter could be a weapon platform. There had also been some limited use of armed helicopters by the French in Algeria, and the USMC in Korea – in both cases rather improvised. On the whole, however, armed helicopters were regarded as not very practicable on the battlefield.

This did not prevent further exploration of the possibilities by a small band of visionaries. One such was Colonel Jay D. Vanderpool, an experienced Korean veteran and advocate for the helicopter. In 1955 he found himself posted to Fort Rucker, commanded at the time by Brigadier General Carl J. Hutton. Hutton had a memorandum originating from the office of General Willard Wyman concerning the training of 'highly mobile' task forces. This document did not actually say 'use helicopters' but then again it didn't rule them out either. Colonel Vanderpool was duly instructed to investigate the possibilities.

Initially with a team of just five, he quickly found there was very little to go on. The USMC had examined the French operations in Algeria and reported enthusiastically, and as far back as 1950 Bell had strapped a bazooka to the side of an H-13 (Model 47) but essentially they started from scratch.

As it was readily available, the H-13 was again selected and the team set about scrounging weapons to try. Test firing of machine guns and rockets with the aircraft fixed to a platform showed no obvious problems and quickly progressed to firing from a low hover.

One or two snags arose; the vibration could burst the H-13's distinctive big canopy, and on one occasion a door shook loose and was riddled. These things were quickly overcome and it became obvious that using helicopters as a weapon platform was perfectly feasible.

Vanderpool and his growing band of converts, now affectionately known around Fort Rucker's weapon ranges as 'Vanderpool's fools', tested anything they could get their hands on, including at one point a trainable gun created by fixing a surplus Boeing B-29 turret under the nose of a Piaseki H-21. At weekends the troops at Rucker enthusiastically tried the new tactics. One technique, eventually called 'Nap of the Earth' tactical flying involved going around and between trees rather than over them – best of all it was legal and the Army paid you for it too!

The Army's higher echelons were not oblivious to the potential of helicopters nor indeed the need to provide armed escorts, and the pioneering work of the men at Rucker had not been wasted. In 1960, at the behest of Secretary of Defense Robert McNamara, General Hamilton H. Howze took the chair of the Army Tactical Mobility Requirements Board at Fort Bragg. What became known as the 'Howze Board' was pretty high powered, including Ed Heineman (designer

The very earliest attempts to arm helicopters in a meaningful way date to the late 1950s. As can be seen here the ubiquitous Bell Model 47 (H-13) was widely available and initially the vehicle of choice. Firmly fixed to a platform, various rockets and guns were fired to determine the effects of blast on the airframe. (*US Army via Ray Wilhite*)

of the Douglas SkyRaider and Skyhawk) and Dr Edwin Paxson of the Rand Corporation. The report eventually issued would shape the future of Army aviation and lead directly to the creation of the Cobra.

The report formalised the Airmobile concept as developed at Fort Rucker. It also made a number of other recommendations regarding the need for armed escorts. Initially it was envisaged that this would be achieved by arming a percentage of the UH-1s. The Army did not at the time see the need for a dedicated weapons helicopter. Notwithstanding, a model of a remarkably Cobra-like project, known as D245, already existed at Bell.

The development of weapons for helicopters was thus a very low-key affair compared to the rapidly expanding 'Sky Cavalry'. As the first UH-1s began to enter service the 'Airmobile' soldiers were very much the thrust of Army doctrine. They were not to wait too long to test the concept in battle, the first US Advisors had been sent to Vietnam in May 1959.

There is always a political dimension to procurement. Secretary of Defense Robert McNamara will be remembered for the concept of 'commonality'. If you wanted the funds you had to come up with a basic vehicle that could fulfil a number of roles with the minimum of change, and therefore cost.

Whilst 'commonality' was a laudable doctrine, it ignored many predictable issues and viewed from today's perspective it was ultimately flawed. The TFX programme for instance was intended

This photo dates from 1961 and shows four stations capable of accepting the French SS-10 missile, a first-generation anti-tank weapon. Bell's highly successful two-blade rotor was proven on the iconic Model 47 (known as H-13 in US Army service). This versatile aircraft was to play a vital part in Cobra development. (*US Army via Ray Wilhite*)

The little Hiller H-23 was also fitted with machine guns and rockets. (*US Army via Ray Wilhite*)

This slightly self-conscious chap is demonstrating that aiming and firing a machine gun when strapped in is not that easy. The large pile of spent cases and links around his feet suggest a major FOD problem too. (*US Army via Ray Wilhite*)

The venerable H–19 also found itself festooned with various experimental rocket mounts. The original caption describes this rig as '10 foot rocket pods' in this case 14–shot 'packs' one on each side. (*US Army via Ray Wilhite*)

The Marines also got into the act, but being Marines they wanted bigger and better. The Bullpup missile was widely used on Naval fast jets of the time and was successfully fired from the H–34. The idea however was not taken up operationally. (*US Army via Ray Wilhite*)

This massive twin gun pod appears to have been created from an Aero–series drop-tank. As Cobra pilots were to discover a generation later with the advent of the M–35 system, firing it was likely to cause more damage to the aircraft than the target. (*US Army via Ray Wilhite*)

The greater lifting power of the Piasecki H-21 'Banana' allowed the trialling of some fairly substantial kit. Described in the original caption as 'ACR kit M' the rack under the nose accommodates four rockets either side as well as at least two machine guns above them. A further .30 cal is mounted in the doorway. (*US Army via Ray Wilhite*)

This rig was later adopted almost exactly for the Huey in Vietnam. Featuring four M-60s it was trainable (in elevation) and reasonably effective at close range. (*US Army via Ray Wilhite*)

The search for fully trainable – turreted – weapons led to this concoction using a surplus B-29 turret. The turret gun was to become a fundamental and very effective feature of the Cobra and most attack types since. (*US Army via Ray Wilhite*)

The much smaller H-25 also found itself festooned with rocket packs. (*US Army via Ray Wilhite*)

to result in a multi-role fighter/bomber which could be common to both the Air Force and the Navy. Unfortunately the naval variant of what became the General Dynamics F-111 quickly proved to be far too heavy for carrier operations.

As events transpired this need to demonstrate minimum change turned to Bell's advantage and was nevertheless to become very relevant to the, as yet, unborn Cobra.

By June of that year there were 685 US personnel in Vietnam. By early 1962 the arrival of two additional Army aviation units in Vietnam had raised American strength there to some 4,000 personnel. Back in Texas, Bell (with UH-1s in full production) had already built a mock-up gunship configuration and was converting an OH-13 airframe to validate the concept.

Meanwhile three distinct Huey variants emerged. The troop carrying 'Slick' with little more defensive armament than a bungee-mounted M-60 machine gun in each doorway; the 'Hog' (an appellation not entirely unconnected with its flying abilities) which was essentially flying artillery carrying two 24 shot Folding-Fin Aerial Rocket pods (FFARs); and finally, for the more general fire suppression role a combination of rockets and guns which could be varied depending on the mission. These aircraft became known to every infantryman by their 'Cobra' callsigns.

As UH-1s were a type new to the inventory, Bell Helicopter had technicians serving with the deployed aircraft to maintain them and deal with the mass of modifications and upgrades that any combat situation throws up. Despite being in full production the flow of new information was already stimulating their development people. They knew that the armed Huey idea had a fatal flaw – hanging all that armament on the aircraft made them slower than the 'Slicks' they were supposed to be escorting. They also knew that sooner or later the Army would need a dedicated weapons helicopter.

A tour of the war zone by Bell President E. J. Ducayat confirmed this belief. The Bell people showed their preliminary ideas to General Westmoreland and other senior Army officers. Their reaction was very positive, but it was also clear that a lengthy gestation was out of the question – troops on the ground were going to need support as soon as possible.

The arrival of the UH-1 heralded an aircraft with much better power-to-weight ratios thanks to its lightweight turbine engine. Once these became widely available at Fort Rucker, armament kits based on the earlier experimental rigs began to appear. (*US Army via Ray Wilhite*)

Chapter 3

Cobra Dawn
Bell beats the Mongoose

Bell Helicopter had been studying armed helicopters for some time. During 1950 Hans Weichsel and Joe Mashman had persuaded the USMC to fit and test fire a bazooka from an H-13 (Bell Model 47). In the mid-1950s this work was expanded by the Army at Fort Rucker. Since the advent of the turbine-engined UH-1, which had provided the performance jump such a machine would need, Bell development engineers had been formulating the requirement.

As early as 1958 Bell proposal D245 showed a sleek, but clearly H-1 based, design with stub wings – the earliest known iteration of the Cobra layout. By June 1962 the project had matured and emerged as a full-scale mock-up, project D255.

Marketed as the 'Iroquois Warrior', the aircraft was still clearly Huey aft of the sail. The forward fuselage however was very different, and all of the Cobra's salient features were already evident.

A big 'fighter' canopy provided superb vision for the crew who were seated in tandem. The pilot was behind and slightly above the gunner, who had a pantograph mounted sight for the turreted gun/grenade launcher mounted in the nose. Externally, stub wings supported no less than six SS-11 anti-tank missiles, three on each side in the then-standard arrangement. A pod semi-recessed in the belly was to house a 20mm gun.

It was decided to build a proof-of-concept vehicle and in December the same year, work started to convert an OH-13 airframe into the Sioux Scout demonstrator.

This nimble little aircraft proved the tandem crew concept. The standard side-by-side 'bubble' was replaced with a sleek nacelle half as wide. Small stub wings contained fuel (and later provided at least a token demonstration that they could carry weapons). Whilst not fundamental to the design they also served to offload the rotor in high speed flight. The pilot sat behind and slightly above the gunner, who was provided with a chin turret mounting a pair of M-60 7.62mm machine guns. As on the D255 the turret was controlled by a pantograph-mounted sight. Because of this, the normal layout of flight controls was not possible and the front-seater was provided with a side-stick cyclic control. This too would become a distinctive Cobra feature – at the time it was simply a practical solution to a problem, but it was to prove revolutionary.

First flown in July 1963, the Sioux Scout was taken on a tour of Army bases by Joe Mashman (pilot) and Phil Norwine (sales engineer) to demonstrate the capabilities an armed scout could offer. It found universal approval.

Dating to 1958 Project D245 is the earliest-known visualisation of the Cobra concept. Clearly Huey-based, the tandem cockpit and stub wings are already apparent. (*Bell via Mike Verier*)

Whilst being demonstrated to the 11th Aviation Division in November 1963, it was flown by Brigadier General 'Pip' Senneff. Having taken the scout for some live-fire flights on Fort Bragg's extensive ranges he came back thoroughly enthused and wanting to know when Bell 'were going to do this with a Huey airframe?' General Senneff, who later became Chief of Army Aviation, was to prove pivotal in getting the Army to accept the gunship concept, and eventually flew the Cobra's first combat mission in Vietnam.

Eventually amassing some 750 hours, the Sioux Scout's demonstration tour served to confirm the Army's increasing battlefield experience and by the middle of 1964 there was a growing acceptance that they needed a dedicated weapons platform for helicopter escort.

Despite the enthusiastic response at the operational level the murky waters of political intrigue were not so easily navigated. There was an element within the Army that felt that they, not commercial contractors, should be doing R&D. (A bigger more complex and technically advanced programme could give rise to an Army Aviation Development Command). There was also a suggestion that too much dependency by the Army on Bell was not desirable. (Doubtless fuelled by other manufacturers who were of course lobbying in their own interests – a tour of Army installations with the Warrior mock-up was abruptly terminated when complaints were made that Bell were circumventing a formal competition process for the order – this despite the fact that no formal requirement actually existed at the time!)

The little Sioux Scout was built as a proof of concept vehicle. It succeeded admirably and today rests in honourable retirement at Fort Rucker. (*Bell via Mike Verier*)

The Warrior was eventually 'killed' at the Pentagon level by writing a requirement for a much more advanced aircraft (which bore a remarkable similarity to an aircraft Lockheed had in development). The problem was that the aircraft the Army thought it wanted was not going to be a quick procurement.

A considerable fuss

The RFP (Request For Proposals) issued in August 1964 called for an Advanced Aerial Fire Support System (AAFSS) designed for deep penetration at high speed and to have capabilities well beyond anything then flying. The AAFSS (the acronym was usually pronounced 'Ay-Fuss') was ambitious in its aims and would take a long time to develop. Seven companies responded, including Bell. Their entry, D262, was based on the Iroquois Warrior. The New Year edition of Bell News for 1965 was upbeat and spoke of projects 'under wraps'

In early 1965 however the competitors were reduced to two, Lockheed and Sikorsky, entering a six month project definition phase before final selection.

Whatever the result the Army was not blind to the growing operational need and a board was convened under Colonel H. L. Bush to consider an 'interim' type that could be fielded pending service entry of AAFSS which was not expected for at least another five years. That contest meanwhile was drawing to a conclusion, the decision eventually going to the Lockheed proposal the AH-56 Cheyenne.

In truth the other manufacturers, including Bell, probably suspected that they were not to get the order, nevertheless, having worked on their proposal six and seven days a week for some six

Immediate precursor to the Cobra was the D255 Iroquois Warrior. Like 245 before it, the Huey origins are very apparent. The crew arrangement, 'fighter' canopy, pantograph sight and nose gun turret (in this case fitted with a 40mm grenade launcher) are already there. The pod under the fuselage was to house a 20mm cannon and six wing stations were projected. The mock-up showed the then current, but essentially useless, AS-40 missiles. (*Bell via Mike Verier*)

months, losing the AAFSS order to a company that had never built a production helicopter came as a blow to the design team at Bell. Many decided to catch up on long-overdue leave,

Still at his desk whilst his boss took leave, Design Engineer Mike Folse found himself pondering the 'must be selected by competition' dictum – had not Bell sold the Army successive Huey developments (UH-1A/B/C/D/E and F Models) without the need for a competition every time? He took a fresh sheet of vellum and began drawing.

Some three days later he had a three view of an aircraft very similar to the Warrior in concept and layout, but optimised as a 'G Model Huey'. The design used 100% of the dynamic components of the UH-1C. 'All I had done', Folse later recalled with some understatement, 'was add a new streamlined fuselage with a retractable landing gear.'

The drawing was spotted by Cliff Kalista (then Director of Military Marketing) who, following a brief questioning asked Folse if he could get some dimensions on the drawing 'by Monday morning.'

The finished drawing was duly whisked away and by 2.00pm on that Monday in March 1965, a meeting in the office of Bell's President E. J. Ducayet had decided to go ahead. 'Duke' had persuaded Textron (Bell's parent company) to give him $800,000 to build a prototype – providing it could be done in six months.

This was the moment of conception for the Cobra – had Bell won the AAFSS order it would not have existed.

Bell's decision to go for the interim type on a Private Venture basis was not without commercial risk. Indeed, Bell senior management effectively staked their careers on building the prototype of the Model 209 with the company's own money; at the time there was no formal requirement for the aircraft. This was mitigated by their knowledge that they had a head start and already knew what the right aircraft for the job should look like.

It was to prove an extraordinary feat of engineering and sheer determination. Chief Experimental Projects Engineer Charlie Siebel had just six months and less than one million dollars to get the prototype flying. Assisted by Bob Duppstadt and the newly promoted Mike Folse, Siebel's team of engineers never exceeded forty-two. Supervised by Shop Superintendent 'Red' Woodall, the project was carried out in the greatest secrecy in a secure 'Green Room' within the Experimental Department's Hanger 45 at Fort Worth. In July 1965, Hans Weichsel (Bell's Senior VP, Product Development) undertook a tour of operational units flying on combat missions, and talking to everyone from mechanics to Lieutenant Generals about gunship requirements. Key officers were shown plans of the still-secret gunship and told that it could be fielded within eighteen months. Several of them were, like Bell's management, to bet their careers on backing an urgent requirement for the new machine.

The reason for the Cobra; a fully armed UH-1 was twice as wide and very 'draggy'. This aircraft carries the 'Cobra' emblem of one of the 114th's two 'Gun' platoons. A callsign that was to become synonymous with armed helicopters. (*US Army via Ray Wilhite*)

By August, construction of the prototype was sufficiently advanced for Bell to make a confident presentation of the 'modified UH-1' to the Bush Board.

This last point was politically crucial. All the contenders had to be based on existing types to minimise development time. The Army was assured that all development had taken place under Engineering Change Proposals (ECPs) and only involved 'some streamlining of the fuselage' and the necessary weapon mounts for what was still a UH-1.

The initial entries were Sikorsky's H-3 Sea King, Boeing-Vertol's H-47 Chinook, Piasecki's Model 16H Pathfinder, the Kaman HH-2C Tomahawk (a modified Sea Sprite and in reality the only serious competition) and the Bell submission. The Model 209 was carefully pitched as an armed scout – it could not be seen in any way as competing with AAFSS.

Unlike the others, Bell did not offer a utility airframe with weapons bolted on. The sleek form that emerged from the experimental hanger in September 1965 – on time and within 5% of budget – was a sports car against pick-up trucks; Bell had got it right.

The Cobra's first flight, with Bill Quinlan at the helm, and the soon-to-be discarded ventral fin fitted. Note that the pilot canopy door has been removed. There are no markings other than 'EXPERIMENTAL' below the cockpit. (*Bell via Mike Verier*)

Now marked with its distinctive registration, the prototype shows its sleek lines with the undercarriage retracted. 'Clean', the Cobra, was a very fast aircraft indeed. (*Bell via Mike Verier*)

The Cobra Described

From the outset the aim was to make the Cobra fast, in fact there was another agenda influencing design.

Industrial designer Richard Ten Eyke was employed to 'tweak' the design with the instruction, 'Make it look like it's doing 200kts even when it's parked.' The sports car analogy was nearer the truth than most realised. In the battle against the Pentagon elements that lobbied against ordering the Cobra (there was allegedly a 'Mongoose' office pledged to kill it) it may actually have proved decisive.

The Army had to have something to make Army Aviation 'sexy'. They were going to need to recruit men who aspired to be fighter pilots, not truck drivers. The conflict in Vietnam was growing but re-enlistment rates were falling. The Cobra design, for all its technical brilliance, owed its aesthetics, at least in part, to an Army recruiting drive.

Technically, the Model 209 was a masterpiece of re-packaging. The systems and dynamics of the UH-1 had to be fitted into a slender fuselage only 3 feet (.91m) wide. Not only that but it had to carry more fuel and weapons and be easily accessible for field maintenance. This was achieved by using a box beam and honeycomb panel construction which provided the necessary stiffness for what became a semi-monocoque fuselage.

In turn this meant that there was ample access to the engine and armament with no need for specialist equipment, ladders or servicing stands. The aircraft retained Bell's characteristic two-blade 'teetering' 540 rotor, but dispensed with the stabilising bar, replacing it with a powerful Stability Control Augmentation System (SCAS). The crew layout envisaged in the Iroquois Warrior, and validated by the Sioux Scout, was retained, including the side-stick cyclic for the front-seater (Originally developed to provide the gunner with limited control in an emergency, the side-mounted stick was actually very effective and was adopted with much fanfare some years later for the General Dynamics F-16. The side-stick now features in many fast jets, and both cockpits of the 'Zulu' Cobra)

Every effort was made to minimise drag. Forward of the tail boom the airframe had flush rivets, intakes were designed to 'inhale' air from the boundary layer rather than act as airbrakes. Even vents and drains were ganged to exit efficiently through a single belly outlet. This aerodynamic cleanliness extended to a spinner-plate to cover the opening in the top of the sail for the main rotor shaft.

The quest for speed also led to a feature unique at the time, a skid-type undercarriage that was retractable. Stub wings were primarily to support the weapon pylons, but these too contributed some lift, offloading the rotor in high speed flight. Similarly the turbine exhaust added a small thrust component.

The tail boom supported the drive shaft for the tail anti-torque rotor, mounted on the port side of an elegant fin; closer inspection of which reveals an aerofoil section designed to further counteract the considerable moment generated by the main rotor. This was a perfectly satisfactory arrangement, but in service it was found that the aircraft sometimes 'ran out of pedal' in rearward quartering flight (when backing out of a revetment for instance). The solution was to reverse the direction of the tail rotor by moving it to the starboard side of the fin. This definitive modification was incorporated into the production line with typical speed at Fort Worth. Most 'early production' aircraft were also upgraded, many of them in the field.

Yaw stability was recognised as a potential source of problems, particularly in autorotation where the upper fin loses effectiveness due to wake from the pylon and rotor hub. Consequently the prototype featured an additional ventral fin that subsequent flight testing found to be unnecessary (although it would re-appear on later variants). Finally two horizontal stabilisers/

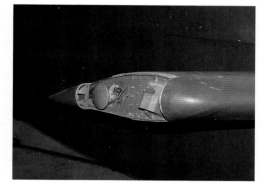
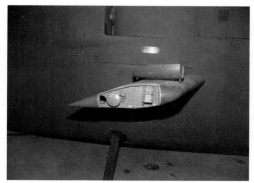

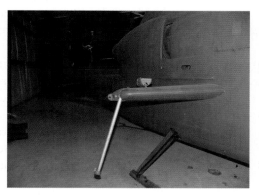

What do you do if the retracted undercarriage fails to extend ? Unlike the flat-bottomed Huey the Cobra would fall over and beat itself to death if a landing was attempted. This never-before-seen sequence shows that someone had thought it through. With the aircraft in a low hover quick release catches reveal a steel tube stowed between the wing spars. Pulled out and clipped into the wing-tip mounts provided, the aircraft could then rest on these supports and the tail bumper. Ingenious, and a very good argument for the fixed skid option. (*US Army via Ray Wilhite*)

elevators were mounted on the boom, forward of the fin. These featured an inverted aerofoil section to impart a balancing moment which increased with forward speed. Consequently movement of these surfaces was limited (around 10 degrees from cyclic 'fully forward' to 'fully aft') but entirely adequate.

Fixed armament was to consist of two pylons on each stub-wing stressed to carry various combinations of gun and rocket pods. The turreted gun at the extreme nose was fundamental to the design as it meant that a considerable field of fire was available either side of the flight path to enable suppression of threats even whilst the aircraft was committed to a weapons run with the fixed stores.

The prototype had a single 7.62mm minigun mounted in an Emmerson Turret. Early production aircraft had the larger TAT-102A, precursor to the more versatile M-28 (then in development) which supplanted it in service. This definitive system could accommodate two miniguns or M-40 grenade launchers in any combination. Ammunition was housed in large drum-magazines sited immediately aft of the turret, below the gunners cockpit. Access to this bay was by downward hinged doors on both sides of the fuselage which were stressed to double as servicing platforms. (Combat service subsequently proved the wisdom and utility of this arrangement, not just for the ground crew either – more than one downed airman was carried to safety courtesy of the gun-bay doors).

Provision was also made for flares and smoke grenades (for target marking) which were carried in the rear fuselage. With the thoroughness borne of operational experience, the magazine for these hinged downwards so that any dropped rounds would fall out of the aircraft.

Early development

There is an adage in aviation circles that if it looks right it flies right. Freshly painted in FS 24087 Army Drab and appropriately registered N209J, the world's first attack helicopter lived up to it impeccably.

At 0730hrs on 7 September 1965, the prototype began its initial engine runs at Carter Field flight test facility. All went well and at 1730hrs Chief Experimental Test Pilot Bill Quinlan lifted the 209 for its twelve minute maiden flight. The following day Quinlan reached 90kts during a shakedown flight, and on 9 September achieved 162kts with the undercarriage still down. The world, including possibly the US Army, did not yet know it, but the 'Snake' had hatched.

N209J tucks its nose down for the classic transition shot as the aircraft translates from vertical to forward flight. This view dramatically demonstrates the Cobra's slender frontal aspect. Note also the position of the stores pylons, subsequently moved outboard. (*Bell via Mike Verier*)

Early in the test programme the ventral tail fin was found to be unnecessary and discarded. The pantograph sight is not fitted. (*Bell via Mike Verier*)

Two more development airframes (YAH-1Gs) were constructed serial number 66-15246 in October 1966 and 66-15247 in March 1967). They featured strengthened stub wings, the larger gun turret, and fixed skids. 66-15246 was used primarily for weapons qualification at Fort Hood, whilst 66-15247 qualified the Stability Control Augmentation System (the only major change to the standard Huey dynamics)

Flight testing quickly revealed that the basic design was sound. The additional ventral fin was discarded, and the benefits of the retractable skids were evaluated. It was found that fixed skids did not unduly impede turret traverse or weapons release. Given the extra weight and complexity, it was concluded that foregoing the few knots of airspeed gained by retraction was a better option. Retractable skids also held a potential for error or accident. Helicopter crews of the time were used to an undercarriage that was 'down and welded' so inadvertent 'skids-up' landing was a real possibility, and of course combat damage might also render them inoperable. Either way landing with the skids retracted was potentially a major problem. Unlike the wide, flat-bottomed Huey, the narrow Cobra would inevitably have toppled with dire consequences.

Unique to the prototype, the ingenious solution was a simple tube prop concealed in each wing that could be pulled out from the tip and locked down by the ground crew or co-pilot whilst the aircraft hovered, thus allowing it to land safely on these and the tail skid. Never required, (at least not to this author's knowledge), they are actually still in place on the preserved N209J. Ultimately this information proved to be at its most valuable when negotiating the final contract with the Army as it enabled Bell to offer a 'cost-reduction' at the appropriate moment.

The definitive undercarriage has endured to this day and consists of skids fixed to curved cross-tubes. The design quest for speed meant that even the cross-tubes originally came with aerodynamic fairings to minimise drag. Often removed in the field however, they were discarded altogether on later model Cobras.

The skid undercarriage is thus a key Cobra feature. Rugged and practicable it will cope with uneven surfaces better than wheels and allow flexure in the event of a heavy landing. Tests to determine exactly *how* heavy were carried out later, and a video exists showing a frankly rather brave test pilot hitting the ground harder with each landing. At one point the belly actually makes contact with the ground without breaking the skids!

Meanwhile the competitive fly-off had shown that the Model 209 was the vehicle of choice for the Army. The Cobra's key supporters, by then fighting an increasingly demanding war in Vietnam, had made their case for an urgent procurement. A sceptical Congress was again assured

This very interesting sequence shows the result of what appears to be a heavy landing by the second YAH-1G, 66-15247. The aircraft is carrying four 19-shot pods so would presumably be near maximum weight on what is clearly a hot day. The location is not given but possibly Fort Hood. (*US Army via Ray Wilhite*)

From the rear it can be seen that the starboard skid has collapsed as has the tail bumper. They appear however to have done their job as the aircraft remains otherwise undamaged. (*US Army via Ray Wilhite*)

The rotors are kept turning whilst a solution is found. Attempting to shut down would result in the aircraft toppling over and beating itself to death. (*US Army via Ray Wilhite*)

The outboard pods have been removed and the crew are now attempting to support the wingtips so that the aircraft can be shut down. Note that the front canopy door has been jettisoned, the pulled cable being clearly visible. 15247 survived this incident, going on to serve in the Cobra NETT. (*US Army via Ray Wilhite*)

Superb study of N209J, possibly at Yuma, before selection by the Army. Still bearing its 'Bell Helicopter Co' legend and absolutely pristine. (*US Army via Ray Wilhite*)

The Cobra only had one serious competitor, Charlie Kaman's UH-2 SeaSprite derivative the Tomahawk. Technically it was a very competent aircraft (H-2s remain in service today) but considered expensive. The two chin turrets are worthy of note. Kaman believed he did not get the order for political reasons, although some small recompense was the contract to supply the Composite K747 blades for the Cobra fleet some years later. (*US Army via Ray Wilhite*)

that they were buying a 'modified UH-1' (which meant that long and costly type certification was not needed, as well as the 'commonality' benefits to maintenance, training and spares inventories). This argument was very attractive to cost-conscious politicians and was destined to be used more than once in the Cobras' long future.

Designation and appellation

Consequently when the first order was placed it was for 'UH-1H' aircraft. The designation was only later changed to AH-1, the 'A' standing for 'Attack'.

The origins of the Cobra name are variously reported. As described above Huey units in Vietnam had acquired various colourful appellations such as the 'Soc Trang Tigers', 'Mavericks' and 'Playboys' (The latter even going so far as to have custom black flight suits with the inevitable 'Bunny' logo).

The first unit to be deployed directly from the US to Vietnam was the 114th Airmobile Company. Their new UH-1B 'guns' adopted the name 'Vinh Long Cobras' and the 'Cobra' call sign had quickly become synonymous with armed helos.

The two pre-production aircraft are seen here in formation with the prototype. Apart from the fixed skids other subtle differences can already be seen in the development aircraft. 66–15246 with the white chequers was the weapon trials aircraft. 66–15247 (farthest from the camera) was primarily used to qualify the SCAS system. (*Bell via Mike Verier*)

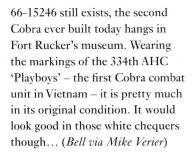

66–15246 still exists, the second Cobra ever built today hangs in Fort Rucker's museum. Wearing the markings of the 334th AHC 'Playboys' – the first Cobra combat unit in Vietnam – it is pretty much in its original condition. It would look good in those white chequers though… (*Bell via Mike Verier*)

Also tested on N209J was this variation on the ventral fin. (*Bell via Mike Verier*)

The Cobra name also had a historical connection to Bell's last fighter aircraft, the P-39 Airacobra and P-63 Kingcobra. At one point the name 'HeliCobra' was considered, but the definitive name for the new aircraft is generally attributed to the influence of General 'Ham' Howze (who had joined Bell following retirement from the Army). He pointed out that 'Huey Cobra' had a nice ring to it, and combined the Cobra name with the almost universally recognised 'Huey' descriptor. (Bell actually considered copyrighting 'Huey' as a company trade mark at one point). Whilst never publicly acknowledged, maintaining the suggestion of a 'Huey variant' was also of course politically savvy.

The marketing department quickly found a definition of the Cobra describing a snake, 'resident in far Eastern climes', that could 'strike quickly, spitting venom with deadly accuracy'. Cobra it was.

Army bureaucrats took some further persuasion, but at the time they were experiencing some litigious difficulty with the Piper aircraft company who were also using Indian Tribal names for their aircraft. Eventually they gave in; the Model 209 would henceforth be known as the 'AH-1G Huey Cobra'.

The pace quickens

Development continued apace, whilst the basic configuration was spot-on, making the aircraft combat ready required some further development. It was quickly discovered that the large canopy, whilst providing superb vision, was also a 'greenhouse'. In an attempt to reduce this, early aircraft had a blue-tinted canopy (which merely served to reduce visibility). The problem was eventually solved by a very effective air-conditioning unit, with an engine driven fan drawing air through a small intake on the port side aft of the canopy to ventilate the cockpit and the crew seats.

Another early change to the canopy was the deletion of the heavy armoured glass windscreen. Research had shown that the chances of a direct hit from head-on were only 4% – so it went. (This was not necessarily seen the same way by those who spent 100% of their time in the 4% zone, but in service the Viet Cong soon found that even attempting to engage a Cobra that was pointing directly at you was foolhardy and quickly desisted).

Conversely the crew were provided with Ausform armoured seats and Boron Carbide side panels that could be raised to provide additional protection from small-arms fire from the side and rear (at the time this was the main threat). The crew also wore personal 'chicken plate' armour which protected the torso. This was felt to be inadequate in some circles and many pilots opted for the massive .45 as their personal weapon, arranging the holstered pistol so that its substantial steel construction sat between their legs when flying.

A factor in the apparently light armour was the Cobra's turreted gun. In the context of the time, the GAU-2B/A 7.62mm minigun was a formidable weapon and a massive improvement on the single M-60s carried by the Huey. Fired for the first time at Fort Sill on 16 January 1966, the turret gun could traverse a 230 degree arc of fire, with an elevation of 60 degrees below and 25 degrees above datum it could suppress a very large area either side of the aircraft even when it was committed to an attack run with the fixed weapons.

Into production and service

On 11 March 1966, the Army had announced the 209 as the winner of the fly-off for an interim type. In the first few days of April a contract was received for two UH-1H pre-production airframes. An order for 110 machines followed on the 13th.

Following the discussion about nomenclature, this was modified on 19 May to change the designation to AH-1G – A for Attack (role), H-1 (type), and G (the next letter in the series). A further modification on 13 July finally conceded that the aircraft was to be known as the AH-1G Huey Cobra, the first helicopter to carry the A for Attack designation and a unique break from the Army's use of Indian Tribe names which was never seriously challenged.

There was a brief flurry of inter-service indignation when the Air Force complained that the new designation intruded on their turf as it denoted an offensive aircraft. This author was once assured by a very senior officer that the Army's position at the time was that, 'It was darn well *meant* to be offensive...' (and not entirely, one suspects, just to the enemy...!)

Even as production was getting under way the situation in the war zone was becoming more urgent and the requirement growing. On 30 September, seven (non flying) airframes were added to the order to serve as system trainers, and on 30 November, a further 210 Cobras were ordered.

With aircraft becoming available a joint Army/Bell NETT (New Equipment Training Team) was formed at Fort Hood in May the following year. Under the command of Lieutenant Colonel Paul Anderson it was tasked with getting the Cobra into active service as soon as possible. The UH-1 heritage proving invaluable in this as much of the engineering and systems common to both types was well established in the Army inventory and experience.

Meanwhile N209J continued to serve the development and sales programme, producing much acclaim at the 1967 Paris Air Show and during a subsequent European tour. The prototype Cobra was demonstrated to several nations during this trip – (the Germans even ordered three for evaluation albeit they later changed their minds, setting something of a pattern). The last leg in the UK, allowed Clem Bailey and Joe Mashman to present the 209 to the Royal Navy at Lee on Solent, the British Army at Odiham, Old Sarum and Middle Wallop, and the boffins at A&AEE Boscombe Down. Whilst all these airfields are relatively close together in southern England it must have been a pretty busy couple of days to say the least. Given that the aircraft only had some 600 hours total 'on the clock' when it reached the UK, that some 150 of them had been flown during this very intensive tour amply demonstrated the aircraft's serviceability when operating away from base.

In this incarnation the 20mm gun turret was also fitted. Effectively the proof of concept for future Cobra armament layout. Whilst the USMC wanted twin-engine safety for their proposed J Model, there was a strong possibility that politics would prevent its acquisition. Had that impasse not been surmounted this would have been what they got. (*Bell via Mike Verier*) (*Bell via Mike Verier*)

Later in its career '209 was modified to test the TOW configuration. This layout was subsequently adopted for all TOW capable Snakes. (*Bell via Mike Verier*)

Interesting in this view are the cheek bulges on the ammunition bay, adopted many years later for the AH-1W. (*Bell via Mike Verier*)

This photo shows the genesis of the Cobra. Lined up are the Iroquois Warrior mock-up, the Sioux Scout demonstrator, a UH-1C and of course N209J. (*US Army via Mike Verier*)

N209J as she appeared at the Paris Salon in 1967. The red numbers are 'show only'. Note that a (fake?) Army serial is carried on the tail (this airframe remained civil registered and was never on the Army inventory.) (*US Army via Ray Wilhite*)

The remarkably detailed report generated during its demonstration to the Army Air Corps at their Middle Wallop headquarters makes interesting reading. Slightly envious in tone (it was to be some four decades later that the British finally received attack helicopters) it nevertheless correctly foresaw that the Cobra would find the European environment (even then dense with sophisticated air defence weapons) rather more challenging than South East Asia.

As an aside it was during this tour that the aircraft sported a genuine Cobra head mounted on the front-seat collective. Guaranteed to get attention as it apparently rose and turned in the cockpit, it was reportedly 'mislaid' at some point (allegedly Munich) and doubtless adorns a trophy cabinet to this day.

The Bell marketing department, as we shall see again later, never missed an opportunity to get a potential customers' attention. Apart from the Cobra-head collective, a supply of realistic rubber snakes proved highly effective, as was a caution light that lit for what one startled British pilot described as 'a heart-stopping moment' shortly after start-up. It said 'BUY COBRAS'...

During August the NETT deployed to Vietnam. Twelve aircraft were flown directly to Bien Hoa on four Air Force C-133 Cargomasters, arriving on the 29th it had aircraft re-assembled and flying within forty-eight hours. Delivered in the standard overall Olive Drab paint scheme,

During its European tour N209Js collective was fitted with a real Cobra Head. Reckoned to be a great 'attention getter' by pilot Joe Mashman, the Spectacle Cobra came courtesy of Fort Worth's Forest Park Zoo. Sadly it went missing 'somewhere in Europe.' (*Bell via Mike Verier*)

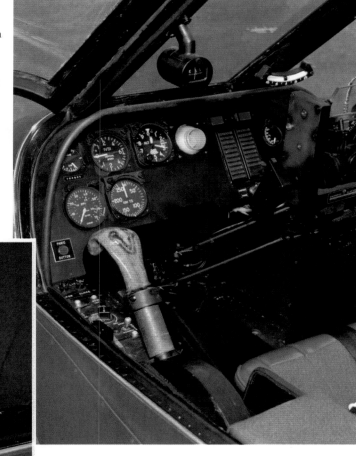

two of the unit's aircraft acquired additional tan camouflage patches and white undersides at this time. Allegedly Army 'C' rations were traded for Air Force paint, a practice quickly stopped by those higher up the supply chain!

As can be appreciated there was much interest in the Cobra's arrival and one of Colonel Anderson's first jobs was to demonstrate the new bird to General Westmoreland and other senior officers who were eagerly awaiting the Cobra's debut in-theatre. To put this in context, because of the length of time needed to qualify a new aircraft, it is very rare for any aircraft to be developed and fielded operationally during the conflict that gave rise to the requirement.

The Army's intended vehicle, the AH-56 Cheyenne, had begun development before the Cobra but was not expected to enter service for at least another 5-6 years. The Cobra arrived in Vietnam just two years (almost to the day) after its first flight, and only seventeen months after the Army had announced that it would go ahead – a truly remarkable achievement.

The Cobras' first blood went appropriately to 'Pip' Senneff – General Senneff had been the first senior Army officer to fly the Cobra and was instrumental in getting the AH-1 in service. He successfully attacked an armed sampan after happening upon a firefight between some VC and UH-1Cs whilst on a 'familiarisation' sortie on 4 September 1967.

Joe Mashman briefs
the Royal Navy on
the Cobra at Lee-
on-Solent during the
British leg of the tour.
(*John Sproule*)

As production got under way the first Cobras were heavily engaged in qualification work – at least two went to Fort Richardson in Alaska for cold-weather trials – at the time the most colourful of Cobras, especially once the already high-visibility Arctic scheme acquired the inevitable shark mouth. (*US Army via Ray Wilhite*)

Two days later a $60 million order added another 214 Cobras to the Army's requirement.

The NETT's first task was to qualify a cadre of pilots from the 'Playboys' of the 334th Assault Helicopter Company on to the type. On completion of the first course on 4 October 1967, six of the twelve aircraft were turned over to them, the 334th becoming operational two days later.

The remaining six airframes, included 66-15247 the second pre-production Cobra (YAH-1G) and the first three production airframes which had all been hand-built resulting in some maintenance issues as parts were not always interchangeable.

It was not to be long before the real baptism of fire. In November, Lieutenant Colonel Anderson had been assigned to 1st Aviation Brigade Headquarters and his place taken by Major Richard Jarrett. Like Senneff, Dick Jarrett had been with General Westmoreland when Bell had first proposed the Cobra. His enthusiasm and belief in the aircraft was to be tested almost before he had got his feet under the desk. The coming New Year was to see the Tet Offensive.

Others went to weapon trials. AH–1G 'Bearcat 15' is seen here at Fort Rucker. 66–15252 was the fifth production Cobra and spent much of its life at Rucker on weapon qualification trials as 'Bearcat 15'. The work done here ensured that weapons and aircraft functioned properly at the 'sharp end'. (*US Army via Ray Wilhite*)

'Bearcat 15' fires the turret gun on the ranges at Fort Hood. The pile of spent cases beneath the turret bearing testimony to the weapon's awesome rate of fire. (*US Army via Ray Wilhite*)

'Bearcat 14' was the third production Cobra. It later went to Vietnam as part of the Cobra NETT. (*US Army via Ray Wilhite*)

Chapter 4

Trial by Fire
Snakes in Vietnam

The Tet 'offensive' was nothing less than a full-scale invasion from the north. Involving some 80,000 North Vietnamese Army (NVA) and Vietcong troops it targeted thirty-six out of forty-four provincial capitals and was timed to coincide with a truce negotiated for the Lunar New Year, hoping to catch the civil and military administration off balance. It may well have succeeded without the Cobras.

Bien Hoa was amongst the bases attacked, In the pre–dawn gloom of 31 January 1968 the first mortar rounds impacted the base at 03.00hrs local time. Simultaneously enemy sappers blew up the USAF ammunition dump at nearby Long Binh. Such was the ferocity of the attack that at one point the perimeter was breached and the eastern end of the sprawling complex overrun.

With no warning of the massive assault, Cobras and UH–1C Hueys of the resident 334th Assault Helicopter Company 'Playboys' were scrambled to try and stem the tide. The fighting was almost hand to hand which meant that air strikes from fast jets were out of the question. The Cobra on the other hand offered a precision that meant fire power could be brought to bear on an enemy the width of a dirt track away from friendly forces. More to the point with the runways

Prior to actual deployment the first production and pre-production Cobras were used to form the Cobra New Equipment Training Team (NETT) tasked with getting the aircraft into service as quickly as possible. This AH–1G actually deployed with the NETT to Bien Hoa. (*US Army via Ray Wilhite*)

The First cadre of pilots trained by the NETT was the 334th AHC 'Playboys' who were quickly engulfed in action when the Tet Offensive burst on Bien Hoa. (*US Army via Ray Wilhite*)

It was only a matter of time before 'sharkmouth' adornments started to appear on the Cobra. Most were painted by hand as can be seen here and whilst a general style common to a particular unit was observed there were many variations.

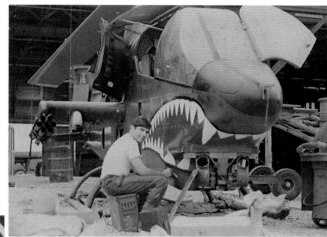

Whilst they were to later to adopt a particularly impressive sharkmouth, at least one aircraft of the 25th Avn Battalion 'Diamondheads' adopted this 'eye' marking. The 'evil eye' was regarded with great superstition in South East Asia and intended to seriously rattle anyone the aircraft was pointing at. (*Via Werner*)

Meanwhile training continued apace. This rather weary Cobra was seen at Fort Rucker.

The extremely smart instructor is explaining the finer points of the XM-35 20mm Gatling guns' ammunition feed to a doubtless high-ranking audience. The 'instructing-whilst-standing-to-attention' stance will be familiar to anyone who has served in the military the world over. (*US Army via Ray Wilhite*)

under sustained rocket and mortar fire, fixed-wing aircraft could not operate anyway. It was down to the helicopters.

With most of the flight crews quartered a good mile away from the base, the first Cobra on the scene was Captain Ken Rubin's 66-15275 which happened to be returning from a 'Firefly' mission just as elements of the Vietcong 274th, 275th and 68th infantry regiments launched their assault on the strong-point at 'Bunker Hill 10'. This redoubt was quickly cut-off and its USAF Security Police defenders were fighting for their lives. Had it not been for the intervention of the Cobras it would almost certainly have fallen.

As the fighting intensified Dick Jarrett and his NETT team waded in too. Not technically a combat unit they actually had to seek permission 'from above' to join the fight. Approval was quickly granted and the extra Cobras joined the fray. The 'book' said that thirty minutes was required to re-arm and re-fuel a Cobra – the task was completed with rotors turning, and shot and shell raining around them in less than ten. Again and again the exhausted crews returned to

The first AH-1G Cobras were airlifted directly to the warzone. Large batches also arrived by sea. Once in Vietnamese waters the aircraft were assembled and flown directly ashore. Also visible on the crowded deck are OV-10s and CH-47 Chinooks. (*Bell via Mike Verier*)

The USMC took delivery of thirty-eight G Models diverted from Army stocks. This Bell photo shows the difference between the Marines' specified 'Marine Green' and the Army's 'Olive Drab' to advantage. (*Bell via Mike Verier*)

An early modification was the deletion of the nose-mounted landing light (which was moved to the belly, aft of the turret) this left a convenient empty space, and (inset) Snoopy rides the Cobra! (*US Army via Ray Wilhite*)

The 20mm M–35 was deployed to give the Snake better 'reach' and firepower. Clearly visible here are the ammunition sponsons and the cross–feed under the fuselage. The 'appliqué' panels on the forward fuselage were necessary to reinforce the airframe locally so that it could withstand the blast effects of this massive weapon. (*US Army via Ray Wilhite*)

Unidentified Cobra, possibly A Company 2/20th ARA in its revetment. The smooth flush-riveted finish of early AH-1Gs is very apparent here. Intriguingly the Cobra in the next bay appears to be painted black overall. (*US Army via Ray Wilhite*)

support the hard-pressed ground troops, after more than thirty-six hours of intense fighting the offensive faltered. Operating under the most extreme conditions the Cobra had proved its mettle. Afterwards Dick Jarrett was to accord particular recognition to the civilian Bell technicians with his unit who had worked tirelessly and without regard for their own safety to keep the Cobras flying. 'The Army,' he wrote at the time, 'should have men like these.'

Following this traumatic introduction to service the increasing number of Cobra equipped units set about honing their tactics and forging an identity. Their cavalry lineage was very apparent with much use of markings involving crossed sabres and lance pennants on the aircraft. Inevitably sharkmouths also started to appear (never was there a more suitable aircraft for the adornment). The crews in turn sported black Stetsons with yellow cords in recognition of their heritage. Most famous and distinctive of these units was the 1st Cavalry Division (Airmobile), sent to Vietnam in August 1965, whose big yellow and black patch became iconic.

Some idea of the gathering pace of Cobra deliveries and the urgency of the situation in Vietnam can be gleaned from the training programme required. At the time the 'Cobra Hall' at Hunter-Stewart Army Airfield was turning out some forty crews every three weeks.

As the deployment of Cobras continued, the fight was taken to the enemy. One of the most successful (and dangerous) tactics was the Hunter-Killer team of a Cobra and a Hughes OH-6 'Loach' helicopter. The nimble egg-shaped OH-6 was flown low in an effort to scout for signs of enemy activity or draw them into revealing their positions. The Cobra would remain high to cover the scout and be able to roll in on a smoke marker if a target was presented.

In the Cavalry, the different arms are identified by a colour: the scouts are 'Whites'; the guns 'Reds'; and the Aero Rifles (infantry) 'Blues'. Inevitably these scouts and guns combinations became known as 'Pink teams'. Other permutations included 'Purple' (a Cobra and a Huey full of infantry) and 'Heavy Red' (two Cobras and a Loach)

As expected the Cobras immediately made a difference ranging ahead of transports to clear 'hot' LZs (Landing Zones). Its 7.62mm turret gun was ideal for this. An area weapon it could famously 'fill a football pitch' with bullets. The gunner, seated in the front cockpit right over the turret, was provided with Bell's ingenious pantograph-mounted sight and an unrivalled field of view. The M-28 turret could also mount the XM-129 grenade launcher. The two weapons were interchangeable and the most common fit was one of each.

For engagements requiring longer range or more hitting power, wing mounted seven or nineteen-shot rocket pods were carried. The rockets were unguided 2.75 inch FFARs with scarfed nozzles to impart spin stability. (Necessary because of the low speeds typical of helicopter usage). Theoretically they were capable of longer range engagements, but their accuracy tended to depend on a crew's ability to allow for 'Kentucky windage'. At least one crew also discovered to their cost that unscarfed rockets scrounged from the Air Force were downright dangerous when fired at low forward air speeds.

Additional gun pods could also be mounted. After experimenting with M-18 gun-pods borrowed from the Air Force it was decided that something of larger calibre (and therefore longer reach) was necessary. This need became more pressing as the 'Snakes' suffered increasing losses from heavy .51 cal guns used from beyond the range of their own guns by the Viet Cong. The massive XM-35 20mm 'Gatling' was the result. Derived from the Vulcan gun fitted to fast jets it was so big that only one could be carried, slung under the port wing, with ammunition in sponsons mounted over the skids. The whole system with ammunition weighed nearly 1200lb severely limiting the Cobra's ability to carry much else. Usually two aircraft in every unit were XM-35 equipped.

This was very much an interim solution but it did provide much needed additional firepower and greater stand-off capability. Often described as being more dangerous to the user than the recipient, firing it caused so much vibration and blast effect (overpressure) that instruments toppled, rivets popped and the front seater often had to hold his canopy shut. This was at least partially addressed by reinforcing the fuselage and ammunition bay door on the port side, M-35 capable aircraft being readily identifiable by the resulting 'applique' panels.

Meanwhile the USMC had concluded that sacrificing some of their precious lift capacity for attack helicopters would be worthwhile. In the long term they needed more capable aircraft than the Army versions and the necessary AH-1J development was under way. In the interim thirty-eight 'Gs' were loaned from Army stocks, the first aircraft going operational at the Marble Mountain Air Facility in April 1969. Despite some difficulty with spares and the Army communications fit, the Marines also quickly found the aircraft invaluable. As well as fire-support missions the USMC were heavily involved in the riverine warfare of the Delta region, Cobras supporting the 'Brown Water Navy' to considerable effect.

Despite the fact that night operations had to be flown in Vietnam, they were very much 'seat of the pants' and relied solely on the pilot's night vision. First generation Snakes were daytime/ VFR (Visual Flight Rules) machines with no true night/bad weather capability. Consequently a number of night-vision devices were trialled during the Vietnam conflict including Infra-red and Low Light Level TV. The technology of the day was not up to operational use however and it would be many years before a true night-capable Cobra was fielded.

Two of the oddest-looking were CONFICS and SMASH. Both of these aircraft were developed under ENSURE programmes, the latter acronym standing for Expedite Non-Standard Urgent Requirement for Equipment. Of the two, SMASH is perhaps the better known.

As acronyms go the 'Southeast Asia Multi-sensor Armament Subsystem for Hueycobra' was rather contrived but it had an effective ring to it. What resulted was an AH1-G which had a nose mounted FLIR, (Forward Looking Infra-Red), AN/AAQ-5J known at the time as SSPI (Sighting Station Passive Infra-red) and a podded moving target indicator radar (AN/APQ-137)

The spectacular 'sharkmouth' sported by this AH-1G from the 25th Aviation Battallion 'Diamondheads' replaced the earlier 'eye' design. (*US Army via Ray Wilhite*)

SMASH was another attempt to marry a night sight to the Cobra. Whilst this too was unreliable for operational use it was the beginning of what we now know as FLIR technology and was to eventually lead to today's sophisticated sighting systems. (*US Army via Ray Wilhite*)

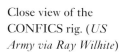

Close view of the CONFICS rig. (*US Army via Ray Wilhite*)

CONFICS was an early attempt at a night-vision system for the Cobra. It proved too cumbersome and unreliable to be fielded. (*US Army*)

which was mounted on the starboard outer pylon. Displays were available in both cockpits, and permitted the detection and engagement of both vehicular and personnel targets at night or in bad visibility. The FLIR also enhanced the pilot's ability to navigate in darkness. The aircraft retained the M-28 turret and was equipped with the M-35 20mm cannon. The only other thing that room could be found for on the aircraft was a seven-shot M-155 launcher. SMASH was tested at Redstone arsenal but never worked satisfactorily and wasn't deployed to Vietnam.

CObra Night FIre Control System on the other hand was a slightly simpler if no less cumbersome attempt to provide night vision by use of low light TV. Developed under Ensure 100, the system was derived from the Huey mounted INFANT (Iroquois Night Fighter and Night Tracker) rig. It was intended to control the turret guns and the sighting station was therefore built into the front cockpit. One aircraft (67-15761) was converted and underwent testing at Redstone and Fort Rucker. Again testing proved disappointing and the Army went back to flares and searchlights pending the arrival of more viable technology.

An equally prescient realisation was that the post-Vietnam Cobra fleet would need an anti-armour capability as demonstrated by the difficulty Cobras had in dispatching the small numbers of NVA tanks they encountered towards the end of the conflict. A pair of Hueys hastily armed with TOW (Tube-launched, Optically-sighted, Wire-guided) missiles, showed that weapons potential, but again it was not to be during the Vietnam fighting.

The final act of the conflict, operation 'Frequent Wind' (the evacuation of the last Americans from Saigon in April 1975) was covered by USMC Cobras, operating from offshore. Thus the Cobra was operational from the moment it arrived in theatre until the very last American aircraft left the skies of Vietnam.

Chapter 5

Cold War and Hot Deserts

Sharpening the Fangs –
Post-Vietnam single engine development

Following withdrawal from Vietnam there was a period of retrenchment for the Americans. The long war in South East Asia had to a certain extent taken the eye off the fact that they still faced a number of potential enemies around the world. From the US Army's perspective a re-focus was needed towards anti-armour capabilities, especially in Europe where NATO forces still faced hordes of WarPac armour poised just a few miles away in Eastern Europe.

The answer should have been the AH-56 Cheyenne, but that programme was already behind schedule and even on the most optimistic estimates was unlikely to be available for service for several years. The G Model Cobras, effective though they had been in Vietnam, were (as the British had correctly surmised a decade earlier) not really suitable for the European scenario.

In the short term the success of the TOW missile in the closing stages of the Vietnam conflict had provided an appropriate and effective anti-armour weapon for helicopters. It had a genuine one-shot 'kill' capability and a reach of some 3 kilometres. It came 'pre-packed' and could consequently be treated as a round of ammunition, re-loads simply being clipped into the launcher assembly on the aircraft.

AH-1Q – the first step

In 1973, under the Improved Cobra Armament Programme (ICAP), eight 'G's were equipped for TOW under the designation YAH-1Q. The nose-mounted M-65 sighting turret made them easily distinguishable from 'standard' 'G's. The same installation was also adopted for the Iranian J Models and subsequently the USMC's AH-1T.

The original Pantograph sight was replaced by the M-65's big TSU (Telescopic Sight Unit) that now dominated the front cockpit. Also new was the HSS (Helmet Sight System) that enabled either crewman to point the guns or the sighting turret at whatever was in their line of sight. The system had a mechanical linkage to each helmet with the two polished rods in the roof of the cockpit being a distinctive recognition feature.

A total of ninety-eight ICAP conversions were re-designated AH-1Q, albeit this was only ever to be an interim configuration as the additional weight rendered the aircraft marginal on power.

The Army however had an aircraft that could nevertheless defend the Fulda Gap – the corridor across the German plains which a large armoured formation would have to cross heading for the Channel – if only in daylight.

The power deficiency was of course recognised and in 1975 the next step was taken under the Improved Cobra Agility and Manoeuvrability programme (ICAM). Two aircraft received uprated (1800shp) T53-L-703 engines and the same drive train as the Iranian 'J'. (Derived from the Huey Tug and qualified on the Model 309 KingCobra). One airframe was a straight 'G', becoming the YAH-1R, the other a 'Q' becoming the YAH-1S (*see 'Historic Cobras 2' page 121*).

The sole YAH-1R ICAM test bird, AH-1G 70-15936, received the engines and drive-train intended for the next Cobra improvements. The black and white circles are for photo calibration, whilst the dayglo areas denote 'Test' status. The new tail rotor gearbox cover is still in primer. (*Bell via Mike Verier*)

AH-1S – towards the ultimate

Commencing in 1976 the resulting upgrade, brought 378 airframes (including all the 'Q's) to a configuration known as AH-1S(Improved) – they were also sometimes referred to as 'Modified S'. Meanwhile the Cheyenne had been cancelled and at the same time the Army was defining its next generation helicopter (AAH). This would ultimately result in the AH-64 Apache, but again the goal posts had moved ten years into the future and the Army would have to not only manage with its existing Cobras but order some more to bridge the gap. Consequently the Snake continued to develop.

The next, and certainly the most visual change was the so-called 'flat-plate' canopy. The classic Cobra canopy offered superb visibility from the cockpit. Its curved surfaces however also meant that 'glint' from the canopy could give away the helicopter's position from several kilometres. The 'flat-plate' appellation is actually something of a misnomer as only the three centre panels are actually flat. Both front and rear side panels are slightly bulged to improve crew visibility. Access remained as on the old canopy with the front port and aft starboard panels opening.

The much heavier framing reduced visibility from within the cockpit, and rain clearance was sometimes a problem, but compared to compromising your position it was considered a reasonable trade-off. Interestingly the USMC concluded the exact reverse and stayed with the 'round' canopy for its better view and aerodynamics. Glint was a big issue if you were trying to hide amongst German trees. The Marines however generally expect to encounter very few trees between the boat and the beach so it was the least of their worries.

AH-1G at Fort Apalachicola in April 1970. Hastily added following early Vietnam experience was the massive XM-35 20mm cannon system. For all its limitations it gave the Cobra better 'reach' and hitting power. This gun was the full six-barrel 'Vulcan' used on jet fighters. The developed three-barrel XM-197 remains the Cobra weapon of choice to this day. (*US Army via Ray Wilhite*)

The first priority was to give the Cobra a true anti-armour capability. Ninety-six airframes were modified by simply adding the TOW/M-65 system to G Models. This is 70-16055, one of the YAH-1Q test aircraft. (*US Army via Ray Wilhite*)

The early M-65 sighting 'bucket' was typified by the two teardrop-shaped bulges. The yellow rod is simply to give the gunner a visual reference to the turret's alignment. The original caption states that the aircraft is fitted with 'laser amplifiers'. (*US Army via Ray Wilhite*)

Other AH-1G Models soldiered on. This undated photo clearly shows the 101st Airborne's 'Screamin' Eagle' patch. (*US Army via Ray Wilhite*)

Given the Army doctrine that the attack helicopters' airspace extended 'from the top of the grass to the top of the trees' wires and cables were a real hazard in the European operating environment. The opportunity was taken therefore to add cable-cutters to the aircraft, the Wire Strike Protection System being primarily visible as 'horns' above the canopy and beneath the nose.

The 100 airframes produced from 1977 incorporated all the earlier ICAP/ICAM improvements and the new canopy, these were known as 'Production S'. Until this point the original M–28 turret gun had remained unchanged. Its rifle-calibre guns and their short range, however, made it increasingly unsuitable and the adoption of the J Model's M–197 20mm turret was also undertaken with the production of ninety-eight 'Upgun' S Models also known by the programme acronym ECAS (Enhanced Cobra Armament System) from 1978. Unlike the Marines, the Army did not use the aerodynamic cowling for the otherwise identical installation as it makes maintenance (often undertaken in a muddy field at night) much more difficult. The ECAS Cobras also received the rocket management system and a 10kva alternator/generator which necessitated a distinctive teardrop bulge on the port side cowling immediately forward of the intake.

Towards the end of the Vietnam conflict, shoulder-launched heat-seeking missiles had reached the battlefield. The interim solution for the Cobra had been the adoption of an up–turned exhaust shroud (variously known as the 'toilet bowl' or 'sugar scoop') intended to dissipate the exhaust plume by directing it into the rotor disc. A more effective answer was needed if the Cobra was to survive improved 'heat seekers'.

Consequently a new exhaust shroud and cooled-plug type suppressor was developed by Garret Air Research. It cooled the exhaust gasses by mixing them with ambient air and passing them through a system of baffles. Even the paint was changed from the Army's beloved Olive Drab to a darker more matt finish designed to absorb IR radiation (the effectiveness of this almost sandpaper-like finish can be attested to by anyone who has tried to photograph it; light just falls into it making it very difficult to see the aircraft at any distance). These passive defences were augmented by an active system, the AN/ALQ 144 IRCM jammer. Colloquially referred to as the 'disco-lights' it is actually a heat source. Mounted immediately aft of the rotor pylon, the multi-faceted unit works by swamping a seeker with constantly changing heat signatures. Unable to maintain a steady lock, the seeker head will eventually give-up and go ballistic.

The final major airframe change that transformed the Vietnam-era Cobra into a more capable anti-armour type was a new rotor. The 540 metal blade had served the Cobra and Huey well but it was heavy and limited to about 1,000 hours. At the time composite technology was finding its way into rotor blade development and Bell rival, Kaman, found themselves with a contract to supply new blades for the Cobra fleet.

The K747 blades are easily distinguished by their wider chord and tapered tips. Completely interchangeable with the old blades they were lighter, quieter and had a design life in excess of 10,000 hours. They could also tolerate hits by rounds of up to 23mm without failure. Importantly they were also easily repairable at unit level in the event of minor damage such as tree or bird strikes.

Inside the cockpit many more changes were made. With the arrival of the TSU (Telescopic Sight Unit) 'scope', the front office had been re-designed, the new canopy having provided more headroom and a deeper instrument panel. The rear station received a modern HUD (Head Up Display) in place of the old gunsight. Radar Warning Receivers (RWR) provided information on threats, giving both the bearing and type of radar that was scanning the Cobra. Provision was made for the later inclusion of laser detection/warning.

Ballistic accuracy of both the gun and unguided rockets was greatly improved by the addition of a British-developed Air Data System which fed accurate information to the computer about wind direction and strength when the helicopter was moving at low speeds or hovering. Finally the Cobra crews had something more reliable than 'Kentucky Windage' with which to aim their ballistic weapons.

The Helmet Sight System (HSS) also proved to be extremely effective, especially at bringing the guns to bear quickly on off-axis threats. This capability gave a measure of air-to-air defence if the Cobra crew saw the threat first. The Soviet Mil Mi-24 'Hind' had a bigger gun but it had to manoeuvre to bring it to bear and it was a much larger target than a Cobra. As an aside, crews had to learn not to link the HSS and guns on the ground – a careless nod down into the cockpit would depress the big six foot long barrels and jack the nose up!

The Army had intended that all these improvements would be retrospectively applied across the fleet, and that ultimately all Cobras would reach a common standard to be known as AH-1S(MC) (Modernised Cobra). Compared to the Vietnam era 'G's the fully developed 'S' was more powerful, better armed and harder to detect and 'kill'. Furthermore it could bring weapons to bear at almost double the effective range and with much greater accuracy. The fully modernised 'S' was also to become the baseline model for the increasing number of export orders secured for the Cobra as US production was completed, and capacity became available.

The upgrade programme was ambitious, with earlier machines returned to Bell's Amarillo plant and stripped back to the basic structure before re-building. In the event it was never completed. By the early 1980s, with the AH-64 just entering service and Bell's 249 Advanced Scout rejected, the Army's thoughts were turning towards the future LHX, which was intended to eventually replace the Cobra in the scout/attack role. Funds were not going to be available to do all three things.

During September and October 1981, trials were carried out with the FIM-92 'Stinger' IR Homing Missile. Originally a light, shoulder-launched, MANPAD it was adapted for helicopter use. Although trialled on the Cobra, and remaining in service today, the Army chose not to arm its Snakes with this very effective weapon. (*US Army via Ray Wilhite*)

A simple box structure held two Stingers. The device on the outboard pylon appears to be a camera. The airframe is an AH-1G, 70 -15972. (*US Army via Ray Wilhite*)

All change – alphabet soup

This left the Army with a nomenclature problem. The fleet now consisted of aircraft in widely different mod-states, but all called 'AH-1S'. In 1988 therefore, it was decided to accept the *status quo* and re-designate the different 'S' variants. The fully modernised machines were to become AH-1Fs, remaining ECAS airframes became AH-1Es, and the flat-plate 'Production S' became the AH-1P. The surviving ICAP/ICAM Cobras (which were at one time to be designated AH-1M) retained the 'S' designator and ten of these were given the AH-64 Apache Pilot Night Vision System (PNVS) to serve as 'Surrogate' Apache trainers at Fort Rucker and were known as TH-1Ss.

Unsurprisingly, this has led to a great deal of confusion as time has gone by, with some sources stating with great authority that so many AH-1Es or Ps 'were built' when in fact none were – they were all re-designated 'S' variants. The distinctions between the various sub-types were not always obvious either and the exact designation of a given airframe remains a question with several possible answers depending on the date it was asked.

Whilst major development of the single-engine Cobra had effectively ended, a number of operational modifications became necessary in the ensuing years. The long awaited night capability was fitted to some aircraft with the adoption of the Tamam/Kollesman CNITE (Cobra Night Imaging Thermal Equipment) FLIR upgrade.

The deployment of more powerful Mk 66 2.75-inch WAFARs (Wrap-Around-Fin Aircraft Rockets) led to problems with engine surging and compressor stalls. This was cured with a rather Soviet-looking inlet flow diverter to prevent the airflow disturbance that firing these caused.

Through the 1980s and 1990s US Army Cobras continued to patrol frontiers from Germany to Korea. They saw combat from Panama to the first Gulf War and they helped preserve the fragile peace in the Balkans. Gradually however, the Apache matured and took over the front line duties carried out for nearly four decades by the faithful Snake. Finally leaving the regular

BACK TO THE FUTURE - THE TRANSITION FROM AH-1G TO AH-1F

SERVICE DESIGNATION	AH-1G	AH-1Q	YAH-1R / YAH-1S 'IMPROVED S'	AH-1S 'PRODUCTION S'	AH-1S 'UPGUN S'	AH-1S(MC)
ACRONYM		ICAP	ICAM		ECAS	
POST-1988 DESIGNATION			AH-1S	AH-1P	AH-1E	AH-1F
TURRET ARMAMENT	M-28 7.62MM / 40MM				M-197 20MM	
SIGHTING (TURRET)	PANTOGRAPH	M-65 TSU HSS				
FIXED ARMAMENT	ROCKETS M-35	ROCKETS TOW				
SIGHTING (FIXED)	XM-73 REFLECTOR					HUD
ENGINE	1400 SHP		1800 SHP			
TRANSMISSION	1134 SHP		1290 SHP			
MAIN ROTOR	540 METAL					K-747 COMPOSITE
CANOPY	'ROUND' CANOPY			'FLAT PLATE' CANOPY		
OTHER						IR EXHAUST / AN/ALQ-144 / AIR DATA SYSTEM
GROSS WEIGHT	9500 Lb		10,000 Lb			
EMPTY WEIGHT	5809 Lb	6249 Lb	6300 Lb	6278 Lb	6419 Lb	(MIN) 6598 Lb
LATER MODS						RADAR JAMMER / LASER TRACKER / C-NITE / INLET DIVERTER

The ICAM modifications applied to a 'Q' produced the baseline AH-1S – the enlarged tail-rotor gearbox being characteristic. Notable in this photo are the rarely-seen 'Bear Pad' snow-shoes fitted to the skids and the additional light fixed to the turret grenade launcher. (*US Army via Ray Wilhite*)

This unidentified Cobra is involved in early trials of the 'flat-plate' canopy. However, it also features an early M-197 20mm turret but not the M-65 nose-mounted sighting unit. It may be the AH-1S trials aircraft 70-16019. (*US Army via Ray Wilhite*)

This appears to be an AH-1Q with a trial canopy installation, apparently photographed at Fort Rucker. (*US Army via Ray Wilhite*)

Army's inventory in 1999, Cobras soldiered on with Air National Guard units until 2001 when nearly 500 remaining aircraft were finally gathered at Fort Drum to await their fate.

History will probably record that the 'interim' single-engine Cobras served the US Army for over thirty-five years, most of them on the front-line. Arguably it continues to benefit the Army well beyond official retirement however. A single example continues in development work and sales generated from reclamation of the old airframes have even given money back to the taxpayer.

Far from being an epitaph, the silent lines of redundant airframes at Wheeler-Sack Army Airfield marked only the opening of another chapter in Snake history. As is noted elsewhere many of them still live, flying with other air arms and civilian owners to this day. Old Cobras die? Never!

Fort Rucker in Alabama is the home of Army aviation, and where the test squadrons live. This photo dates from March 1983 and may, or may not, be a TAH-1F. The term was used rather loosely and is a very subtle distinction involving a booster for the front-seat 'side-stick' cyclic designed to give the instructor the same leverage as a student in the back. Novel at the time, 70-15339's sand paint-job was to become popular some years later. (*US Army via Ray Wilhite*)

AH-1F, 70-15603, sporting another experimental camo scheme, this time using the standard colours applied to ground vehicles. This aircraft is illustrated in the colour section. (*US Army via Ray Wilhite*)

Given that all the markings have been painted over this may be a 'temporary' trial paint-job. The colours appear to be the same as the 'Asia Minor' shades applied to Jordanian cobras. (*US Army via Ray Wilhite*)

Rucker's Cobras then became involved in Apache development. This aircraft features an early iteration of the Pilot's Night Vision System (PNVS) system that folded neatly into the nose. Note that the crew are also wearing the Apache Integrated Helmet Data Display System (IHADDS) helmet, a first generation 'integrated' helmet. (*US Army via Ray Wilhite*)

The PNVS test aircraft in flight. (*US Army via Ray Wilhite*)

Following trials ten S Models were converted to 'surrogates' so that students, (under the 'bag' in the back seat), could master the art of landing and take-off using the PNVS without risking an expensive new Apache. (*Mike Verier*)

Photographed at Fort Ruckers' Mattesson Ranges in 1987 these TAH-1Fs have had the performance-reducing Garret exhaust removed but are otherwise 'stock' fully upgraded AH-1S(MC) airframes, complete with the new K-747 composite blades. They were re-designated 'AH-1F' after 1987. (*Mike Verier*)

The new blades are shown to some advantage here, as is the protruding arm of the gimballed Air Data System. The only piece of British kit on the Cobra, it provides accurate wind and drift information for the ballistic weapons, finally replacing 'Kentucky windage'. (*Mike Verier*)

As three AH-1F Cobras settle at the re-arming pad, the big white identification numbers become apparent. These help find the individual aircraft on the flight-line and discourage un-authorised low-level flying. (*Mike Verier*)

Known colloquially at the time as 'ECAS' birds (later AH-1E), this AH-1S belonged to the 82nd Airborne at Fort Bragg, NC. Pictured on the live ranges, the gun is being fired with cases and links falling from the turret. (*Mike Verier*)

Fort Bragg's Simmonds flight line in 1989, with two ECAS Cobras showing changing fashion. The aircraft in the foreground has the old 540 metal rotor (yellow Tips) whilst the one behind it has the then-new (and interchangeable) K-747 composite blades. (*Mike Verier*)

Another trials aircraft shows what was to become the last major mod before the Army Cobras were retired. The Inlet Flow Diverter, seen here in prototype form, was needed to prevent engine surges caused by local pressure surges caused when the new and more powerful WAFFR rockets were fired. (*US Army via Ray Wilhite*)

In the mid-1980s F Model Cobras were still holding the line in Europe. This aircraft is from B Company, 503rd Attack Helicopter Battalion. (*Floyd Werner*)

This AH-1P is from the 1-7th Cavalry and is seen on exercise at the Bicycle Lake National Training Centre. It is equipped with the MILES rig which uses lasers to simulate and register fire. (*US Army via Ray Wilhite*)

AH-1F, 78-23113 'Betsy', was decorated sometime around 17 January 1991, whilst the unit was waiting for orders, once again proving the Snake's natural affinity for shark teeth. (*Floyd Werner*)

The Starboard side of 'Betsy' shows evidence of earlier chalked artwork. Unlike other units who had even resorted to domestic paint for 'desert' camouflage 1–7th Cavalry retained their 'green' paint throughout the conflict. (*Floyd Werner*)

This AH-1F Cobra was found apparently abandoned in a Wadi by members of 1st Cavalry, who promptly claimed it, flew it back to their assembly area, and downloaded the armament. When 1st Infantry eventually arrived to claim their aircraft back, (it had suffered a compressor stall and been left behind in the advance), they found that tradition had been observed – and it had acquired a 1st Cavalry patch and a considerable range of graffiti from the ground crew, and (insert) The new nose-art that comes from landing in the wrong place! (*Floyd Werner*)

AH–1F, 78-23221 'Vivacious Vonnie', Floyd Werner's 'own' aircraft resting quietly just after the Desert Storm hostilities ceased in 1991. (*Floyd Werner*)

One of the last operational deployments for the Army's Cobras was keeping the peace in Bosnia during the winter of 1995/96. The opposite climatic extreme to service in the Iraqi desert, this photo of an AH–1F was taken at Taszar in Hungary in December 1995. (*Floyd Werner*)

CW2 Perry Scachetti loading up at Kaposuar, providing an indication of both how big a 20mm round is, and how cold it was in the Bosnian winter. (*Floyd Werner*)

Top of the Range and end of the line. Seen at Budlingen Germany this Snake has all the upgrades the F Model Cobra ever got, including the Inlet Flow Diverters. Until the day they retired, the Cobras in Europe remained fully capable of taking on any threat that might emerge from the East. (*Floyd Werner*)

The very last Cobra to leave Germany was flown into honourable retirement at a military college in England by Floyd Werner (left) and Captain Jud McCrary. Just visible are the ground-handling wheels packed into the ammunition bay. (*Floyd Werner*)

Chapter 6

Semper Fi

Marines meet Cobras

During the Korean conflict the US Marine Corps had been amongst the first to experiment with armed helicopters. They kept a watch on later developments too (there was a permanent USMC liaison office at Fort Rucker). Initially however they displayed little more than academic interest in the armed helicopter.

This was because the USMC's primary mission, Seaborne Assault, is fundamentally different from that of the Army. They are often the first into battle and likely to confront an enemy at close quarters; consequently the Corps has its own air assets, including fast jets and transport helicopters. Thus if a Marine could not be supported by fixed-wing aircraft, he would be within range of naval gunfire (NGF) – either way the sole function of the helicopter was to get the troops and their supplies to where they were needed.

There were other reasons for the Marines' reluctance to over-specialize. They had to be prepared to deploy anywhere in the world, jungle or desert, arctic or equator. This meant that funds were inevitably and invariably stretched leaving little room for what was seen as the unnecessary luxury of armed helicopters.

Likewise arming existing types was seen as a non-starter. In the era of the Sikorsky UH-34 Seahorse, payloads were very limited, every machine gun you put on the aircraft meant one less Marine inside, and the only place you could mount a machine gun was in the one doorway the 'HUS' had. This would slow down egress of the troops at the very time the aircraft was most vulnerable – whilst it was on the LZ. Finally, and probably the most powerful argument against the armed helicopter, was that it was widely felt that specialized weapons helicopters would not only have to be traded off against fixed-wing procurement, but would put pressure on the limited lift capability that the Corps had at its disposal.

Almost unnoticed, an event took place in March 1962 that was ultimately to bring about a change in doctrine, and lead to the acceptance of the attack helicopter elements as we know them today. On 1 March the Secretary of the Navy approved adoption of Bell's UH-1B for light reconnaissance and utility duties. In Marine service it was to be known as UH-1E and differed from its Army equivalent in having a rotor brake, Navy avionics and radios, and a basic construction of aluminum rather than the customary magnesium which was readily corroded by salt water.

Although they were not required by the Marines, Bell left in the airframe the provisions that the Army had incorporated for weapon mounting, avoiding the necessity for structural re-design.

On 19 March 1962 the JCS (Joint Chiefs of Staff) decided that a squadron of Marine Corps helicopters could usefully be substituted for an Army unit scheduled for deployment to Vietnam.

In 1968 the first USMC Cobra squadron, HMA-367 'Scarface' fielded G Model Cobras diverted directly from Army orders. The Marines lost no time in applying their own distinctive scheme to the aircraft. '367 have had a continuous association with the Snake ever since and today fly the Zulu variant. (*Buck Simmons*)

Herb Silva with TV/25 showing the full and spectacular snake head decoration in all its glory. This scheme is illustrated in the colour section. (*Via Buck Simmons*)

The first J Models arrived at Marble Mountain around 1970. This brand-new AH-1J features a full-colour Scarface patch. The black painted tail adds a rakish touch but was actually a practical response to the Cobras exhaust plume which blackened that part of the aircraft anyway. (*Hank Perry*)

Out in the field the patch has been toned down and the aircraft now looks 'operational'. (*Hank Perry*)

That the Cobra was derived from the Huey is clear in this photo of an AH-1J. In the USMC the two types formed a symbiotic relationship that continues to this day. This pair wear the full-colour insignia and markings of 'Stateside' aircraft at the time. The location is Kanehoe Bay, Hawaii in about 1969-70. (*USNAM*)

Consequently on 22 March, the 1st Marine Aircraft Wing (1st MAW) was ordered to prepare to deploy one squadron for an operation that was to be codenamed SHUFLY. The selected unit, HMM 362, commanded by Lieutenant Colonel Archie J. Clapp, commenced operations from Soc Trang on 15 April, and by the 22nd the first aircraft had received combat damage.

It very quickly became apparent that the transport helicopters needed suppressive fire over and above that which could be provided by available resources, and by July Commandant of the Marine Corps, General David M. Shoup, was asking the Chief of Naval Operations to furnish him with six North American Aviation T-28 Trojan fixed-wing aircraft for helicopter escort (the use of jets not being politically acceptable at the time).

The JCS prevaricated; the rules of engagement stated that the enemy must fire first. In February 1963 they gave temporary permission for helicopter crews to shoot first but only against 'clearly defined VC elements considered to be a threat to the helicopter and its passengers'. Less than a week later they changed their minds and again returned to the 'defence only' posture. This did not prevent the men of HMM-362 proudly announcing on 13 March that for the first time, three UH-34s had successfully provided close air support during a landing.

Finally, in April, after yet another request from General Shoup for armed T-28s, the SHUFLY squadron received the support of six Army UH-1B gunships. The Marine Corps was finding out the hard way that it did after all need armed helicopters.

Whilst this was going on, UH-1E Iroquois production was under way, the first aircraft being handed over to VMO-1 at Fort Worth on 21 February 1964. As if to remind them, the JCS again stated in May of that year that armed helicopters were not a substitute for close air support.

In August, North Vietnamese Fast Patrol Boats upped the stakes by attacking two American destroyers in the Gulf of Tonkin. Within a fortnight the then Commandant of the Marine Corps, General Greene, had ordered work to begin on a 'high priority' basis to develop an armament kit for the UH-34. A similar directive covering the UH-1E followed in October. By December, the first TK-1 (Temporary Kit 1) groundfire suppression armament kits were issued to the SHUFLY squadron, and in January 1965, VMO 6 at Camp Pendleton had the modified TK-2 sets for its UH-1s. Thanks to the unplanned but fortuitous existence of airframe hard points incorporated into Huey variants since the UH-1B, each kit could be installed in less than a day without making any holes in the aircraft.

The UH-1E was to prove useful and effective in the armed role, unfortunately its very success compounded the Marines problems. The aircraft were assigned to the VMOs, squadrons whose duties were concerned with observation, forward air control (FACA), and general liaison. Constant involvement in the escort role placed tremendous pressure on these resources. The planned arrival of the OV-10 (not due until 1968) would go some way to alleviating the problem, but there were already those within the USMC who could see that a fundamental shift in doctrine was needed.

The gunship emerges

An incident that occurred towards the end of 1967 dramatically highlighted the effectiveness of armed helicopters. On 19 August, a VMO-6 pilot, Captain Stephen W. Pless and his crew, flying an UH-1E gunship as chase aircraft for an emergency MEDEVAC in Southern Quang Ngai Province, won a Congressional Medal of Honour and three Navy Crosses, for a dramatic rescue of soldiers trapped by an overwhelming Viet Cong force. His lone aircraft, the only support close enough to help, used its rockets and guns to drive the enemy away from the wounded and almost exhausted Americans before landing under heavy fire to extract them.

Eventually the pace and scope of operations in South East Asia and the success that the Army was having with the Cobra convinced the Marines that it was about time that they had some of these too, albeit modified for their mission. Operating from ships, Marine helos needed twin engine safety, rotor brakes, EMP (ElectroMagnetic Pulse) resistant 'Navy' radios, and protection against salt damage and corrosion. The Marines also correctly concluded that a larger calibre turret gun would be required to increase stand-off from any target. Because they may find themselves the only air support available to deal with a variety of threats, Marine Cobras would need to be able to carry a much wider range of weapons than their more narrowly-focussed Army cousins. Those decisions were to prove crucial in Cobra development. The aircraft was to be designated AH-1J.

The political in-fighting that surrounded this acquisition is beyond the scope of this narrative, save to record that whilst continuing to press for the twin engine machine (which Bell were

30th November 1974.
Nothing toned-down about
this 'J' about to come aboard
the USS Vancouver (LPD-
2) off Palawan Island in the
Philppines. (*USNAM*)

AH-1J 157772 served in the MARHUK operation and went on to see Deployment in Desert Storm before finally retiring in 1990. (*USNAM*)

more than happy to provide, but which utilized a politically sensitive Canadian engine, and was expensive for such a small production run) the USMC reluctantly accepted a reduced total of thirty-eight 'standard' Army G Model aircraft finally allowed for in the FY 69 budget.

In February 1969, the first USMC Cobras were handed over by Bell and sent straight to Hunter Army Airfield where they were to be used to qualify increasing numbers of Marine pilots on the Cobra. Three months later, out of a class of thirty-nine, the four Marine pilots on the course graduated in the first four places.

The Command Chronology for VMO-2 for the month of April records laconically that, 'The first Marine Corps AH-1G in Vietnam went operational 18 April 1969'. The Mission followed a week of test flights and was a MEDEVAC escort flown by Major Donald E. P. Miller (later to become Commanding General 3rd MAW) with 1st Lieutenant Tommy L. James in the front seat. It was to be the first of many. The arrival of the first Cobras aboard USAF Douglas C-133 Cargomasters at Da Nang was recorded by 'Leatherneck' Magazines' reporter, SSgt P. L. Thompson. At the conclusion of an article reporting their enthusiastic acceptance by the hard-pressed Marines, Thompson speculated that the Cobra, like the F4U Corsair before it, may well have 'the soul to become legend 20 years hence' – his prophesy was to prove entirely correct, albeit a little out on the timing.

During the ensuing months the aircraft continued to give a good account of themselves, hampered by the Army communications fit and the consequent difficulty in obtaining spares. The Marines nevertheless took to the aircraft exactly as their Army counterparts had. It still needed a bigger gun, and of course whilst acceptable for Vietnam the lack of a rotor brake made shipboard operations something for another day, but there was no denying the thing had potential and, being Marines, they exploited it to the full, flying their Cobras higher, lower, faster and more aggressively than their initial (Army) training had envisaged.

Matters were in fact already in hand. At the same time that VMO-2 was deploying its first aircraft, Bell was flying the first prototype 212 for the Canadians. This Huey derivative featured the same TwinPac engine that was planned for the J Model, and the economics began to look better. Politically things were moving too. Following the Tet offensive the Marine Corps resorted to a persuasive argument known as the 'attrition buy'. Roughly it ran, 'If we have to buy the aircraft anyway (to make up combat losses) they might as well be the ones we want'. The ones they wanted were twin engine Hueys and twin engine Cobras.

A large order for 212s from the Canadians finally broke the political and economic log jam. The USMC eventually procured the 212 as the UH-1N and the engines it shared with the J Model were therefore no longer a problem as the Marines could also play the 'commonality' card.

Such was the pace of deliveries that the unveiling of new types was becoming something of a routine at Fort Worth, but the ceremony that accompanied the official hand-over of the first AH-1J to its proud owners on a windy day in October 1969 was something more. It was the point at which the Cobra family diverged on two very different paths.

The sleek machine, gleaming in its fresh coat of FS14097 'Marine Green' on Bell's flight line that day was a great leap in capability from the original Cobra. Few present however, could have imagined that over forty years later its descendants would still be defending front-line Marines and still be sharing a remarkable symbiosis with the UH-1N as their 'Yankee' and 'Zulu' variants enter a service that may well see the 'interim' Cobra exceed sixty years at the sharp end.

The AH-1J described

The AH-1J was structurally unchanged from the G Model save for the new engine installation. The two engines neatly packaged into what the manufacturers referred to as a 'TwinPac' was officially designated T400-CP-400 and offered a 400shp increase in power over the original T53 of the G Model.

As the rotor and drive system were retained almost unchanged the 'J' was transmission limited (which meant that the engine could produce more power than the drive train was designed to handle). This very useful margin gave the 'J' the ability to hover on one engine and permitted more flexibility when flying in 'hot and high' conditions. Marginally heavier empty than the 'G', the J Models retained a 10,000lb gross weight.

Designed from the outset with shipboard operations in mind the 'J' had the long-awaited rotor brake as well as appropriately naval avionics and radios. Critical components in some areas had also to be changed from magnesium to aluminium as saline corrosion was a very real problem. This too would stand the Cobra in good stead in the future.

As far as weapons are concerned the 'J' also marked a milestone as the first Cobra variant to mount the M-197 20mm turret gun. The standard wing stores capability of the earlier version remained but was quickly expanded to cover a much wider variety of ordnance than the Army machines, a reflection of the rather more diverse missions that Marine Cobras would be called upon to perform. The Marines eventually cleared the Cobra for virtually every weapon in the inventory that it could actually lift. (This even included 'iron' bombs, although this author has yet to speak to anyone who ever actually dropped one in anger!)

This requirement for 'droppable' (as opposed to merely jettisonable) stores led to later machines having the standard inboard weapon pylons replaced with distinctive outboard canted units to ensure clearance of the skids. Together with a ballistic canopy jettison system these were eventually retrofitted to the entire fleet, (adding another 100lb or so to the empty weight). Other than details of equipment and the later addition of a jammer and chaff/flare dispensers, the basic J Model served the Marine Corps unchanged into the 1990s.

In at the (very) deep end

Unlike the G Models which had required no pre-service testing the 'J' was a 'new' aircraft. Four aircraft thus went to 'Pax River' (Patuxent River Naval Air Station, Maryland) in July 1970 for trials, with the next seven arriving at New River in North Carolina for crew and maintenance training in September, still lacking some components that were yet to be installed by Bell.

In January the following year, as preparations were made to deploy the first 'J's to Vietnam, 1st Lieutenant J. W. Gallo of HMA-367 was celebrating becoming the first Marine aviator to complete 1,000 hours on the AH-1G. HMA-367 was shortly to begin participation in Operation 'Dewey Canyon', and on 8 February turned its attention to the huge incursion into Laos known as 'Lam Son 719'.

The combat evaluation of the J Model was to prove the most severe of tests. Four 'J's were airlifted directly to Da Nang and quickly deployed to Marble Mountain. Lam Son was to see some of the most intense fighting of the war, the four 'J's expending vast amounts of ammunition and ordnance in the process and more than proving the worth of the 20mm gun.

Later, use of the 'J' in Vietnam was to validate its design ability to operate from offshore platforms, including the unprecedented MARHUK (MARine HUnter-Killer) interdiction of Hon La anchorage in North Vietnam, and Operation 'Frequent Wind' the last desperate evacuation of Saigon. The AH-1J thus also gained the sad distinction of being the last US combat aircraft out of Vietnam.

There were only sixty-seven J Models built for the USMC, as production was switched to the AH-1T 'Improved Sea Cobra' for the rest of the batch. Because it was not economical to re-manufacture the J Models to 'T' configuration, they actually went on to serve the USMC for many more years in the training and reserve squadrons. When Operation 'Desert Storm' was initiated in 1990, both Reserve Squadrons HMA-775 and HMA-773 deployed their fully operational 'J's to back up the 'T' and 'W'-equipped squadrons.

This was to prove their swansong, almost all being retired in the early 1990s as the fleet transitioned to an all AH-1W force, most going in to storage at Davis Monthan AFB, others to museums. The very last 'J' produced, Bu 159227, had spent its entire service as a test and evaluation machine at Patuxent River Naval Air Station, where it continued to serve until 1997. Since then, it has been preserved there in 'honourable retirement', a testament to a type that was to prove the progenitor of all subsequent Marine Cobras.

AH-1J 157788 was bailed to Bell for demonstration to the Shah of Iran. So successful was it that the largest ever export order for Cobras was placed. In this author's opinion this shot of '88' in formation with a Huey as the cloud builds over Fort Worth is one of the best Cobra pictures ever taken. (*Bell via Mike Verier*)

Old and new colours. These two HMLAT-303 AH-1Js basking in the midday heat at Camp Pendleton in 1987 show the transition from the Vietnam-era green to the three-colour scheme then coming into service. The nearest aircraft is 157762 which was one of the first Js in Vietnam. It served in the 1972 MARHUK operation and went on to see action in Desert Storm in 1990, finally retiring in 1991 – a true warhorse. (*Mike Verier*)

Pictured at MCAS New River in 1989 resplendent in its new Camo scheme, AH-1J 157768 was serving with the East-Coast squadron HMLA-167 'Warriors' as 'TV/12'. (*Mike Verier*)

AH-1J 'TV/12' hover-taxies away from the Warriors' flight line at New River in 1987. This view shows to advantage that the twin-engine Cobra retained the slender frontal aspect of the G Model it was derived from. (*Mike Verier*)

Introduced with the J Model was the 'canted' inboard pylon unique to 'Marine' Cobras. This was to allow 'droppable' stores to clear the skids. (The Army had no requirement for gravity weapons and a simple 'kicker' was sufficient if stores had to be jettisoned in emergency). (*Mike Verier*)

This AH-1J, 150214, belonged to HMLA-367 'Scarface' Camp Pendleton's resident squadron at the time. The late 1980s were a time of change for the USMC and the new Whisky Cobras can be seen in the heat haze. (*Mike Verier*)

This freshly-painted AH-1J, 15788 'QT/431', was serving with HMLAT-303 at Pendleton. (*Mike Verier*)

Marine Cobras participated in many weapon trials. Here an AH-1J qualifies the HellFire as part of the 'Supercobra' programme that would see the weapon adopted for the AH-1W. (*Bell via Mike Verier*)

Also supporting the W programme this AH-1J, 147769, totes a live Sidewinder. Note the 'warts' visible on the 'doghouse' which appear to be a laser detection rig as fitted to Army AH-1F Cobras. (HMLA-167 via *Mike Verier*)

As the J models were deployed the surviving Gs were put to other use. At least two served with the Test Pilot School, wearing the full 'peacetime' glossy green and full-insignia paint job. (*USNAM via Ray Wilhite*)

The TPS was a joint service operation and this G Model qualifies as one of very few Cobras to wear 'NAVY' titles. (*USNAM via Ray Wilhite*)

The AH-1Js served the Marines for many years, finally going to the two reserve squadrons as the fleet received AH-1Ws. On the eve of their retirement they nevertheless put on full warpaint and headed for the Gulf to back up the hard-pressed front-line squadrons involved in Desert Storm. This aircraft is from HMLA-775 and is sitting on the alert pad at FOB 'Lonesome Dove' 'somewhere in the desert'. (*Via DeHart*)

Chapter 7

A Royal Legacy
The brief reign of the Kings

The 'KingCobra' has remained a little known project primarily because only two aircraft were built. This belies the importance of the programme in terms of the effect it was to have on Cobra development.

The decision to proceed with the construction of two flying prototypes was partially prompted by the difficulties that the much vaunted AH–56 AAFSS was running into, Bell was not alone in the industry in suspecting that cost and complexity escalations would eventually kill the Cheyenne and had initiated studies into the requirements of a second generation attack helicopter. Sikorsky were also working on a Private Venture AAFSS contender, the S–67 Blackhawk.

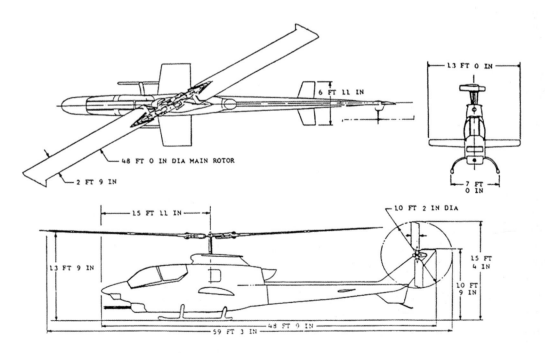

Bell drawing showing the basic dimensions of the Model 309 KingCobra. Note the tail rotor shown on the port side. (*Bell*)

Sikorsky also pitched for an alternative to AAFSS. Their solution, the S-67, being a much larger machine that could also carry an infantry squad. As can be seen from this view it bore a remarkable similarity to the Soviet 'Hind'. The prototype crashed not long after this photo was taken during the Farnborough Air Show in September 1974. (*Dick Ward*)

During the period 1969 to 1971, a veritable plethora of design ideas emerged from the Projects Office, some were destined to go no further than models or drawings, others reached the hardware stage and were test-flown. In any event Bell designers felt that they could not only offer the Army a useful increase in capability at modest cost, but, whilst they were at it, could add all of these improvements to the twin-engine variants, which would open up further sales potential, primarily with the Marines.

In order to more fully demonstrate these improved capabilities, Bell teamed-up with a number of suppliers to finance the two KingCobras. This was essential as the airframe itself, whilst of primary importance, was only the vehicle into which had to be integrated the various sub-systems that would make the whole thing viable.

In January 1971, as Joe Gallo was celebrating 1,000 hours on the G Model Cobra, and before the J Models had seen their first combat, Bell decided to go ahead with the construction of the two 'second generation' demonstrators. Less than nine months later, on 10 September, the first aircraft flew. On the 28th, the appropriately registered N309J was publicly unveiled to the world's press and a high-ranking military delegation.

The presentation was spectacular, Gene Colvin, Bell's project pilot for the 309, held the aircraft in the hover a mile-and-a-half or so from the gathering shielded by trees, and completely unseen. At the appropriate moment he performed a 100 foot pop-up, diving towards the display area to arrive from behind the 200 or so invited guests. A steep, maximum power climb and wingover (what would now be called a 'return to target' manoeuvre) was followed by a high speed simulated gun-run on the crowd centre before a 270° turn brought the King to the hover for a '360' that allowed them to appreciate the elegant lines of the new gunship. The demonstration concluded with a maximum power vertical climb out, the wing-over at the top followed by a landing in front of the suitably impressed audience.

For the press members present it was a superb display of agility. That the 'target' had at no time been out of sight of the aircraft was a point not lost on the military personnel either. After shutdown a presentation of the aircraft's capabilities was made, backed up by hanger displays

A standard G Model Cobra alongside the first KingCobra (N309J). At this stage the standard wings are still fitted but the longer cross-tubes and wide-chord blades are very apparent. (*Bell*)

which included all the sub-contractors, and a full scale mock-up of an AAFSS configured aircraft. During this, the Marine Corps people present were provided with an eighteen page brochure describing a whole range of optional improvements that would enhance their AH-1Js.

As an aside, also carried out that day was a small ceremony in which Bell's first proof of concept type, the Sioux Scout, was turned over to General William J. Maddox, director of Army Aviation, for permanent display at the Army Aviation Museum Fort Rucker, where it can be seen to this day.

The number one aircraft whilst clearly displaying its Cobra origins was a very different animal to its forbearer. Structurally it had a strengthened airframe to cope with the higher gross weights, and a lengthened tail boom, complete with new ventral fin to both improve directional stability and make provision for the increased (48 foot) diameter of the rotor; the main rotor featured a new high lift aerofoil section developed by German aerodynamicist Professor Franz X. Wortman. Compared to the standard blade it had wider chord and an asymmetric section. It also had what (at the time) were very odd-looking forward swept tips designed to delay the onset of compressibility and reduce the very distinctive thudding beat that heralds the arrival of a Huey or Cobra.

In order to cope with the increased thrust available, the uprated dynamics and drive train from the already tested Model 211 Huey Tug were used, with power coming from the standard T400-CP-400 'TwinPac' as used on J Models (although it was envisioned that growth models would provide an increase in power from the 1800shp of that model to 1970shp, and ultimately to 2400shp).

The 'King' had also grown a large bulged housing under the belly, and a prominent nasal extension carrying the 'visionics' turret. Both in fact illustrated the Bell doctrine of utilizing existing hardware. The bulge was to house a new high-capacity ammunition drum for the 20mm turret. The drum was a shortened but otherwise standard unit from the General Dynamics F-111, whilst the nose turret was actually the bottom half of the AH-56 Cheyenne system. Unlike Lockheed, Bell had decided not to use the complete turntable mounted sight and seat (which could track targets through a full 360 degrees) primarily to save weight and complexity, but it had also been reported that gunners using the system had been in third degree vertigo by the time they had tracked 180 degrees, due to the disparity between the visual and physical inputs they were receiving!

A stabilized sight incorporated a range of optics and sensors whilst a low–light TV provided the pilot with an independent real–time image directly forward when the gunner was engaging a target with the turreted system. All of which added up to a capability for 'around the clock' operation, available over a decade before the men at the front line actually began to receive it in the shape of the AH-64 .

It was also envisaged that the weapons capability be greatly enhanced. Encounters in Vietnam with an enemy capable of deploying heavy calibre AAA and heat–seeking anti–aircraft missiles had already indicated that NOE (Nap Of the Earth) tactics and greater stand–off ranges would be the order of the day if an attack helicopter was to stand any chance of survival in the anti–armour role. The demonstration aircraft retained the standard FFARs, and the proven 20mm M-197 turret, but prophetically it also sported 'boiler plate' mock–ups of what became the standard TOW launchers. Also foreseen was the wing–tip mounting of self–defence (i.e. air–to–air) missiles such as 'Stinger' and provision for the advanced 'Hellfire' anti–armour weapons.

The Marine Corps were enthusiastic about any increase in capabilities that an 'improved Sea Cobra' could offer, but in the light of the omnipresent budgetary strictures that they worked under, knew that at best they would only be able to afford parts of the system. No such financial restraint applied to the Shah of Iran however. Just before Christmas the same year, a contract was signed for the largest ever export order for helicopters; the aircraft specified incorporated a number of features validated by the KingCobra.

The 'Army' (single engine) version of the 'King', N309K, did not fly until some four months after its twin engine sister ship. Structurally it was identical to the number one airframe (both aircraft were built to production, not fabrication, type drawings and had a high utilization of AH-1 jigs and tools in assembly, demonstrating that a retro–fit programme was entirely feasible if required).

Powerplant for the number two ship was a Lycoming T55-I-7C. Capable of 2,850shp it was flat–rated to give 2,000shp at 4,000 feet on a 95°F day. This meant that the 'King' could hover OGE (out of ground effect) under these conditions at take–off weight (around 14,000lb compared to the 9,500lb of the 'G' version) a significant improvement that brought 'hot and high' operations well within its capabilities.

The single–engine machine was intended to be fully instrumented and equipped. It is worth looking at the sub–systems in detail as some of the capabilities demonstrated were not to fully

The second KingCobra prototype, N309K, as first flown. As was later to prove valuable, the airframes could have either single or twin-engine 'power packs' interchanged. (*Bell*)

Published here for the first time, this previously lost sequence show the 'Army' configured N309K during gun trials at Fort Hood in 1973. Head-on, the dramatic increase in wing span can clearly be seen. The so-called 'Big Wing' held more fuel whilst also moving the stores pylons clear of the skids. (*George Nicholas*)

N309K's wing was also to be a 'six-point' mount with four conventional pylons and tip-mounted 'Redeye' or 'Stinger' missiles for self-defence. (*George Nicholas*)

mature for nearly two decades. In the late 1960s and early 1970s only the entirely fictional crew of the Starship Enterprise had 'sensors' of sufficient reliability and accuracy to be of real use to the military!

Aside from power plant suppliers the major sub contractors were:-

General Electric: Primary fire control system and gunners' sighting station. Laser range finder, HUD, and computer. (Burlington Vermont handled the 20/30mm gun system as well)
Litton Guidance and Control Systems: Inertial navigator and fire control
Sperry Univac: Helmet sighting system
Dalmo Victor: Pilots night vision system(LLLTV)
Honeywell: Radar altimeter
Itek: Radar warning system
Texas Instruments: FLIR night vision system
Hughes Aircraft: TOW Missile system

Heart of the KingCobra weapon system was the Stabilised Multi-sensor Sight (SMS) which combined with a fire-control computer and displayed both through the gunner/co-pilot's TSU and the pilot's new HUD. Both crewmen had helmet sights, slaved to the turret gun and SMS, to assist rapid target acquisition.

The SMS featured a stabilised mirror and optical bench. Mounted on the bench were day and night optics, a neodynium laser ranger/designator, FLIR and TOW missile tracker. On the 'King' it displayed a 2x or 6x magnification in both the gunner's eyepiece and, if required, on the pilot's HUD. Operating in the far infrared region it could, give a high resolution picture in total darkness. Alternatively it could be used by day to penetrate light fog or smoke and reveal camouflaged vehicles invisible to the naked eye.

Independent of this system, the pilot also had a fixed forward looking LLTV camera which was mounted in the sail above and behind his head. This gave real-time imagery which was again superimposed on his HUD and greatly aided low-level night flight. Provided with a wide range automatic light control, the camera had a useful operating span which ran from starlight to bright sunlight.

Navigation centred on the Litton inertial navigation system (INS) which provided the pilot with precise current location whilst giving bearing and range-to information for any of up to sixteen pre-set destinations. The INS also supplied primary attitude reference to the gunner, the fire control computer, and the TOW electronics. Other equipment included VHF/FM homer, ADF and IFF transponders, a gyro magnetic compass and a radar altimeter with low-altitude warning.

The 'King' therefore had an unprecedented ability to find and attack its target in the most adverse conditions. The communications suite was also extremely complete covering UHF/FM, VHF/AM, and VHF/FM with provision for a high frequency SSB radio and the KY-28 secure voice system.

As originally conceived the KingCobra was to feature a number of items that were either not proceeded with or which fell by the wayside during development. This has led over the years to some disparity between published descriptions of the aircraft and the actuality.

Chief amongst these is the so-called 'big wing'. Of 13 foot (3.95m) span and much greater chord, the new wing was intended to be 'wet' and thereby increase fuel capacity by some 50% to 2,300lb. It also provided greater clearance for the weapon pylons, which would no longer be

As N309K starts-up, the 'visionics' turret can be seen mounted under the extended nose. This unit was in fact the lower half of that designed for the AH-56 Cheyenne. (*George Nicholas*)

In this view, N309K's greatly increased wing chord can readily be seen. The orange panels indicate a 'Test' aircraft. (*George Nicholas*)

sighted directly over the landing skids, and in so doing make room for a Jamming pod (possibly AN/ALQ 87) which was to be pylon mounted to the 'corner' of the fuselage between the skids. Bell drawings show either side depending on their date, but port would be more logical as it would be less likely to conflict crew access on that side. Hardpoints were to be incorporated at the tips providing a further two weapon stations intended for self defence missiles such as 'Redeye'.

Concurrent with the introduction of the 'big wing', the tail rotor was to be returned to the port side of the fin. Until recently the only known photographs showed what appeared to be a mock-up wing fitted to the 'twin' KingCobra (N309J). Despite many years of research this author had never come across anyone at Bell who remembered the wing flying and indeed it was widely believed by many interviewees that as development had not been pursued it had never gone beyond the mock-up stage.

Reproduced here for the first time is a recently discovered sequence of photos showing that the wing *was* flown, on the single engine airframe N309K. It would appear that all the photos were taken on the same day, probably at Fort Hood during gun trials, and they may represent the only surviving images of the fully AAFSS-configured KingCobra.

What is certain is that this aircraft subsequently crashed and was written off; its very short life presumably accounting for the lack of pictures and knowledge of it, even within Bell. With Army trials looming a decision was made to convert the other aircraft which had its TwinPac replaced with a Lycoming unit so that it could take part in the fly-off against the Sikorsky submission and the AH-56. The change of power plant also served to illustrate the adaptability of the design. This unexpected turn of events effectively terminated development of the big wing at the time.

Ultimately the Army decided that none of these aircraft would fit the bill, cancelled the Cheyenne and embarked on the AAH contest instead. What remains of the KingCobra now reside in rather forlorn storage at Fort Rucker's museum, giving no indication of its pivotal role in the Cobra story.

Almost everything about the KingCobra found its way onto later Cobra variants however. The uprated engine, transmission and TOW capability formed the basis of the Iranian 'J', and the USMC's AH-1T which also incorporated the bigger rotor and lengthened fuselage.

Essentially then the KingCobra was the basis of the 'Iranian J International', and the de-facto prototype AH-1T 'Improved SeaCobra'. In due course the 'T' was itself improved to become the AH-1W 'Whisky' and ultimately grown again to become today's 'Zulu'.

Amongst its many improvements, the new AH-1Z features a long-span, 'wet', six point, wing. All told an impressive legacy for two proof-of-concept prototypes that flew over forty years ago.

The photographer stands his ground as N309K transitions away. Unlike the rather chunkier AH-1T that it sired, the KingCobra exhibited considerable elegance of line. (*George Nicholas*)

Above: N309K's wide-chord blades, if not the experimental tips, gave a very stable ride and were subsequently adopted for the Tango Model and (inset) Close-up view of the unique forward-swept tip of N309K's Wortmann rotor. Not carried forward at the time, such aerodynamic improvements are common nowadays. (*George Nicholas*)

Left: N309K's beefed-up tail boom and wide span wings are very apparent in this view. (*George Nicholas*)

The basic Cobra design already featured a side-stick cyclic in the front cockpit, so finding room for the sighting system presented no difficulty. Note the 'mission grip' sight controls, a feature of today's Zulu Model. (*George Nicholas*)

The rear cockpit on the other hand was virtually unchanged from production Cobras. 'Test' instruments are mounted in the orange-painted panel. (*George Nicholas*)

Whilst the gun barrels are changed, the enlarged wing and ventral bulge can be seen more clearly. The orange painted box above the wing is a camera mounting. (*George Nicholas*)

Out on the range shell cases can be seen falling away from the M-197 20mm gun. This was taken unchanged from the AH-1J already in production. N309K was badly damaged in a crash soon after these photos were taken. Consequently they may be the only surviving images of the Big Wing 309. (*George Nicholas*)

Chapter 8

Sea Snake Evolution
Marines get more muscle

The arrival of the AH-1J was a huge boost to the USMC and it quickly proved to be an excellent aircraft. The Vietnam scenario was not typical of what could be expected in the future however.

For most of the conflict, engagements had been against Infantry within visual range, mostly in daylight and with rifle-calibre guns or short-range rockets. Towards the end of the war the arrival in theatre of Soviet SA-7 'Strella' shoulder-launched surface-to-air missiles (first generation MPADS – Man-Portable Air-Defense Systems) and the difficulty Cobras had in killing tanks amply confirmed that improvements would be needed.

The first KingCobra, N309J was the de-facto prototype for the AH-1T 'Improved Sea Cobra'. (*Bell via Mike Verier*)

The TOW anti-tank missile, with a range in excess of 3,000 metres and a useful secondary ability against bunkers and other hard targets, was an improvement that both the Army and the Marines wanted for their Cobras. A night/adverse weather capability was also highly desired but delivering it with the technology of the day would take a little longer.

Meanwhile the faltering AAFSS programme had resulted in the two KingCobra (model 309) prototypes described in Chapter 7. Intended to demonstrate the potential of an upgrade to existing airframes, the 309 featured a new transmission, more power, a new rotor, TOW main armament and an advanced night vision/target acquisition capability. Whilst the largest potential market would be the Army, Bell kept one eye firmly on a possible buy for the Marines, and the first KingCobra to fly featured an up-rated TwinPac engine installation.

In the event the KingCobra *per se* did not proceed into production for the Army, who went back to the drawing board and began the Advanced Attack Helicopter (AAH) programme competition. The Marines, with new 'J's still being delivered, opted for further consideration.

Bell's investment was not to be wasted however. When they proposed an improved J Model for the Iranians it featured the power plant, transmission and TOW armament qualified during the KingCobra programme. The Iranians ordered 202 'J Internationals' in 1972. Eight also went to South Korea. At the time they were the most potent Cobras in service anywhere.

Nothing daunted, Bell went on to pitch for the AAH contest with the Model 409, the YAH-63. The significance of this seemingly unconnected event to the Cobra's evolution would only become apparent later.

The USMC could therefore have simply upgraded their aircraft to the same configuration as the Iranians. The Corps however felt that a heavier and more capable aircraft would be needed, albeit the 'J International' (sometimes also referred to in Bell publications as J+) would be

AH-1T 159228, the first AH-1T, was built as a 'slick' without the TOW provision. (*Bell via Mike Verier*)

This overhead view of 159228 shows to advantage the wide chord rotor adopted with the AH-1T. (*Bell via Mike Verier*)

159229, the second AH-1T, was provided with the full TOW/M-65 and was used for weapon qualification. (*Bell via Mike Verier*)

This view of 159229 clearly shows the fuselage extension which has moved the cockpit forward and lengthened the skids. (*Bell via Mike Verier*)

The first AH-1T, 159228, was retained at Bell for trials of early FLIR systems. The equipment was still bulky and necessitated considerable modification to the nose. (*Bell via Mike Verier*)

Such were the improvements offered by the AH-1T that production of the remaining Js on order was switched to the new model. The early Ts were delivered as 'slicks' to get them into service. They were all eventually fitted with TOW. (*Bell via Mike Verier*)

This immaculate AH-1T was photographed at China Lake in October 1981 for Sidewinder trials. The USMC qualified the aircraft for everything in the inventory that the Cobra could actually lift making it an extremely versatile platform and contributing to its longevity. (*DoD/S Wyatt*)

The additional power of the AH-1T meant a greater ordnance load. Seen here is a Zuni pod inboard, a 100 gallon fuel tank outboard, and the first iteration of the 'six-point wing' with a Sidewinder mounted overwing. The SideArm anti-radar missile (which had a different seeker head) was also qualified for the Cobra. (*Bell via Mike Verier*)

Much heavier than the first-generation Cobras the AH-1T had an altogether more substantial look to it. This aircraft, 160812, was sadly lost in Grenada in 1982. (*Bell via Mike Verier*)

the baseline for development. At a time of post-Vietnam budgetary strictures, the advantage the Marines had over the Army was that effectively the Shah of Iran had already paid for all development and qualification to that point. Consequently, when the next-generation AH-1T 'Improved SeaCobra' was finally announced it proved to have a remarkable similarity to the KingCobra.

For reasons now lost to history these two AH-1T airframes were delivered in what appears to be 'Israeli Tan'. They participated in camouflage trials at Camp Pendleton at some point, but neither the base colour nor the exotic camouflage were adopted. (see colour section in Appendix 2). (*Bell via Mike Verier*)

Introduced on the AH-1T (and retro-fitted to the 'J') was the AN/ALE-39 chaff/flare dispenser designed to give protection against the increasing threat of heat-seeking missiles. The rough grey coating is called 'Flexfram'. It is an epoxy coating to protect the aircraft skin from the efflux of rockets fired. (*Mike Verier*)

AH-1Ts saw considerable combat. This example from HMM-261 was pictured on the USS Saipan in 1990. (*DoD*)

At the end of the eighties the arrival of the Whisky in the fleet signalled a progressive switch to the 'new' three-colour camouflage, 'T's and 'J's adopting it as they went for maintenance. This AH-1T carries a Sidewinder acquisition round inboard and two TOW tubes outboard. (*USMC*)

In their final years in service the Tangos succumbed to the inevitable Grey scheme. This AH-1T, 160819, 'HF/17' is from HMLA-269 'Gun Runners' home-based at MCAS New River. The photograph was taken on the USS *Nassau* (LHA-4) during the Desert Storm operation. Historically this was the only time that J, T, W and F model Cobras were operational in the same war zone. (*USN*)

The USMC works hard and their aircraft don't remain pristine for long. This battered AH-1T example was pictured at Camp Pendleton. (*USMC*)

Old Cobras never die… 160805 was built as an AH-1T more than half of them survived to be converted to AH-1Ws, subsequently upgraded to NTS aircraft. Seen here emerging from the paint shop at New River in 2011 this example from HMLA-167 'Warriors' looks set to carry on for some time yet. (*Mike Verier*)

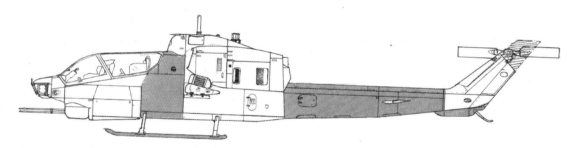

The AH-1T model represented a major airframe change from first-generation Cobras. The larger main rotor meant extending the tailboom. This was balanced by a one-foot extension to the forward fuselage which moved the cross-tubes and required longer skids. Finally the tail fin was truncated to reduce overall length, this was compensated by the increased keel area below the tail. (*Mike Verier*)

The Tango described

It was decided that the last two 'J' airframes of the first batch would be converted on the production line to serve as prototypes for the Improved SeaCobra. The first aircraft (c/n 26068 BuNo 159228) was started in 1975, flying for the first time on 20 May 1976 as a 'Slick' (ie without the TOW fit). The second (c/n 26069 BuNo 159229) was delivered fully TOW-configured some time later.

The conversion was extensive. The AH-1T featured a much bigger and heavier main rotor blade (48 foot span with chord increased from 27 inches to 33 inches). This necessitated extending the tail boom by inserting a section aft of the main fuselage (resulting in the distinctive 'kink' that 'T's and subsequent Models display). Balance was maintained by adding a 12 inch plug forward of the wing root which moved the cockpit and front cross-tubes forward, necessitating longer skids. The space created was used for additional fuel and avionics.

Unlike the 309, the tail fin was truncated to keep height and overall length down, the missing keel area replaced by a compensatory ventral fin. To match the main rotor a new, more powerful, tail rotor was provided and both the main and tail rotor hubs were improved. The hydraulic system was improved and made more damage resistant and a completely new transmission (essentially the Bell Model 214 transmission) handled the increased power from the 1,970shp (1470kw) Pratt & Whitney Canada T400-WV-402 TwinPac. Finally the Stability Control Augmentation System (SCAS) was upgraded and improved.

Along with the all-important TOW provision came the M65 Telescopic Sight Unit (TSU) and another novel feature, the Helmet Sight System (HSS). HSS provided both crewmen with a helmet-mounted monocle sight which could be slaved to the TSU and the gun turret. Thus if the pilot was committed to an attack with the fixed (wing mounted) stores the front seater was able to scan for off-axis threats. (*vice versa* if the 'gunner' was head-down on the TSU). As the gun was pointing where he looked reaction time was very fast.

Originally intended as a 'quick-look' system, HSS actually proved to be remarkably accurate. Active defence against heat-seeking missiles consisted of an AN/ALQ-144 IRCM Jammer mounted on the Dog House aft of the main rotor, and a pair of AN/ALE-39 chaff/flare dispensers, one mounted above each wing. Passive defences included the low-reflectance paint and RWR 'pimples' at the nose and tail.

The opportunity was also taken to address some in-service deficiencies that had surfaced; the time needed for an engine change for instance had been an issue on the 'J' and Bell made particular effort to reduce it, demonstrating that two men could remove an engine in 20 minutes.

In order to permit the 'indiscriminate' loading of stores the wing attachment points were strengthened so that any combination of fuel, rocket or missile stores could be accommodated, asymmetrically if required.

All-up weight rose from the 'J's 10,000lb to 14,000lb. The heavier main rotor also gave a very smooth ride making the 'T' an excellent weapon platform.

The 'Tango' was amongst the first aircraft programmes to have to conform to stringent Naval Air Systems Command (NAVAIR) performance requirements with regard to reliability and maintenance standards as well as the more obvious requirements. An arduous NPE (Navy Preliminary Evaluation) phase demonstrated that the attention Bell paid to feedback from the squadrons had paid off. The 'T' demonstrated an unprecedented servicing to flight hour ratio of 0.0225 (at a time when many military aircraft routinely required tens of hours per flight hour).

The promise shown by the AH-1T was such that only sixty-seven (of the planned 124) AH-1Js were delivered, production being switched to the AH-1T. The first machines began coming off the assembly lines at Fort Worth by mid-1977, and in May 1978 the first of thirty-three 'Slicks' began arriving at Camp Pendleton. A follow-on batch of twenty-four 'T(TOW)'s began deliveries in January 1979. Eventually all 'T's were brought up to TOW standard and the distinction was dropped.

During this period Bell made a paper proposal to the Iranians for a 'T+' using the T700 engines first flown on the unsuccessful Model 409 (YAH-63). Proposed to the Iranians at the same time was the Model 214ST Huey derivative. The engines and transmission were to be common to both aircraft. Whilst neither project was to proceed at the time, the modern reader will recognise the birth of a concept that was to reach fruition with the AH-1Z and UH-1Y over three decades later.

Earlier work for the Iranians had already benefited the USMC's Cobras. This included a 'nodalised' gunner's seat, an improved recoil compensator for the turret gun, and a stabilised sight. Collectively these measures dramatically reduced vibration and enabled effective use of the TSU out to the full range of the 20mm gun without the unfortunate gunner suffering a black eye!

Sensing further Iranian-funded development potential, the Marines agreed to bail the last production 'T' (BuNo 161022) back to Bell for T700 development work. Unfortunately delivery coincided almost exactly with the fall of the Shah and the abrupt end of US involvement with Iran. As it transpired however, it too proved to be a wise investment.

The Marines made no secret of the fact that they desired Apaches to replace their Cobras. Notwithstanding, they agreed to allow qualification of the T-700 engine for the AH-1T to continue on a low-key basis. Ultimately the cost of 'marinising' the AH-64 was considered prohibitive and in 1981 Congress formally refused to countenance their procurement – despite a determined sales drive by the manufacturers with dramatic brochure illustrations depicting a navalised 'Gray Thunder' lifting off a heaving deck toting four AGM-84 Harpoons.

Nothing daunted, the Marines turned to Plan B – upgrading the Cobras. Once again the Snake was about to evolve into something bigger and more powerful.

A total of fifty-seven AH-1Ts were built for the USMC which turned out to be the sole customer. The 'Tangos' served with considerable distinction well into the 1990s, being involved in a number of conflicts around the world. Eventually they were not so much replaced as transformed. More than half of them survived to be upgraded to 'W' standard and quite a few consequently continue to serve today.

The Bell Whale

The mid-1970s were a time of great activity and innovation at Bell. Post Vietnam the US Army was re-focussing its mission and, following the demise of the AH-56, re-starting its search for the definitive second generation attack helicopter.

The resulting Advanced Attack Helicopter (AAH) competition was a prize major helicopter manufacturers were keen to win. Bell had offered the 309 KingCobra as an entirely practicable upgrade of the Cobra but the Army felt it wanted something bigger and better. Ultimately the two finalists were granted contracts to build prototypes for a competitive evaluation. Bell's entry was the model 409 which was allocated the designation YAH-63. Its competitor was the (then) Hughes Model 77 which became the YAH-64.

Designed to the same specification with the same engines and armament package, both aircraft were of course very similar. The major point of difference between the contenders was the rotor system, albeit there were also some fairly fundamental differences in design philosophy too.

Whilst Hughes went for a new-design, four blade, semi-rigid rotor, Bell stayed with their successful and combat-proven two-blade system. On the YAH-63 the 5ft 6in (15.7m) main rotor had a massive 3ft 6in (1.06m) chord to allow for twin-spar construction (to enable the blades to meet the requirement for tolerance of up to 23mm strikes).

Survivability was another key feature of the AAH specification and much attention was paid to battle damage resistance. The cockpit and other vulnerable areas were armoured and the airframe was designed so that even a direct hit in the ammunition bay would result in any explosion being directed out of the aircraft. The gear box featured flat helical gears again designed to survive battle-damage.

A unique feature of the gearbox was that the mast could be retracted down in to it so that the aircraft could more easily be transported by air with the minimum of dismantling. Getting the aircraft into a C-141 was further aided by a 'kneeling' undercarriage.

A wheeled undercarriage was a major departure from the Cobra's skids. The YAH-63 featured a nosewheel arrangement which improved both ground handling and the pilot's view when taxiing. This in turn flowed from the decision to reverse the traditional 'pilot' and 'gunner' tandem crew arrangement so successful on the Cobra.

In first-generation aircraft the gunner relied on direct-vision optics and had to be in the front. With the development of electronic vision devices this was no longer essential and the pilot could be moved to the front seat where he would be better-placed for 'nap-of-the-earth' flying. This feature was much-liked by all who flew the aircraft, many commenting on the improved view.

The YAH-63 also marked the first appearance of a 'flat-plate' canopy. Easier to manufacture and maintain than the 'curved' type it was also intended to reduce 'glint' that could betray the helicopter's presence on the battlefield at considerable distance.

Rather more controversially, Bell placed the turret gun in the extreme nose with the sighting 'visionics' below it, reversing the accepted practice. Their reasoning was sound enough, on the TOW Cobras the gun muzzles were immediately below the TSU 'bucket' which consequently sometimes suffered vibration and blast damage as well as being degraded by smoke and muzzle flash.

This was perfectly logical as an engineering solution (mast-mounted sights were still some years away) but it didn't find favour, possibly because the delicate electronics were now very near the ground and therefore harder to access for service in the field. Detractors argued that that the aircraft had to be 'more exposed' for the turret to have line of sight, but in reality either arrangement required the same amount of aircraft to be raised above the trees in order to bring the gun to bear. In the case of firing TOW missiles an extra 3 feet is hardly relevant at 3 kilometres from the target.

Bell built a mock-up, two flying prototypes and one ground-test airframe. The two flying airframes carried the serials 22246 and 22247 (as a piece of trivia the 'last three' numbers were the same as the two pre-production Cobras 15246 and 15247) Following testing and evaluation the YAH-64, later to become the Apache, was declared the winner, the YAH-63 programme being cancelled in December 1976. What had become affectionately known amongst the test crews as 'The Bell Whale' was seemingly consigned to a footnote in history. Today one surviving airframe (22247) languishes at Fort Rucker's museum.

Like everything Bell does however, the programmes lessons and developments were not wasted. The other significant link to the Cobra story was the first use by Bell of the T700 engine. An excellent powerplant it was a significant improvement on previous engines. After the 409 programme was terminated, qualification was continued on a bailed AH-1T, initially with Iranian production in mind, but ultimately to power the developed 'Whisky' and 'Zulu' models that continue in use to this day.

This overhead view possibly shows the most similarity between the model 409 and the winning AAH contender, the Apache. Unlike Hughes, Bell stayed with the two-blade rotor. It lacked the agility of the Hughes aircraft but was very stable. (*Bell via Mike Verier*)

Whilst the design logic was sound, it resulted in the YAH-63 having a very portly profile. It nevertheless pioneered some important features that were to prove relevant to future Cobras including the 'flat-plate canopy, and of course the T-700 engines that have proved so successful since. (*Bell via Ray Wilhite*)

The YAH-63 mock-up was presented with a number of markets in mind. This iteration, bearing the fake but helpful tail number '73409' bears a camouflage remarkably similar to a later USMC scheme, despite the 'UNITED STATES ARMY' legend. As was the fashion at the time the rotor blades were also camouflaged. (*Bell via Ray Wilhite*)

Head–on the YAH-63 looked very much the attack helicopter. (*Bell via Ray Wilhite*)

A year later, now marked '74409' sales in the Middle East were on everybody's mind and this 'desert' scheme emerged – possible the best the 409 ever looked. (*Bell via Mike Verier*)

Historic Cobras

161022 – a singular T

The last 'T' off the production line, BuNo 16122 was destined to be pivotal in Cobra development. Bailed to Bell in December 1979 to serve as a development airframe its first job was to qualify the T-700 engines in support of a proposed update for the Iranians (and at one time was known as the 'T+'). The USMC was happy to loan the aircraft as they would ultimately derive much benefit from a programme paid for by someone else. (Improvements to the Iranian 'J' models had already qualified the TOW missile, its associated sighting system and 'nodalised' gunner's seat – all improvements taken up for Marine Cobras).

The fall of the Shah in 1979 put paid to plans for licence production by an Iranian equivalent to Westlands or Agusta; the development effort however was not wasted.

The AH-1T 'Improved SeaCobra' was just such but lacking power to lift its considerable increase in weight it was marginal in some conditions. The Marines consequently coveted a 'marinised' AH-64 but were not going to get the funds from a parsimonious Congress. The improvement that new engines would bring to the Cobra fleet on the other hand would produce a aircraft with similar performance on a budget. Qualification was allowed to quietly continue.

Thus '22 continued in its role whilst a case was put together for a 'low cost upgrade' of the 'T' which would, amongst other things, bring supply chain and support cost savings as the T-700 was already in fleet service (H-60 SeaHawk).

Gradually the airframe morphed from a re-engined 'T' into the 'T+'. Effectively it became the prototype 'Whisky'. The one improvement that the USMC had to postpone for the 'Whisky' Cobra was a four blade rotor. Once again '22 was to be the development vehicle becoming the '4BW' (shorthand for 'four blade Whisky')

Once the rotor was qualified the aircraft again underwent modification to represent an operational '4BW' configuration, with improved sighting system and a six-station wing that allowed wingtip mounting of AIM-9 Sidewinder missiles. In this form it was shown at Farnborough in 1990.

This programme was eventually to lead to the much more ambitious 'H-1 Upgrade' and the development of the 'Zulu' model.

BuNo 161022 was refurbished and finally returned to the USMC as a 'Whisky' model, serving in Bosnia amongst other places. After such a long and distinguished career the old warhorse was finally written off in a crash at Camp Lejeune in May 1996 whilst serving with HMM-266 from MCAS New River, a sad end for a great aircraft.

Seen here in its original configuration AH-1T 161022 was bailed to Bell in order to qualify the T-700 engine for what was then a proposed 'Improved Iranian Cobra'. Had it proceeded it would have looked very much as seen here. The project was also sometimes referred to as the 'T+'. (*Bell via Mike Verier*)

Following the demise of the Shah of Iran it was decided to continue qualification of the engine installation and develop other improvements which could be retro-fitted to the USMC's AH-1T fleet. Discreetly the aircraft received a new paint job and the title 'Supercobra'. (*Bell via Mike Verier*)

Firing the mighty Zuni rockets generates potential problems with blast damage (overpressure) and engine surging from ingesting the exhaust gasses. Sidewinder, Hellfire and TOW missiles were fired. No problems were found. (*Bell via Mike Verier*)

With trials complete, 161022, was completely stripped down and refurbished. Whilst still unannounced 161022 had become the de-facto prototype for the AH-1W the first of which was by now under construction. (*Mike Verier*)

At one point this stunning scheme was applied in order to publicise the improvements that could be offered to the USMC by adoption of the new engine and other upgrades. (*Bell via Mike Verier*)

With the W qualification completed, 161022 was retained for further development work on the four-blade rotor. A significant improvement the Marines coveted but lacked the funds for. The new rotor was also a key technology for the forthcoming LHX competition. (*Bell via Mike Verier*)

The aircraft was treated to the then-current USMC three-colour scheme and quickly became known as the '4BW' (Four-blade Whisky). The new rotor fully lived up to expectations, the combination proving fully aerobatic as demonstrated here. (*Bell via Mike Verier*)

Shown at Farnborough Air Show with other improvements including the 'six-point' wing and what would become the NTS sighting upgrade, the 4BW was also offered to Germany to meet their anti-armour requirements. (*Mike Verier*)

Chapter 9

It's a Cobra Jim – But Not As We Know It……
Tango becomes Whisky

Cobra lineage may well have finished with the AH-1T had the USMC got Apaches. Funding however was not forthcoming, and the Corps was told it would have to continue with its Cobras, albeit augmented by forty-four previously-funded attrition replacements. Once again however the 'attrition buy' would prove a useful device for a service adept at getting the best from whatever opportunity presents itself.

The AH-1T, good though it was, was marginal on power in hot and high conditions. It was proposed therefore that the aircraft be re-engined using the T-700 – the same engine as the Apache and the SH-60 Sea Hawk and thus already in the inventory. This, the persuasive argument ran, was a low–cost/low risk proposal as the engine had also already been

Newly delivered around 1987 to HMLA-267 'Stingers' at MCAS Camp Pendleton, this AH-1W models the Sidewinder rails that gave the Cobra a serious air-to-air capability. Also clearly visible are the bulged cheeks that created more space in the ammunition bay. (*Mike Verier*)

Just leaving the fuel pits, this HMLA-367 'Scarface' AH-1W carries a Sidewinder drill round (the blue colour means 'inert'). (*Mike Verier*)

Much bigger and heavier than its predecessors the AH-1W needs two sets of ground wheels to move it along with men on the ammo bay doors and a tail-walker to keep it steady when towed. (*Mike Verier*)

The rig on the nose of this aircraft is to bore sight the TOW system. (*Mike Verier*)

Pictured around 1987 this HMLAT-303 AH-1W gives a good view of the then-new three-colour camouflage scheme. The characteristic exhaust staining has already rendered much of the tail boom darker than the rest of the aircraft, a problem not resolved until some 20 years later. (*Mike Verier*)

Meanwhile manufacture of new-build AH-1Ws and conversion of existing AH-1Ts was in full swing at Bell. At the time Fort Worth were producing AH-1Fs as well and the production line was a busy place indeed. (*Bell Via Mike Verier*)

qualified on a 'T' airframe (161022 originally bailed to Bell as part of the Iranian development programme)

Although the Iranian proposal had foundered with the fall of the Shah, the development aircraft, known as 'T+', was still (by the merest co-incidence) in use as a trials aircraft and in 1983 Bell were awarded a contract to complete the qualification of the T-700 engine, 'While we are at it,' continued the Marines' pitch, 'we may as well incorporate a few small improvements.' Quietly and without fanfare 161022 began to evolve into the de-facto prototype for the, as yet, unannounced AH-1W.

The basic 'T' airframe, rotor and transmission were retained. The new engines, two GE T-700-GE-401s being mounted as podded units (the –401 was the navalised version already in use on the SeaHawk). After some aerodynamic changes the final cowling shape featured a 'scoop' arrangement aft (later discarded) designed to direct airflow over the jet pipes which themselves incorporated heat suppressing baffles. The engine cowlings, designed to provide easy

Fashions change in camouflage. These two aircraft from HMLA-167 'Warriors' illustrate the change from the green/grey/black era to greys. The grey aircraft is carrying the massive Zuni rocket (so big the pod only holds four rounds) The grey scheme served to emphasise the effect of the exhaust plume. (*Bell via Mike Verier*)

maintenance access, were split horizontally with the lower section stressed to double as a work platform when open.

The other external changes were cheek bulges that resulted from widening the ammunition bay behind the gun turret. The extra space allowed the ammunition box to be moved to one side making room on the port side of the bay for the TOW 'black boxes', previously sited inconveniently in the tail boom. This restored the centre of gravity (which the new engine installation had moved aft) and also saved the weight of several long cable runs.

Uniquely amongst attack helicopters, the Marines decided to not only retain the TOW missile but also wire the aircraft for the AGM-114 Hellfire air-to-surface missile. Both missile types could be carried at the same time giving the new Cobra unprecedented flexibility on the battlefield. A further standard option in place of either of these on an outboard pylon would be either AIM-9 Sidewinder (air-to-air) or the derivative AGM-122 SideArm (air-to-surface, anti-radiation, anti radar) missile. All four pylons were also 'plumbed' to accept long-range fuel tanks.

The performance of the new variant was seriously impressive. The twin engines developed a total of 3,380shp (compared to the 'T's 1,970shp) giving the Whisky the best power to weight ratio of any attack helicopter then extant. The extra power provided a considerable safety margin and the AH-1W could even take off and climb out at 800ft/min (4.1m/sec) on one engine. Bell

HMLA-269 bird on the USS Guadalcanal (LPH-7) somewhere off Puerto Rico in May 1993, this aircraft has had an interesting paint job with black patches over the grey scheme. The aircraft carries a 100 gallon ferry tank. The purple shirts denote fuelling crew. (*Robert Scoggin*)

continued to drive down maintenance man hours with the 'Whisky', and much attention was paid to access as noted above.

Carried over from previous AH-1T development were the AN/ALQ-144 IRCM jammer, wing-mounted AN/ALE-39 chaff/flare dispensers and the Helmet Sight System. The pilot (rear seat) received a modern HUD to replace the old gunsight.

Gradually the final shape emerged. The aircraft flew for a while with a fairly anonymous Field Green (FS34097) paint scheme save for the word 'SUPERCOBRA' marked in black on the cowling. Once development funding was secure it again went to the paint shop, emerging with a stunning black and gold scheme with a stylised 'striking cobra' design running the whole length of the fuselage. Bell and the Marine Corps were ready for the world to see their few small improvements.

Even then the very considerable changes to the aircraft were not fully acknowledged until the first production machine was rolled out on 27 March 1986. Resplendent in its brand new three-colour Marine camouflage scheme, BuNo 162532 was officially designated AH-1W. The 'Whisky' had arrived.

As deliveries of the new aircraft began to reach the fleet, surviving 'T' airframes were withdrawn and upgraded to 'W' standard (the 'J's could not be economically converted, but continued to serve with Reserve and training squadrons), together with new builds the USMC acquired a total of 225 AH-1Ws. 'Whisky' Cobras were also supplied to Turkey (12) and Taiwan (63).

More than twenty-five years later the 'Whisky Cobra' is claimed to have flown more combat hours than any other Cobra variant. USMC machines have served in Bosnia, Iraq, Afghanistan and many other inhospitable spots around the world. Turkish 'W's have seen prolonged combat in the high mountain passes too. It will not escape notice that most of these locations are a long

Modern for its day the AH-1W cockpit was becoming crowded by the 1990s. The first major modification to the airframe introduced a new front panel and larger FLIR turret. In order to make more room the front panel was enlarged and the canopy changed in what was known as the NTS (Night Targeting System) upgrade. (*Mike Verier*)

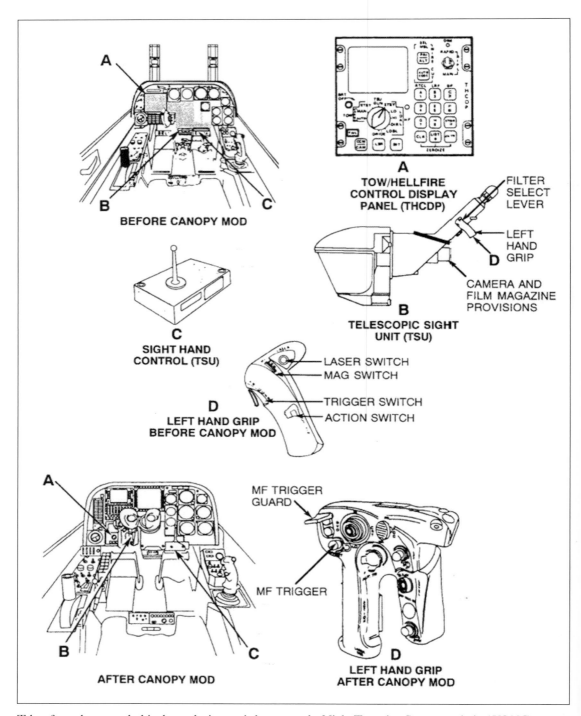

Taken from the manual, this shows the internal changes to the Night Targeting System cockpit. (*USMC*)

The Night Targeting System front cockpit. (*Mike Verier*)

way from the sea. Strangely enough it is the very fact that USMC Cobras were designed for a maritime environment that has made it so successful in other extreme operating conditions.

The USMC is an expeditionary force, it has to have aircraft that can cope with being operated from a ship in all weathers, and from austere bases once they get ashore. Furthermore they frequently do this for six months at a time. Consequently a great deal of effort goes into keeping corrosive salt-laden moisture out of the sensitive bits of the aircraft. If the seals can cope with salt water then snow or sand are far less of a problem. Marine Cobras achieved an exceptional 92% mission readiness rate during 'Desert Storm' where the talcum powder fine, but highly abrasive, dust was constantly grounding other helicopters. In these punishing conditions the 'Whisky Cobras' flew over 50% of the attack force hours despite being only 20% of the deployed force.

Bell never lost an opportunity to emphasise this ruggedness. At one point during the hotly fought British attack helicopter competition in the mid-1990s, most of the contenders were gathered for a display at Middle Wallop (the home of Army aviation in the UK). At the end of each day many of these 'battlefield' helicopters, including the European Tiger and South Africa's Rooivalk were cosseted away in a nice warm hanger. In the morning teams of men swarmed over them to get them ready to fly. Not so Bell.

The 'Whisky Cobra' on show, 165056, an absolutely standard production example, was always left outside overnight. In the morning, whilst the other teams were rushing about preparing their charges, a single Bell technician would stroll with studied nonchalance out to the aircraft, remove the engine covers, wipe the dew off the windscreen, and start it up. Point brilliantly made!

Even the 'W', like all before it, could be improved. As various bits of kit were added the cockpit began to show its age, becoming increasingly crowded and demanding to operate. This took on a new urgency after 'Desert Storm' and during the early 1990s a Tactical Navigation System (TNS) was added, as was a new restraint system featuring inflatable harness and head protection. Also added were better communications, radar/laser warning and Global Positioning Systems (GPS).

Much of this was integrated into a mod that changed the external look of the aircraft. The NTS (Night Targeting System) upgrade (AN/AWS-1(V)1) was based on the same US/Israeli system the Army adopted and finally gave the Marines a true night capability. It has a larger turret 'bucket' than the old M-65 and needs more space. This resulted in a deeper nasal contour which had the effect of slightly shortening the forward canopy glazing. The extra space created, however, allowed a re-design of the front seat panel. All AH-1W Cobras (including some or all of those exported) have been upgraded to NTS standard.

The NTS upgrade also gave the Cobra the ability to take on the role responsibilities of the OV-10, which was withdrawn from use following 'Desert Storm'. Whilst this increased the value of the Cobra as an asset, it again added to the crew workload.

Another long-standing concern has been the effect of heat from the exhaust plume on the tail boom. The 'Whisky Cobra' exhaust suppression system had its limitations and during the long and tortuous development of the 'Zulu' many configurations were explored to try and resolve the problem. In about 2007, a layout was finally achieved that featured slightly odd-looking exhausts which vented outboard through 'letterbox' tailpipes with a flattened oval cross section. Developed as part of the H-1 upgrade programme (AH-1Z and UH-1Y), the fix was so successful that it was fielded fleet wide without further delay.

At the time of writing, the 'Whisky' fleet continues to give outstanding service supporting the 'grunts' on the ground. A generation of pilots not born when the first Cobra flew regard it as still an outstanding machine. In the war-torn Afghan landscape the Cobra can get in close, most engagements are within 1,000 metres, and the gun, long-since cured of its early unreliability, is cited as 'the best weapon on the aircraft.'

Whilst still fitted, the now rather 'clunky' mechanical HSS is seldom used. Fixed to the gun however is a boresighted laser spot pointer which delivers superb accuracy via the magnification available from the TSU.

A pair of Snakes from HMM-264 'Black Knights' landing-on in distinctly murky weather. (*USMC*)

Dated August 2005 this 'Ragin' Bulls' AH-1W has a most artistic set of teeth. The aircraft is presumably operating from the LPD in the background. (*USMC*)

Another 'Bulls AH-1W operating onshore. It would seem that the squadron artist at the time favoured a more realist approach to the traditional 'evil eye' and sharkmouth embellishments than hitherto employed. (*USMC*)

Back in 1969 Staff Sergeant Thompson of 'The Leathernecks' had watched the first Marine 'G's being unloaded in Vietnam and speculated that the Snake might serve for 'twenty years' and enter into legend. He could not have imagined that nearly half a century later this rugged, reliable old 'raptor would still be on the front line and still 'makin' history'.

A beautiful day as this HMM-162 'Golden Eagles' NTS 'Whisky' turns towards the LPD. (*USMC*)

One of very few Cobras to wear 'NAVY' titling, this AH-1W from test squadron VX-5 was involved in the initial development work for the NTS upgrade. The same rather inelegant nasal contours also appearing on the 4BW demonstrator around 1990. (*USMC*)

Sporting the familiar XE tail code, this VX-5 aircraft has a 'greys' scheme achieved by lightly overspraying the green/black/grey original. This technique was used by at least two of the West Coast squadrons when hastily deployed for Desert Shield. (*USMC*)

Stealth Cobra! Originally developed for the F-22 Raptor this metallic paint is designed to reduce detectability of the aircraft. It has been trialled on a number of aircraft which are decidedly less than stealthy including the V-22 Osprey. Not to be outdone VX-5 has also applied it to a Snake at a location 'somewhere in the desert'. The results remain classified. (*Bell*)

Passive defence has also included attempts to render the aircraft less visible to Night Vision devices. This 'Digital' scheme echoes the success of such designs for combat uniforms – albeit it must absorb many happy hours of paint-shop time and lots of masking tape! (*Floyd Werner*)

The WR tail code reveals the aircraft to be from HMLA-775, a Reserve Squadron. As such they would have had the time to construct this elaborate scheme. (*Floyd Werner*)

Not to be outdone 775's Atlanta based Det A came up with a creative variation that managed to include a 'digital' Globe & Anchor enclosed by the initials USMC. (*HMLA-775 Det A via Peyton DeHart*)

160108 was a AH-1T conversion. When this photo was taken she was serving with HMLAT-303, the training squadron for all Marine Cobra pilots. (*Greg Davies*)

160108 from above. This view emphasises the cheek bulges and engine configuration. The aircraft is carrying a pair of TOW missiles and a full AN/ALE 39 chaff/flare pod overwing. The AN/ALQ 44 'Disco Lights' IR jammer is also clearly visible. (*Gregg Davies*)

The chaff and flares offer additional defence against MANPAD shoulder-launched missiles and form part of the Cobra's defensive suite. (*Bell*)

The Whisky's massive exhaust caused more than just darkening of the tail boom, with heat damage to the structure becoming apparent over time. This problem was addressed as part of the H-1 upgrade programme and many different configurations were tried, including deflecting the exhaust plume both upwards and downwards. (*Mike Verier*)

The eventual solution was to turn the exhaust through 90 degrees, directing it out and away from the tail. Intended for the Zulu, the mod was so successful that it was adopted fleet-wide without delay. The distinctive exhausts have become the defining feature of late-model Ws. (*Mike Verier*)

Cobras prowl the oceans of the world. Seen here in the Gulf of Thailand in February 2009 an AH-1W is directed to its spot on the USS Harpers Ferry (LSD 49). (*USMC/31st MEU*)

The flight line at MCAS New River is home to the East Coast squadrons. This view of a 'Gunrunner' (HMLA-269) AH-1W shows to advantage the fixed trim tab that the truncated tail fin requires. This important fix is known colloquially as the 'Gurney Flap'. Close inspection will reveal that the fin is an aerodynamic shape (as on all Cobras) designed to reduce the effects of tail rotor torque. (*Mike Verier*)

The other squadron at New River is HMLA-167 'Warriors'. Shown to advantage in this view is the AH-1W's massive 2' 9" (.84m) chord of the main rotor. (*Mike Verier*)

For all the bulk that development has added to the Snake over the years, it still retains its youthful slimness from the frontal aspect. (*Mike Verier*)

The red/black chequers and TV tail code proclaim this a 'Warrior' call sign. Photographed in 2011, this aircraft also sports the, then new, 'double' over wing chaff/flare pack. (*Mike Verier*)

Sitting quietly on the flight-line is 'TV/33'. One of the first T Models built, 160805 has been through the Whisky conversion and NTS upgrades and has thus served continuously for over thirty years. (*Mike Verier*)

Captured at Miramar whilst serving with HMLA-369, 160821 is another AH-1T conversion. This is a particularly significant airframe as it served in the Grenada operation in 1983, flown by Peyton DeHart. Operation 'Urgent Fury' had only the four 'Ragin' Bulls' AH-1Ts available initially and two of these were sadly lost. (*Matt Lyons*)

In recent years it has become common for a squadron to have one aircraft (usually the CO's) fully marked in squadron colours. The Warriors are no exception. This aircraft is illustrated fully in the profile section. (*Mike Verier*)

More elaborate nose-art also finds its way onto a Cobra, usually in combat zones when officialdom isn't looking too hard. This is one of the less risqué renderings of a classic decoration and was applied to another T conversion, 160815, a 'gunrunners' bird attached to HMM-365 during Operation 'Enduring Freedom' in 2002. (*USMC*)

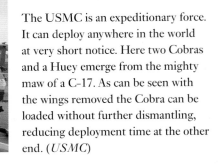

The USMC is an expeditionary force. It can deploy anywhere in the world at very short notice. Here two Cobras and a Huey emerge from the mighty maw of a C-17. As can be seen with the wings removed the Cobra can be loaded without further dismantling, reducing deployment time at the other end. (*USMC*)

Chapter 10

Two Good – Four Better
Four-blade Cobras and the long road to the Zulu

The one upgrade the Marines coveted for their 'Whiskys', but could not find the funds for was a new four-blade rotor. Even worse they already had it flying and qualified in prototype form and knew the advantages it offered. Getting it for the fleet was to prove an exceptionally long and rocky road.

For very good reasons the classic Bell two-blade rotor has been hugely successful, many thousands of helicopters of many different types, over many decades are testament to that. Like any technology however there is always another way to do it, and because the rotor system is fundamental to a helicopter Bell have explored most of them over the years.

By the mid-1970s they had perfected an advanced four-blade rotor which was in production for the Model 412 Huey derivative. The advantage of the new rotor was primarily its vibration reduction which gave a smoother ride, clearly desirable from the commercial point of view. It also had less moving parts than a conventional rotor and a wider G tolerance. Fairly obviously these factors would also have benefits in the military context.

The marriage of the 412 rotor and the Cobra was not long coming. Flying for the first time in 1979, the Model 249 demonstrator was produced to explore the possibilities. This was a sound commercial decision in the context of the time. The AAH competition had been won by the AH-64 Apache, but that was still in development and a long way from production and fielding. The Army's existing Cobra fleet was going to have to hold the line for some time, but single engine development had almost reached its zenith with the various upgrades and improvements leading to the AH-1S (latterly F) Models. The one remaining way to offer a significant improvement was a new rotor system.

The 249 performed extremely well. A number of four-blade options were proposed to the Army, and to potential export customers, notably Germany. Ultimately however, the Army decided not to spend the money and without a production order from them, the export prospects were limited and further major development of 'Army' model Cobras effectively ended. The now redundant 249 was put to work under the ARTI (Advanced Rotorcraft Technology Integration) programme in support of work on the Light Helicopter Experimental (LHX) combat helicopter programme.

In the meantime Bell had continued four-blade research and by 1982 the more advanced 680 rotor was flying on a Model 222. (A very sleek machine with a retractable undercarriage, it achieved considerable public recognition as the star of the TV series 'Airwolf'). Its primary function was to qualify the rotor as the system of choice for the LHX contest. LHX had the

The model 249 demonstrator was the original marriage of the Cobra with a four-blade rotor. It lives on in the AH-58D Scout. (*Bell via Mike Verier*)

The faithful 161022 development airframe in its guise as the '4BW' served to prove the rotor system. (*Bell via Mike Verier*)

This early 'artist's impression' shows the intended layout for the British Cobra Venom proposal. The four-blade rotor was added later. (*Bell via Mike Verier*)

Left: The final version of the Venom cockpit, developed by GEC, proved to have most of the features later adopted by the AH-1Z programme. (*Mike Verier*)

Below: This early development Zulu airframe shows the original end–plate fins on the elevators, as well as the early exhaust configuration with added inlets to try and cure the effects of heat on the tail boom. (*Bell via Mike Verier*)

Once again the symbiotic relationship between the attack and utility versions of the H-1 series is shown in this shot of two HMLA/T-303 birds up from Camp Pendleton. (*Greg Davies*)

potential to be a vast order with some 6,000 aircraft in prospect and the 222/680 was flown and evaluated by many service pilots during its life, including the Marines.

Impressed by the rotor the USMC – at the time in the middle of developing the 'T+/W' upgrade – could see the potential it also had if applied to that machine, but as ever had no funds for its development. They reasoned however that if LHX went ahead they would be able to acquire a fully developed system at a much reduced unit cost and retro-fit it to the fleet.

The 'W' programme reached fruition in 1986 when the first aircraft was delivered. By 1987 the 'T+' development airframe (161022) had completed its work and was back at Bell for refurbishment. The merits of a four-blade 'W' variant were already clear and Bell lost no time in canvassing support, including proposing just such a combination to the Germans as PAH-90 in 1987. Whilst the USMC had no funds to put into the project, it could renew the loan of the aircraft for qualification of the rotor. On 24 January 1989, 161022 flew for the first time with the 680 rotor at Bell's Arlington test facility.

Rapidly becoming known as the '4BW' (four-blade Whisky) qualification continued at a steady pace while Bell set about selling the idea. Brochure proposals of the time include some interesting concepts including a Gull-winged '4BW' with a retractable wheeled undercarriage. By the time that the '4BW' appeared at the Farnborough air show in September 1990 it had demonstrated that the new aircraft was fully aerobatic and Bell's marketing people were talking about the 'Viper'. Prophetically 161022's Farnborough incarnation included a six-point wing and much improved sighting/targeting systems.

Priorities

The talk at Farnborough however was of events unfolding elsewhere. On 2 August 1990, Saddam Husain's forces had invaded Kuwait. The Cobras were going to war again. The 'Desert Storm' campaign the following year was to be the first major test of the 'Whisky Cobra'. It acquitted itself well.

A testimony to the ruggedness of Marine Cobras was their almost legendary serviceability during the conflict. Consequently they flew a very high number of combat hours in relation to the force deployed. When the smoke cleared they had accounted for ninety-seven tanks, 104 APCs and other vehicles, sixteen bunkers and two AAA sites. Whilst emphasising the strengths of the Cobra however, the intense operations also revealed some shortcomings.

Chief amongst these was the need for a true night capability, and the obvious limitations of an increasingly cluttered 'old technology' cockpit. The four-blade rotor was going to have to wait.

The 'Desert Storm effect' rippled out in other ways. The undoubted success of attack helos in general, and the AH-64 Apache in particular marked the swansong of the US Army's fleet of 'legacy' AH-1s. It also convinced the British Army that the Westland Lynx/TOW combination they were using needed replacement with a dedicated attack type. Given a free hand they would have ordered AH-64 Apache on the spot. In the way of these things however, an evaluation and competition was required, the result depending as much on the creation of jobs in the UK as the technical merits of the aircraft. The Cobra was seen as a serious contender for this, potentially very large, order (ninety-five aircraft at one point).

A British partner was required, but in this case it could not be the only helicopter manufacturer in the UK (Westlands) as they were committed to the Apache. Crucially, as it turned out, Bell teamed with GEC/Marconi, an avionics, rather than an airframe company. Marconi were the manufacturers of the XM-143 Air Data System (in use on the AH-1F and the Apache), the company thus had the distinction of supplying the only British piece of kit on a Cobra.

The need for a more modern cockpit was quickly identified as a key factor. The basic airframe and dynamics of the AH-1W already met the performance criteria specified, so in conjunction with Bell, work commenced on bringing the Snake into the 21st Century. In adopting this approach it was also calculated that success would mean new technology flowing in the other direction as the solution to the USMC's requirements which almost exactly paralleled those of the Venom proposal.

The new cockpit that emerged was a transformation. Gone were the 'steam' gauges and the intrusive TSU. In their place were large multi-function display (MFD) screens. Both front and rear stations were almost identical, meaning the 'pilot' could be the front seater if required (the one really successful feature trialled on the abortive YAH-63). Third generation Forward Looking InfraRed (FLIR), Radar Warning Receiver (RWR) systems and Laser technology also superimposed imagery directly onto the visor of a new integrated helmet giving the crew a clear view of the terrain around them on the darkest night.

The new cockpit also fully embraced HOCAC (Hands On Cyclic and Collective) principles, and both stations featured a pull-out yoke for weapons control. The Cobra Venom as it became known would have provided a level of situational awareness and systems integration a generation ahead of that in the A Model Apache. Whilst the airframe was essentially unchanged, the Venom proposal did make provision for the addition of an APU (auxiliary power unit) and a 'baggage pod' to allow true self-deployment capability. Again, whilst not strictly within the specification, it was proposed to wire the wing for future addition of additional stores stations (the so-called 'six-point' wing).

This author was privileged to 'fly' the fully functioning simulator built at GEC's Rochester works. It was extremely impressive and would have transformed the Cobra. Sadly, and despite the late addition to the bid of the '4BW' rotor, the order went to Westlands. The work however was not wasted and virtually all of the features developed for the Venom are now to be found in the 'Zulu'.

In the aftermath of 'Desert Storm' meanwhile, the 'Whisky' had been the subject of a number of upgrades and improvements which had certainly added to its abilities, but had served also to increase the already high cockpit workload. The US Army's chastening experience in Somalia had also shown that the battlefield had changed again. Tactics designed to deal with heavy armour from significant stand-off distances were of no use in a dense urban environment.

By the time of the second Iraq war, and a year later the Afghan deployment the 'Whisky' was a much more capable animal and more than justified the Marines' faith in it. As its capabilities increased so of course did the demands for its services. Bell still lacked a launch customer for the '4BW' which the USMC could piggy back on and the situation now demanded a more radical approach.

Because of their unique role, the Marine Light Attack Helicopter Squadrons (HMLAs) operate a mix of UH-1s and AH-1s. This combination is flexible and effective but it also meant that increasing demand and pace of operations was taking its toll on the Huey fleet too.

In 1996 therefore, it was decided to launch the H-1 upgrade programme. Drawing on the historic commonality between the Utility and Attack machines, the upgrade programme will see the Cobra story come full circle – the AH-1G was a Huey with a Cobra body, the UH-1Y is a Cobra with a Huey body.

Zulu takes shape

The aim of the programme was to ensure the long-term viability of the two aircraft. The four-blade rotor would be adopted for both types, and both would receive completely new 'state of the art' cockpits (based on the work done for the Cobra Venom). A guiding principle was that there should be a very high degree of genuine commonality between the two so that engines, dynamics, drive train and much equipment should literally be identical. This would have benefits in the supply-chain as well as training, maintenance and support advantages.

As with earlier incremental improvements it was envisaged that a mixture of new-build and refurbished machines would be procured. In the case of the UH-1Y 'Yankee' it was eventually concluded that new-build was more cost effective. The 'Zulu' fleet was originally to have consisted of 168 remanufactured and fifty-eight new-builds. This would subsequently change in the light of operational demands on the 'Whisky' fleet.

In September 1998, Bell had delivered seven new AH-1Ws to the Marines, bringing the inventory to 201 aircraft. A month earlier, four AH-1Ws had been returned to Bell for conversion to 'Zulu' configuration. The first of these (162545) was delivered to the USMC on 7 December 2000, entering flight test in April 2001. Amongst the early airframe conversions was 162532 the first production AH-1W.

The heart of the H-1 upgrade is the new rotor system. It confers higher speed, greater agility, and a smoother ride on the aircraft. Being of composite construction with vastly fewer moving parts than conventional rotors, it is lighter and requires less maintenance too. The new aircraft is therefore a better weapon platform with a greatly improved payload. It will also be much less costly to maintain.

From below, the wider wings and tailplane can easily be seen. Not so obvious is the deletion of TOW racks in favour of the more advanced HellFire missile. The rocket pods may look ancient but nowadays they house precision-guided munitions many times more accurate than their merely ballistic predecessors. (*Greg Davies*)

The 'production' Zulu has done away with the end–plate fins and adopted the distinctive out–turned exhausts which finally proved so effective that they were fielded fleet-wide to the Whisky squadrons. (*Greg Davies*)

The opportunity has also been taken to move the chaff/flare dispensers to more permanent housings on the fuselage. The wing-tip station is covered on this aircraft the Zulu being designed from the outset with a 'six–point' wing. (*Greg Davies*)

This view demonstrates that the Cobra's original elegance of line hasn't been completely lost. The AH-1Z is however something like twice the weight of an early AH-1G. (*Greg Davies*)

The four-blade rotor was married to a new drive-train and a more powerful (four-blade) tail rotor. This required structural strengthening of the tail boom and pylon, a larger and more effective tailplane (stabilizer) and 'beefed-up' landing gear – the cross tubes are now of a more substantial square section, and the tail skid has been transformed from a protective bumper into part of the landing gear. The structural changes made during manufacturing/conversion are expected to add 10,000 hours to the lifetime of each airframe.

Just as important as the airframe and dynamics is the new generation cockpit, the design aim again being to achieve as much commonality as possible. The layouts would of course reflect the tandem or side-by-side configuration of the two types, but as far as possible system presentation and operation is intended to be identical. Given the Corps' doctrine of the 'Zulu' and 'Yankee' operating in combination, pilots should be able to fly either aircraft albeit with the necessary role-specific training required. This makes the HMLAs more flexible and greatly reduces hours previously required for conversion-to-type.

Many aircraft in the past have claimed commonality but achieved little more than a similar general configuration. The H-1 programme has reached 84% of identical components, a truly remarkable achievement.

Zulu described

The advanced composite rotor is bearingless and hingeless, and is claimed to have 75% less parts than a conventional four-blade articulated system. The fibreglass yokes are multi-functional structures that accommodate flapping, lead lag and pitch change motions as well as retaining the rotor blade. To save weight and complexity, two identical two-arm yokes are stacked one above the other rather than having one large four-arm unit. The cuffs are also composite construction and have an infinite life.

The blades themselves are primarily composite, built around a spar and honeycomb core. The leading edges are protected by a stainless steel abrasion strip. The blades are individually interchangeable and design life is quoted as 10,000 hours. They are also designed to be tolerant of hits by up to 23mm calibre rounds. To facilitate shipboard stowage and reduce hanger space required, the 'Zulu' has a semi-automatic blade fold system which aligns the blades fore and aft in the same way that the two-blade was stowed. Folding can be accomplished without any crewmen having to climb on the aircraft, a vital feature on a pitching and rolling deck.

The tail rotor has been moved to the pusher (port) side of the fin, and whilst it appears as a four-blade unit it is actually two 'stacked' teetering blades with titanium yokes and elastomeric flapping bearings, shear restraints and pitch horns. Again target design life is 10,000 hours.

The 'Zulu' retains the reliable and efficient T700-GE-401 engines, and adds a Sunstrand APU generator which allows full system checks to be carried out prior to start-up without draining the aircraft battery. The APU also serves to charge the battery and the 'Zulu' is therefore capable of operating without external power. This is an extremely important feature for the expeditionary Marines who regularly deploy their Cobras to austere forward operating positions.

In another echo of the 309 KingCobra, the 'Zulu' has an enlarged wing. Spanning some 14 feet 3 inches (4.36m) it is approximately 4 feet (1.2m) wider than the original wing and moves the inboard stores pylons clear of the skids. Two additional stores stations are available at the wingtips, making it possible to carry AIM-9 Sidewinders without compromising the offensive stores. A 'podded' Longbow fire control radar unit has also been demonstrated mounted on the wingtip station. The additional volume within the new wing also allows it to contain additional

The first operational deployment came aboard the new USS *Makin Island* (LHD-8) ion November 2012. These two 'Scarface' birds are carrying Sidewinders, nineteen-shot rocket pods and 100 gallon fuel tanks. The deck chains are being released prior to take-off. The very last items to come off are the yellow 'noddy caps' on the Sidewinders which are to prevent the seeker-heads going into a frenzy trying to acquire all the heat sources around them. (*US Navy*)

The new technology extends to the pilots' helmets. The 'Top Owl' replaces the HUD, NVG goggles and the clunky HSS. (*US Navy*)

fuel cells, again a feature first proposed for the 309's 'Big Wing' design. All four underwing stations are 'plumbed' for fuel tanks, giving the 'Zulu' an impressive ferry range.

The full range of ordnance applicable to the Cobra can be carried with the exception of the now ageing (but still very effective) TOW. The decision to drop TOW was seen as controversial in some quarters as the AGM-114 Hellfire is an expensive way to take out a truck or bunker. This apparent gap will be narrowed by the introduction of 'smart' laser technology, small enough to do the same for the accuracy of hitherto unguided 2.75 inch rockets that it did for iron bombs a generation before. The APKWS (Advanced Precision Kill Weapons System) will transform the Hydra 70 family WAFAR (Wrap-Around Fin Aerial Rockets) from shotgun to sniper and is seen as very relevant in close urban combat scenarios.

Cockpit and avionics

Both front and rear cockpits in the 'Zulu' are almost identical so that either crewman can serve as pilot or Battle Captain/Gunner as the tactical situation dictates. The traditional control column cyclic has been deleted from the rear seat and both now feature side-stick cyclics. This clears space for the pull-out Mission Grips which are used by whichever crew member is functioning as Battle Captain. The Mission Grip is reminiscent of a games controller and has the switch-control functions for the Target Sight System (TSS) – field of view, slew, track and acquire – and the weapon system's select and launch options.

The instrument panels are now dominated by two multi-function 8 inch x 6 inch LCD displays with a 4.2 inch x 4.2 inch dual-function display centrally mounted below and between them. The system is designed to only display relevant information as required, greatly reducing crew workload.

The crew also use the 'Top Owl' helmet which displays FLIR, video and other information directly onto the visor. The helmet also incorporates a head tracking system so that guns and/or the TSS can be pointing where the crew member is looking. This replaces both the old HSS with its mechanical links and the earlier generation cumbersome NVGs.

For the H-1 programme, Northrop-Grumman are responsible for the IAS (Integrated Avionics System). The IAS uses dual redundant mission computers and synthesises all aircraft functions, including communications, navigation, sensors, weapons, cockpit system controls, electronic warfare functions, warnings, cautions and advisories.

A key component of the IAS is a new targeting system. The programme suffered some set-backs in attempting to field this, but in 2010 the first new units were delivered. The new TSS uses third generation FLIR and charge-coupled device (CCD) technology and can operate day, night or in adverse weather. The system provides multi-mode, multi-target tracking and allows engagement from distances outside the threat envelope of most opposing weapons. Eventually further upgrades will allow video and data linking so that information gathered can be streamed to ground units. Corresponding uplinks will ensure that close air support really does have meaning.

The AH-1Z went through a number of difficulties which delayed its fielding. Having completed a first-stage OPEVAL (Operational Evaluation) in 2006, a second stage was abandoned in 2008 due to system difficulties. These were eventually resolved and the resumed second phase in late 2010 resulted in the 'Zulu' gaining IOC (Initial Operational Capability) in March 2011.

AH-1Zs were first fielded with HMLAT-303 at Camp Pendleton to begin the training of another generation of 'Snake Wranglers'. What would become the first operational 'Zulu' squadron, HMLA-367 (call-sign 'Scarface'), also based at Camp Pendleton, successfully deployed

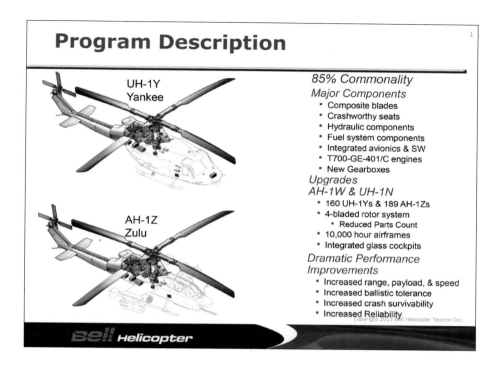

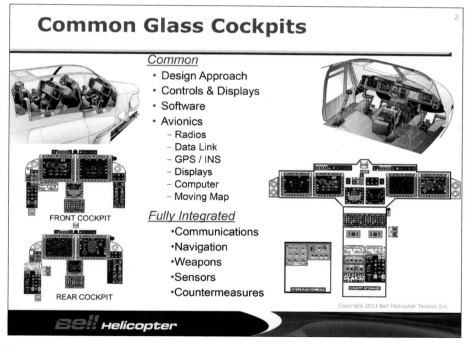

The H1 upgrade has achieved a genuine (identical by part number) 85% commonality between the two types. These Bell CGIs dramatically demonstrate this achievement which directly benefits both training and the support costs for the fleet. (*Bell*)

UH-1Ys to Afghanistan in 2010, adding many more hours to the fleet's operational experience, (by March 2012, the combined 'Y/Z' fleet had flown some 44,000 hours). The first all 'Yankee/Zulu' operational deployment was, appropriately enough, combined with the first operational cruise of the USS *Makin Island* (LHD-8) which departed San Diego on 15 November 2011.

As is customary, the various aviation elements of the Marine Expeditionary Unit (MEU) come under the auspices of an 'umbrella' unit when deployed, in this case, HMM-268 (reinforced). The fifth generation of Cobras to serve the Marine Corps had begun operations.

In march 2012, it was announced that such were the demands on the existing attack helicopter assets in the USMC, (ie the 'Whisky' fleet), that the shortfall created as airframes were withdrawn for re-manufacture was not viable. the marine Corps had decided to keep the 'W's in place and opt for an enhanced 'Zulu Build New' (ZBN) programme. Whilst the total number of airframes (189) was unchanged, the original 131 remanufactured/fifty-eight 'ZBN' mix was revised to just thirty-seven remanufactured and 152 'ZBN'.

Thus began a chapter that has yet to be written in the Cobra story. There are still many improvements 'in the works'. Even now, new targeting, communications and weapons technology is under development for the 'Zulu', and constantly evolving to meet new threats. The grandsons of the first Cobra pilots are now flying Snakes, and their sons may yet follow – by any standards that's an impressive achievement for a type originally envisaged as being required for no more than 5–10 years.

70-16019/Model 249

Another remarkable individual airframe that demonstrates the evolutionary development of the Cobra, 70-16019 was originally built as an AH-1G; one of ninety-two airframes upgraded in 1974 under the ICAP (Improved Cobra Armament Programme), which added TOW capability to the Snake, and as such it thus became an AH-1Q.

The AH-1Qs were always a stop-gap solution as the additional weight left them seriously underpowered. 70-16019 found itself re-designated as the sole YAH-1S prototype under ICAM (Improved Cobra Agility and Manoeuvrability) which gave the aircraft a new, more powerful, engine and drive train. (Sister airframe 70-15936, which was a standard 'G', became the sole YAH-1R under the same programme, the eventual result was the 'Improved S' Cobra.

70-16019, complete with TOW and the uprated engine and dynamics was then further modified in 1979 to trial the four-blade rotor that had been successfully developed and flown on the Model 412 Huey derivative. The converted aircraft was given the Bell Model number 249.

By this time the AAH competition had produced a winner in the shape of the AH-64, which was to be the Army's next generation attack helicopter. The Apache however was still in development and Bell felt that an enhanced 'Army' Cobra had considerable potential both as a low cost/risk upgrade for the US Army (eventually becoming the scout for the Apache), and for the growing number of export customers using the type.

The export customer Bell had in mind particularly was Germany. They had a contest underway for an attack type and Bell pitched the Model 249 for it under the designation PAH-II. *PanzerAbHauber* II was offered with a number of optional extras apart from the four-blade rotor. It could use the then-current M-65/TOW fit, or the sighting group could be mast-mounted. The final option was to graft on the TADS/PNVS (as used on the Apache) system, deleting the gun turret.

The aircraft was offered in a number of forms to the Army and other potential buyers, and at various times was also referred to as 'Cobra 2000' and 'Cobra ASH' (Advanced Scout Helicopter)

The ASH configuration would have featured truncated stub wings with AIM-43 'Redeye' or AIM-92 'Stinger' air-to-air missiles for self-defence at the tips, but no underwing stores. The M-197 20mm turret was retained together with the M-65 'bucket' and TSU. In addition to this, a mast-mounted sight was also proposed to allow reconnaissance from cover. The Amy didn't buy the Model 249 which effectively killed the Foreign Military Sales (FMS) prospects too. The concept however did not die, finally finding very successful form using another Bell airframe, the OH-58. Developed as a scout under the AHIP (Army Helicopter Improvement Programme) initiative, begun in 1981, the OH-58D Kiowa Warrior, was a four-blade, armed scout with a mast-mounted sight. Its considerable success in the 1988 Persian Gulf operation 'Prime Chance', justifying Bell's investment and demonstrating again the value of an armed scout that could not only see, but reach out and touch, at a considerable distance.

70-16019 however was not finished as a technology demonstrator. In 1983 it became part of the LHX development under the ARTI (Advanced Rotorcraft Technology Integration) programme, which aimed to prove the essential automated flight control technologies needed for the single-pilot LHX to succeed. The Model 249/ARTI was able to demonstrate perfectly stable hands-off flight throughout the flight envelope.

With the conclusion of this programme 70-16019 was refurbished to AH-1S standard and returned to the Army. Its subsequent service history is a little vague, but it survived to reach Fort Drum for disposal in 2001. 70-16019 eventually became part of a batch of airframes acquired by the Israelis to provide a source of spares for their Cobras. As ever with the Israelis, detail facts are hard to come by, (numbers between 30 and 100 airframes have been reported) but it can be assumed that they picked the best airframes, and 70-16019 would have had relatively low hours. It is entirely possible therefore that at least parts of this important machine are still flying, re-incarnated yet again as a *Tzefa*. As with all snakes, it has simply shed its skin and started a new life.

AH-1Q: 161019, was originally built as a G, subsequently it became a Q and eventually the YAH-1S prototype. (*Bell via Mike Verier*)

AH-1S: 161019 eventually received the full 'S' upgrade, including the the-new 'flat-plate' canopy. (*Bell via Mike Verier*)

The basic Model 249: 161019, was offered with a number of sighting options including the Apache TADS/PNVS grafted directly onto the nose. This would mean the deletion of the turret gun and the aircraft was routinely flown without it fitted. (*Bell via Mike Verier*)

Offered to the US Army as a product upgrade, the Model 249, 161019, was highly manoeuvrable. (*Bell via Mike Verier*)

The Model 249 shown with the turret and a range of armament including TOW, Hellfire, FFARs and wingtip-mounted Stinger or Redeye. (*Bell via Mike Verier*)

ASH APPLICATIONS

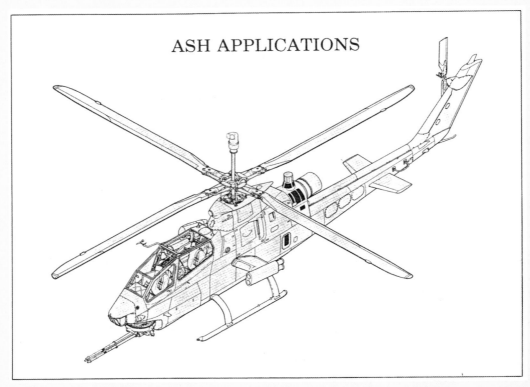

The Model 249 was offered to the US Army as a scout for the Apache and is seen here in a possible ASH (Advanced Scout Helicopter) configuration with mast-mounted sight and stub wings fitted with Stingers for self-defence. The role was eventually filled by the very successful AH-58 Kiowa Warrior which remains in service alongside the AH-64. It uses the rotor, MMS and Stingers first mooted for the 249. (*Bell via Mike Verier*)

Before being returned to the Army as an AH-1F, 161019 served as the ARTI demonstrator. Both pilots can be seen to have their hands off the controls in this picture. (*Bell via Mike Verier*)

Chapter 11

Over the Hills and Far Away

Export Snakes

Cobras have been widely exported, indeed in recent years the availability of ex-US Army machines has if anything increased the number of countries using various marks of Snake. Bell continues to seek customers for 'Zulu' upgrades too.

The first export customer was **Spain** acquiring eight new build G Models in two batches of four in 1971 and 1972 for service with the Navy's *Escuadrilla 007*. These aircraft were equipped for the M–35 20mm cannon system and could often be seen with the prominent ammunition sponsons fitted. Known in Spanish service as Z-14s, they served for many years, operating from both shore bases and the Spanish VTOL carrier *Dedalo*, as well as various LSTs.

The four surviving machines finally retired in 1985, as leased airframes, three were returned to the USA, the original airframe (Z-14-01/71-15090) is preserved at Fort Rucker, masquerading as a 'Vietnam' G Model. The other two were reportedly converted to serve as electrical/systems trainers. The remaining aircraft '01-708' (Z-14-08/72-21464) is preserved in remarkably complete condition outdoors at the Spanish Naval Museum.

Spain was the first export customer taking eight AH-1Gs in 1971/1972. Known in Spanish service as the Z-14 they served or many years. The first aircraft, Z-14-01 is shown here. (*Francisco Andreu*)

Z-14-01 still survives. Returned to the US it is preserved at Fort Rucker wearing its genuine serial (68-15090) and a representative Vietnam scheme. (*Bell*)

Z-14-08 Also survives, preserved at the Spanish Naval Academy. (*Bell*)

Iran

By far the largest export order ever was that for the Shah of Iran who ordered 202 improved AH-1Js and 287 Model 214s for the Imperial Iranian Army in December 1971. These aircraft owed a great deal to the Model 309 KingCobra prototypes having the same engine (T400-WV-402 with a rating of 1,673shp), and the same transmission system (derived from that of the Model 211 HueyTug flying crane). This gave the 'J International' much improved hot-and-high performance, essential in the Iranian case. Early deliveries were externally indistinguishable from USMC 'J's save for the addition of a scoop intake to increase airflow through the engine compartment. Later machines were delivered with the full TOW/M-65 system and at the time were the most potent Cobras in the world. Further improvements, particularly to the gun/sighting system, were developed for the Iranian 'J's and subsequently adopted for other Cobra models. Deprived of technical support following the fall of the Shah, the Iranians nevertheless managed to keep a sizeable fleet in service, and the Cobras gave a good account of themselves

During the sales campaign leading to the Iranian order, AH-1J 57788 was bailed to Bell and went to Iran as a demonstrator painted in this most attractive 'desert' scheme (believed to be FS30257 and FS302400). (*Bell via Mike Verier*)

The first Iranian airframe, 3-4401, was externally indistinguishable from standard J Models, save for the enlarged intake scoop on the engine cowling. 34402, the second airframe, was fully TOW configured. (*Bell via Mike Verier*)

The first of the re-
furbished Iranian Js.
(*Vahid Reza Alaei,
Fars News Agency*)

Ten 'new' Js lined up for the press-launch. Close examination of this picture will reveal several aircraft without TSUs and various panels still in primer. The second aircraft from the camera also seems to be still in it's original paint scheme and markings. (*Vahid Reza Alaei, Fars News Agency*)

This head-on view clearly shows the amount of metal that needed replacing, (these airframes have been in service for three decades). The sighting turret appears to be a dummy, there is no TSU visible in the cockpit and the 'gun' is suspect too. (*Vahid Reza Alaei, Fars News Agency*)

The hybrid 'new build' design seems to be a 'J' airframe mated to a new 'flat-plate' canopy. Also apparent is the nose-mounted FLIR turret. Many improvements however are inside the new 'glass' cockpit. (*Vahid Reza Alaei, Fars News Agency*)

Some Js have been fitted with a FLIR ball mounted centrally beneath the skids. The script reads 'Islamic Republic of Iran Army'. (*Vahid Reza Alaei, Fars News Agency*)

South Korea received eight 'J International' models which were the same as those supplied to Iran. They were TOW capable and much more powerful than USMC AH-1Js. The South Koreans subsequently purchased a large number of AH-1F models. (*Bell*)

during the Iran-Iraq War in the 1980s; that conflict seeing the first Cobra versus Hind combats, and a MiG-21 shoot-down apparently claimed using the 20mm gun. Reportedly somewhere between fifty and seventy-five aircraft remain in service, a remarkable achievement.

Production of the Iranian 'J' (Also known as the 'J International') concluded with a further eight TOW-capable aircraft supplied to **South Korea**. The Korean border remains a potential flash point and the ROK Army currently operates a fleet of some ninety 'S/F' Cobras. There is a requirement for some thirty-six replacement aircraft with the AH-1Z a contender.

Prior to the fall of the Shah, Bell had planned to partner with the Iranians in the production of helicopters for the Middle East market. Bell formed a separate company to oversee both the training of Iranian technicians and pilots and the eventual manufacture of helicopters in Iran. At one point there were more than 5,000 Bell employees (and 8,000 dependants) in Iran. A production facility was nearing completion, development of an improved Model 214, the 214ST, with T-700 engines (50% funded by Iran) was underway and a similarly powered Cobra projected (the AH-1T+ or 'Improved Iranian Gunship').

Started in May 1977, this project echoes in the 'Yankee' and 'Zulu' models of today in that the 'T' airframe was to be married with the engine and dynamics of the 214ST Huey derivative. The 214 was to be produced in Iran, whilst 200 or more Cobras were to be manufactured at Bell, deliveries being planned to start in 1979. This all ended abruptly with the revolution that year and all support for US military equipment was terminated.

More than three decades later a good deal of the equipment the Iranians already had is however still in use with the **Islamic Republic of Iran Army**, kept going initially by cannibalisation and purchase of black market spares. Gradually however the Iranians have managed to reverse-engineer spares, weapons and latterly whole aircraft. Effectively they are now producing unlicensed copies of Bell products, including it seems, the Cobra.

In 1998 the Panha 2091 was revealed. An upgraded/reverse engineered hybrid reportedly known as *Shabaviz* carried out under the auspice of HESA (the Iranian Aircraft Manufacturing

Industry Co). Externally the aircraft looks like a 'J' but with a Flat Plate canopy (or an 'F' with a 'J' power pack). This evolved into the P4 in 2004 which is believed to be a new build. Internally a number of avionic and defensive upgrades have been incorporated, most apparent of which is a completely new front cockpit with a large MFD screen in place of the old optical TSU. On some aircraft what appears to be a FLIR ball is mounted on the belly, between the skids. The manufacturers have suggested (but not confirmed) that the aircraft is night-capable. A clue might be the name, which alludes to 'something that comes with the night' (in the West that would read as 'Night Stalker' or similar).

A parallel programme has produced the *Toofan* (Storm) which appears to be a refurbished/ upgraded 'J' (TOW). The first ten 'new' airframes were delivered with much publicity on 5 January 2010. Photos show a great deal of saluting with both military and political 'brass' at the ceremony. Study of these images however reveals some airframes with panels still in primer, missing TSUs or apparently fitted with dummy turrets. At least one still displays its original tail number and heavily exhaust stained original paint (all the new aircraft are freshly painted). Presumably there were no volunteers to tell the Important Persons that their aircraft weren't all ready...

Iran has also had to develop a number of local copies of US weapons, including an AGM-65 Maverick equivalent. Maverick has been fired from Cobras, notably by the USMC, it was not however a capability delivered with the Iranian Cobras and its apparently operational use in the Iran-Iraq War speaks of Iranian ingenuity.

Israel

Despite the much larger number of airframes acquired by Iran, **Israel** has been by far the biggest user of the Cobra apart from the Americans. Ever sensitive about security, at one time even the FS number for the paint was secret, being known only as 'Israeli Tan' in Bell's paintshop. The author therefore gratefully acknowledges the detailed research of Ray Ball and his Israeli colleagues for the following:-

It was the dark days of the October 1973 'Yom Kippur' War when Syrian and Egyptian armour stormed over Israeli positions that initially led to the IAF acquiring Cobras. In 2011, after nearly four decades of continuous IAF service, the Snake remains a key asset.

The hard lessons of war pointed to the need for a weapon system to respond quickly to major threats and powerful enough to stem the flow of armour and troops. Attack helicopters seemed to meet this need and the lessons from service in Vietnam, pointed the IAF towards an interest in the Bell AH-1 Cobra. In April 1974, Israel sent a small evaluation team to the USA to look at attack helicopters and whilst they were impressed by the Cobra, the Hind-like Sikorsky S-67 Blackhawk (which could also carry a squad of infantry) also captured their attention. However, the unfortunate crash of the S-67 prototype at the Farnborough Airshow that year, ended any further development on the type and Israeli interest centred solely on the Cobra.

At the end of 1974, Israel purchased six Vietnam War surplus AH-1G Cobras at a cost of $2 million and after a full refurbishment at the US Army's Corpus Christi Maintenance Depot, in Texas, these were shipped to Israel. Each Cobra had an XM-28 chin turret housing the GAU-28 Minigun and XM-129 Grenade Launcher. These aircraft were also configured to accept the M-35 six-barrelled 20mm 'Gatling' gun.

The Cobra's arrived in Israel in April 1975, equipping a newly formed Test and Evaluation Squadron, under the command of Major Joshua Livnat at Tel Nof Air Force Base. These helicopters retained their US Army Olive Drab paint scheme and were given serial numbers '109', '115', '118', '124', '126' and '130'. In IAF service, the Cobra was given the name *Tzefa* (Hebrew for Viper) and a Squadron badge of a snake's head was painted on each side of the tail.

Following a programme of training and conversion courses, the squadron began their test and evaluation exercises, working with other branches of the Israeli Defence Forces, particularly Armoured Brigades, simulating attacks against tanks and other vehicles. From these exercises, it was quickly determined that the Cobra could be an effective 'tank killer', but that would mean having better target acquisition systems and the capability to carry and fire anti-tank missiles.

Realising the potential, the IAF funded a full upgrade for the six *Tzefas* to 'Improved AH-1S' standard and in 1977, these were returned to the US for conversion. At the same time Israel ordered a further six 'Up-gun' AH-1S/ECAS Cobras.

The converted helicopters arrived back in Israel in August 1978, with all six now painted in Brown FS30099, with smaller national insignia, but retaining the squadron badge. Externally, these helicopters (often mistaken for AH-1Qs) retained the 'round' canopy and Vietnam era 'sugar scoop' exhaust outlet, but had more powerful engines, the M-65 TSU turret and TOW missiles. The new squadron had no *Tzefa* helicopters for its first nine months, having a few OH-58Bs attached to them for basic flight and tactical training, so their arrival was long awaited. The IAF designated these six helicopters *Tzefa As* and they all kept their original IAF tail numbers, but with a different prefix, becoming '309', '315', '318', '324', '326' and '330'.

The new squadron, (No 160 Squadron according to published sources), continued its training programme and was declared operational on 7 May 1979, still with six Cobras. Two days later, the squadron was called to action in an offensive against terrorist bases at Beit Al-Halil in Lebanon. The base was hit with four TOW missiles and destroyed.

The six AH-1S/ECAS Cobras were delivered to Tel Nof in June 1979 and were designated *Tzefa Bs*. These carried the chin mounted M-197 three-barrel 20mm gun, upgraded avionics and a helmet mounted sight system which greatly improved the *Tzefa*'s capability. The new helicopters, with their distinctive 'flat-plate' canopies, were revealed during the IAF pilot graduation air show at Hatzerim Air Force Base the following July.

With a full complement of twelve *Tzefas* and three OH-58B helicopters, the squadron moved to Palmachim, south of Tel Aviv, on 19 September 1979. This base was designated to become a hub for helicopter operations and grew rapidly during the ensuing years, starting with a new squadron of MD500 Defenders in March 1980.

Following further conflicts along the Lebanese border areas, in which the Cobras played only a small part, the Israeli Defence Forces launched Operation 'Peace for Galilee' on 6 June 1982. Operating from advance air strips, the Cobras supported troops as they moved through South Lebanon and on to the outskirts of Beirut. In this support role, they acted as forward reconnaissance scouts and brought added firepower when needed to aid troops in combat.

Although they did face Syrian armour, attacking tanks and rocket launchers, their main function was not in the anti-tank role and their full capabilities were not exploited due to lack of training, particularly in night operations. Much of the success against the Syrians tanks came from the Defender helicopters, perfectly at home in the narrow valleys, where their agility came to the fore.

Working closely with ground troops also meant the Cobras encountered enemy ground fire and *Tzefa B* '337' was shot down on the night of 5 June 1982, killing the crew, Captain Yossi Keller and Captain Amichai Spector.

Tzefa '130' was one of the first batch of AH–1Gs to arrive in 1975. It retains the 'sugar scoop' exhaust deflector and US Army paint scheme. The appliqué panels and sponsons for the M–35 are clearly visible. Close study also reveals a flare dispenser strapped under the Rocket pod. (*Ray Ball*)

Above: A very nice study of the a second batch ECAS/S Cobra (Tzefa B) which arrived in Israel around 1979. (*Ray Ball*)

Left: One of fourteen AH–1E Tzefa Fs delivered in 1996, (note the IDF 50th anniversary sticker). These airframes came directly from US Army stocks and this airframe (665) retains its original FS 34031 paint and inlet flow diverter. (*Ray Ball*)

A 'Southern Squadron' Tzefa displays its distinctive 'snake' emblem. (*Ray Ball*)

Not to be outdone, the 'Northern Squadron' painted an even bigger serpent on their aircraft. (*Ray Ball*)

Syrian Gazelle helicopters were also spotted over the battlefields, leading to confusion and unfortunately, on 11 June 1982, *Tzefa B* '309' was hit by friendly fire from an Israeli tank. The crew, Captain Moshe Cohen and Captain Tal Raviv, made an emergency landing and were rescued, but their Cobra was lost when the Sikorsky CH-53D *Yasur* sent to recover it back to Israel, had problems with vibrations caused by the load and had to drop it into the sea.

Nevertheless, the Cobra did impress the IDF and in September 1982 the American government agreed to allow further Cobra sales to Israel. Israel opted to buy enough new-built AH-1S (modernised) helicopters to equip a further squadron. The new helicopters were supplied over the period 1983 to 1985 and featured Kaman composite main rotor blades, a new and more effective exhaust suppressor, a modernised fire control and navigation system, head up display systems, improved warning systems and Israeli designed self-defence chaff/flare dispensers. All the surviving AH-1S and AH-1E helicopters were put through an upgrading programme to bring them up to a similar standard. (Something the US Army never achieved)

A 'Southern Squadron' Tzefa displays its distinctive 'snake' emblem. (*Ray Ball*)

No 160 Squadron, (the original Cobra squadron) was renamed the 'Southern' Cobra Squadron and carried on with its responsibilities at Palmachim, but also assisted with training crews for the new Squadron. This new name also came with a new squadron badge of a winged snake, painted on the tail.

The new Cobra squadron, No 161, known as the 'Northern' Squadron, was formally established in July 1985 under the command of Lieutenant Colonel Efraim Segoli. It too was based at Palmachim and designed its own snake badge to be painted on the helicopter tails.

An interesting footnote; the ill-fated Sikorsky-67 was a potential candidate for an Israeli order, which explains the colour scheme worn at the time of its demise in September 1974. (*Dick Ward*)

Lessons learned from the Lebanon conflict were also applied, as the Cobras were repainted in a different shade of brown (FS30145) and to aid identification by ground troops, large yellow (FS33434) 'V's were painted on each fuselage side.

On 21 October 1985, whilst on a training flight, Cobra '489' crashed off the shoreline of the Sea of Galilee. A second accompanying Cobra landed nearby and rescued the two pilots caught in the wreckage, earning an award from IAF Commander Amos Lapidot. Although Cobra '489' was heavily damaged the IAF recovered it and began a five year rebuilding task which ended with the helicopter's return to service.

A year later on, 16 October 1986, a No 69 Squadron IAF Phantom attacking Palestinian targets in Lebanon suffered damage from a bomb exploding prematurely following a malfunctioning bomb release. The two crew members were forced to eject from the stricken aircraft. The navigator, Captain Ron Arad, was captured by the terrorists and has been held in captivity since that day.

However, the pilot of the downed aircraft managed to evade his pursuers. A pair of Cobras from the Northern Squadron approached his location, but were fired upon by terrorists on the ground, hampering rescue attempts. Taking a chance, one of the Cobras dashed forward to his position and lifted the stricken pilot away hanging on to the landing skids. Major Assaf Meytiv and Captain Avi Hachmon, the helicopter crew, were later decorated for their bravery.

A similar rescue took place on 9 December 1988 after four Golani Brigade soldiers became stranded during a raid on a terrorist base in Na'ama, Lebanon, following Operation 'Kahol ve-Hoom' (Blue and Brown). Under heavy fire, a pair of Southern Squadron Cobras descended towards the soldiers and carried them on their skids to Israeli Navy vessels off the Lebanese coast. The four Cobra crew members who had performed the rescue, Lietenant Colonel Moshe Cohen (the Squadron Commander), Major Eran Fyer, Lieutenant Dan Laluz and Lieutenant Marcello Yalin received citations from the IDF Chief-of-Staff.

During the 1980s the *Tzefa* Cobra developed into a potent attack and support helicopter, as it became a critical part of IDF operations in Lebanon and when working with troops fighting terrorists on the West Bank and the Gaza Strip. New tactics were developed working with IDF Armoured Brigades, particularly when more advanced versions of the TOW missiles became available, increasing anti-tank capabilities.

Heavy usage began to take its toll on the IAF Cobra fleet, particularly on the early examples, but they had proved the concept of the attack helicopter and the IAF began to look at replacements. In the subsequent evaluation, the IAF decided the AH-64 Apache was better suited to its longer term needs, but in the interim more AH-1F Cobras were purchased and these were delivered in late 1989. These Cobras were designated *Tzefa Es* (tail numbers beginning with '5') and were split between both squadrons. The few Defender helicopters remaining in the squadrons as part of their 'Hunter-Killer' teams, were withdrawn and allocated to No 190 Squadron, the original Defender squadron, known in the IAF as *Lahatut* Hebrew for 'trick') .

On 30 May 1990, two terrorist teams launched a surprise attack along the shore of Israel, using speedboats deployed from a Libyan cargo ship. Fortunately for Israel, they were spotted by a Dornier 28 pilot flying along the coastline, who summoned assistance. One of these speedboats was intercepted by the Israeli Navy, but another with nine terrorist on board successfully landed on the beach at Nitzanim in southern Israel. The IAF scrambled two Cobras from Palmachim who soon spotted the terrorists and after an exchange of fire in which four of them were killed by 20mm cannon shells, the remaining five surrendered.

Although the 1990s started as a relatively peaceful time for the IAF, the attack helicopter squadrons were generally kept busy, being frequently called to action against terrorist organisations in Lebanon, which now included the Hezbollah organization, which acted under the umbrella of Iran.

As the terrorist bases and activists were embedded amongst the civilian population, accurate attacks with low collateral damage were necessary and the Cobra was ideal in this environment. IAF Attack helicopters often entered Lebanese territory in advance of IDF ground force incursions, and for these missions the Cobras again operated from forward locations, near the Lebanese border.

Two major operations against Hezbollah guerrillas, 'Accountability' and 'Grapes of Wrath' took place during the 1990s. The first, carried out during July 1993 saw day and night Cobra missions against guerrilla outposts. During March-April 1996, operation 'Grapes of Wrath', was launched with Cobras seeking and destroying Katyusha rocket launchers directed against northern Israel as well as attacking enemy positions in support of the IDF. The first three days saw over 150 attack sorties, with over ninety targets being attacked and over 170 TOW anti-tank missiles fired.

IAF Cobras have received various upgrades throughout their service. Many of the upgraded avionics installed are from Israeli industries, including their weapon guidance systems. In 1993 the Cobras were updated with the IAI-developed NTS (Night Targeting System) sight. This incorporates FLIR, TV and a Laser designator/rangefinder and has also been supplied to the USMC AH-1W fleet (NTS Upgrade) and some US Army Cobras as 'CNITE' updates.

In June 1994, a distinctive sand-coloured snake was painted on both sides of all the 'Southern' Squadron Cobra helicopters, but squadron rivalry also exists in Israel and the 'Northern' Squadron joked about them having 'worms' painted on their fuselage sides. However, in 2002, an even bigger snake was painted on the fuselage sides of all of the 'Northern' Squadron Cobras.

In 1996, fourteen surplus US Army AH-1E Cobras were air-lifted to Israel in C-5 Galaxy transport aircraft. These were named *Tzefa F* and given numbers beginning with '6'. Most were used to replace the MD500 Defenders in the IAF Attack Helicopter Training Squadron at the Flight School at Hatzerim. Some did go to the Cobra squadrons at Palmachim, leading to the withdrawal of the remaining early (ex-AH-1S) airframes still in service.

On 24 May 2000, the IDF completed its withdrawal from Lebanon and since then, with the invasion of Iraq, the threat of another armoured invasion of Israel on the dimensions of the 1973 war has much diminished. With two squadrons of the more capable Apache helicopter in service, the IAF has had to review the position of the Cobras and consider its future in the Order of Battle. Meanwhile, the Cobras continue to prove their worth mounting precision attacks against terrorist targets on the West Bank and Gaza strip.

Over the years, the IAF shared Cobra operating experiences with the US Army, who continued to provide access to training and support. However in 2001, the US Army withdrew the Cobra from service, raising concern in Israel about increased operating costs and the continued acquisition of spare parts for the large number of Cobras still in service. In 2006 these concerns were alleviated when thirty ex-U.S.Army Cobras from the stocks of retired aircraft at Fort Drum arrived in Israel to provide a source of spares. (Unconfirmed reports suggest that subsequently further shipments may also have been delivered). (These airframes were delivered from the stocks held at Fort Drum as sources of spare parts – and there are unconfirmed reports of much larger numbers of airframes eventually going to Israel).

On 12 July 2006, Hezbollah ambushed an IDF patrol on the Israeli side of the border with Lebanon, killing three soldiers and kidnapping two others. In response, Israel launched an operation against the Hezbollah in southern Lebanon. During this operation, Cobra helicopters mounted hundreds of missions, escorting assault helicopters, destroying mobile rocket launchers and attacking Hezbollah targets.

In December 2008, the IDF launched Operation 'Cast Lead', against Hamas terrorist groups in the Gaza Strip, following attacks against Israeli towns. Cobras from the Southern Squadron were involved in the opening sequence of the operation, by launching missiles at a Hamas parade. More Cobra missions followed until the operation ended with an agreed cease fire.

The future of the Cobra within the IAF is unclear as it is now an old helicopter, with the newest airframes being over 20 years old. Although out-classed and out-performed by the new Apaches, it still provides reliable service and is used for Attack Helicopter pilot training. The Cobra will certainly be seen and heard over Israel for a few years more yet.

Japan

Japan remains unique in manufacturing Cobras under licence. These aircraft are equivalent to the fully updated AH-1F baseline. In Japanese service however these aircraft retain their original 'AH-1S' designation as unlike the Americans the Japanese have only one configuration. (*Bell*)

To date only Japan has manufactured Cobras under licence. Two pattern AH-1S aircraft were delivered during 1977/78 configured with the earlier 'sugar scoop' exhaust and the 540 metal blades (AH-1E under current nomenclature). Fuji Heavy Industries produced eighty-nine production machines which were fully up to F Step 3 standard with the Kaman composite blades (albeit they retain the original 'AH-1S' designation in Japanese service). These aircraft equip five attack squadrons and a training unit.

Jordan/Pakistan

In 1982 Jordan ordered twenty-four AH-1F standard Cobras all of which had been delivered by 1985. At about the same time the Pakistan Army also ordered F Models and have taken delivery of two production batches, and possibly some attrition replacements. There are reportedly twenty in service at present plus six currently undergoing refurbishment.

Jordan ordered its first Cobras in 1982. This AH-1F example is seen leaving Bell's Flightline on the first leg of its delivery. (*Mike Verier*)

Pakistan has received at least two batches of AH-1Fs. This example is again up from Fort Worth prior to shipment. (*Bell*)

Thailand

The baseline export model is essentially an 'F' airframe with some of the more sensitive electronics deleted and intake particle filters added. It is also operated by **Thailand** who purchased four in 1999, one of which was lost. Four more refurbished airframes were delivered from Fort Drum in 2012.

The Royal Thai Army has the distinction of operating a Cobra that is both the oldest and newest airframe in service. Delivered in 2012, this was a 'zero-timed' AH-1F which was originally built as an AH-1G and had served in Vietnam with the USMC. (*Bell*)

Bahrain

Bahrain, received a number of batches between 1995 and 2007 bringing the fleet to thirty, of which six are TAH-1 trainer variants (a very subtle distinction, 'TAH' aircraft are identical to 'AH' apart from a modification to the front seat cyclic which results in a small bulge in the external skin). Illustrated in the colour section.

Turkey

Turkey is currently unique in operating a mix of single and twin-engine models. Turkey purchased thirty-two 'F/P' Models in two batches in 1992/3. In 1994 ten of the more capable AH-1W variant were supplied from USMC stocks as a planned precursor to a much larger order. By all accounts the 'Whiskys' have performed extremely well and the type was selected under the ATAK competition (a requirement for up to seventy-five new attack helicopters) as long ago as 2000. Turkey was also offered the AH-1Z (reportedly with a wheeled option). Political and budgetary constraints seem to have killed the prospect of this order and Turkey is in the process of acquiring Agusta A129 *Mangustas*. Despite this two 'Whiskys' were reportedly delivered in 2010/11 as urgent attrition replacements, (only six of the original ten remaining). Illustrated in the colour section.

Taiwan

Taiwan has sixty-three 'W' Models, deliveries being made in six batches commencing in 1993. The aircraft are fully Hellfire capable and equipped with the NTS upgrade. The Republic of China Army Aviation operates two attack wings, each with two squadrons, and a training wing. These aircraft operate in conjunction with Hellfire equipped AH-58D Kiowas, and as such represent a powerful deterrent to any aggression from the mainland. An upgrade/replacement requirement exists with Zulu Models in the running.

Taiwan is the largest operator of AH-1W model after the USMC. As can be seen here their aircraft are fully updated with the NTS upgrade. (*Taiwan Army*)

Orders that 'almost were', include the often reported one from **Greece** (which was approved but never confirmed) and **Germany** who seem to have a long history of flirtation with the Cobra. They reportedly ordered three for evaluation at the 1967 Paris Salon – an order never confirmed. Nothing daunted, Bell offered them the AH-1S in 1975 to meet the original PAH (*PanzerAbHauber*) requirement, then the four-blade Model 249 to meet PAH-2 in 1981, and subsequently the 4BW version of the 'Whisky' in 1987 as PAH90. Despite the fact that all three met or exceeded the stated requirements (and would have been manufactured by Dornier who had already built UH-1D Hueys) the Germans, having gained a great deal of data from evaluating other people's helicopters, chose to develop a European solution with the French.

Plans for licence production of a 'Whisky-based' model in **Romania**, under the designation AH-1RO *Dracula* originally envisaged a ninety-six aircraft order. Budgetary and political difficulties could not be resolved however and the project was shelved in 1999.

A 'Whisky' variant was also proposed to a number of **Latin American** states in 1998 for ant-narcotics work. Known as the MH-1W it retained the 20mm and rocket capabilities, but deleted the anti-tank TOW/Hellfire options.

More recently **Australia** was offered the 'Zulu' under the designation ARH-1Z for its Attack Helicopter requirements, the order eventually going to the Franco-German *Tigre*. This was actually the second time the Australians had looked at the Cobra. An early 'G' en-route to Vietnam (67-15662) was briefly sent there for evaluation during the Australian involvement in the Vietnam War (gaining a kangaroo 'zap' in the process).

Accompanied by Bud Orpen and an eight-man Bell team, the Cobra left Fort Worth in an Air Force Douglas C-124 on July 15 1968. Along with a JetRanger it was first demonstrated in **New Zealand** before going on to Australia. 67-15662 was airlifted out of Australia on 5 August, going directly to Vietnam. In December 1970, eleven 'G's were ordered for No 9 Squadron RAAF, then in theatre. On 18 August 1971 however, Prime Minister McMahon announced that Australian troops would be 'home for Christmas' and in October the order was cancelled.

The much-travelled 67-15662 survived combat in Vietnam and ultimately served the full span of the Cobra's Army career, becoming an 'F' and finally reaching honourable retirement at Fort Drum in 2001.

The largest effort in recent years went into the 'Cobra Venom' proposal for the **British Army**. This was based originally on the 'Whisky' airframe and would have featured state of the art avionics and sensors in a completely redesigned cockpit. Prime contractor GEC Marconi built a cockpit mock-up/simulator at their Rochester works which placed the pilot in the front, rather than rear, seat, reversing the classic layout (strictly speaking the 'pilot' could fly from either seat, as is the case with the 'Zulu'). The night capability included a helmet system that projected a real-time FLIR image directly onto the pilots' visor, (a huge improvement over the 'tunnel vision' NVGs then in use). A great deal of work went into ensuring that the new layout addressed all the perceived limitations of the 'Whisky' cockpit.

As originally drawn, the British specification was entirely met by an upgraded 'Whisky'. Unlike its primary competitor the 'Whisky' Cobra was already fully marinised too, (unfortunately mis-pronounced by GEC's Lord Weinstock as 'marinated' during one rather enthusiastic press presentation). This very important Cobra feature was ignored in the RFP however, something the MoD was to later regret.

The programme was very cost conscious and GEC were at pains to point out how many Cobras could be acquired (and how quickly) versus the competitors. The two-blade rotor had originally been retained for reasons of cost, but late in the programme the four-blade main and tail rotors were included in the proposal, bringing it fully up to the '4BW' configuration then current.

As described earlier, technical merits are one thing, but politics and co-production agreements quite another. Originally to be a large (about 100 aircraft) order, even Kamov threw their hat in the ring offering the Ka-50 'Werewolf' as did the South Africans with *Rooivalk*. Ultimately however the choice came down to the Cobra (Bell/GEC), the Apache (Boeing/Westlands) and Tiger (Eurocopter/BAe). The order went to Westlands WAH-64 Apache in 1995.

An ironic post-script came in 2012 when the MoD was to discover the cost of ignoring the need for marinisation. In 2011 the otherwise very successful WAH-64 was committed to Operation 'Ellamy' in support of the anti-Ghaddafi movement in Libya. With no land-bases available, the Apache operation had been conducted from the deck of the assault carrier HMS *Ocean*. Landing on a ship of course presents no great problem for a helicopter. Operating an armed one for an extended period from a sea base is however an entirely different proposition.

Quite apart from the obvious problems of salt corrosion and adequately chaining parked aircraft to a rolling deck, the aircraft electronics and weapons need to be hardened against EMP emissions from the ship's radar, which can damage electronics and cause weapons to fire. As the Americans found when they briefly considered it many years ago, marinising an Apache is a difficult and expensive undertaking on the production line. The MoD was seeking retrospective modifications to a land-based airframe – it is not hard to imagine the sharp intake of breath when the estimates came in.

Part of the reason for the success of the 'Marine branch' Cobra variants on the other hand is that they have been fully marinised as standard since the J Model.

The Cobra Venom was an impressive project and had it proceeded the USMC would certainly have benefited directly. Not for the first time the Marines had persuaded someone else to carry out a great deal of development and qualification work. It was not wasted as most of it did indeed carry directly over into the subsequent 'Zulu' programme.

OLD COBRAS NEVER DIE
A remarkable regeneration

Throughout the Cobra story, the AH-1 has, like the eponymous reptile, frequently shed its skin to emerge newer and stronger. This has normally taken the form of evolution, 'G' models becoming 'Q's and then 'S', 'T's becoming 'Whisky' and then 'Zulu'. There is however another, less-well known, regeneration story.

When, in 1999, the Army decided to retire its largely AH-1F fleet from the front line, (Snakes soldiered on until 2001 with National Guard units), it could have scrapped them or parked them out in the desert. Instead a far more imaginative programme was begun in 2000 that would not only ensure that the Cobra lived on, but actually prove profitable to the Army and the taxpayer.

F Model Cobras remain in service with air arms around the world and under the auspices of the FMS 'shop' at Wheeler-Sack Army Airfield, Fort Drum NY, an initiative was begun to collect all remaining Cobra airframes, spares, tools and associated equipment. Survey teams were sent out to evaluate aircraft on site and the first machine arrived early in 2001. Eventually some 469 airframes passed through the facility,

The airframes were drained of fluids and evaluated on arrival. Depending on their condition some were stripped for spares, the airframe hulks going for targets or to museums. The USMC alone purchased some $75 million of these spares.

The better airframes were completely refurbished. At around $1 million and 5,500 man-hours per airframe all the aircraft received new wiring looms manufactured on site and replacement items such as batteries and engines as required.

FMS customers accounted for the bulk of these sales. Aircraft and spares went to Israel, Turkey, Bahrain, Jordan, Thailand and Pakistan. Reportedly up to 100 airframes went to Israel, possibly unrefurbished, as Israel has of course the capacity to carry out its own re-manufacturing.

In 2012, the Royal Thai Army took delivery of the final four re-conditioned 'zero time' AH-1Fs to go through Fort Drum. Responsible for the re-assembly and test flying of the aircraft on arrival in Thailand, pilot 'Mac' McMillan had also carried out the necessary 'post-production' (Return To Service) check-flights. Going through the aircraft records he noticed what appeared to be an anomaly; the oldest of the airframes, 68-17108, was clearly an Army aircraft, but it had undergone maintenance and even battle damage repair with the USMC. His curiosity aroused he dug deeper, the story that unfolded showed the airframe to be no stranger to South East Asian skies and again illustrates the Cobra's remarkable longevity.

68-17108 (c/n 20836) was built as a 'G' at Bell's Hurst plant in 1970 and delivered to the USMC at Fort Hood as part of the batch of thirty-eight 'G' models 'loaned' to the Marines (these aircraft retained their Army serials, hence the odd-looking documentation). Going almost directly to Vietnam it saw considerable combat (both Buck Simmons and Hank Perry actually flew '108 as 'TV-25' during its time there with HMA-367 'Scarface'). Following its combat tour '108 returned to the US and after overhaul at Corpus Christi Army Depot (CCAD) in 1972, it became part of the newly-formed HMA-169 at Camp Pendleton, CA. It continued to serve there until withdrawn to storage at the Davis-Monthan desert 'boneyard' in April 1979 as the USMC's 'J' models were deployed.

In 1981 it was transferred to Bell's Amarillo facility where it received the full AH-1S conversion. Re-designated as an 'F' it re-joined the Army in February 1982 serving with the 1st Armoured Division in Germany. Following a further update at CCAD in 1988 it went to Korea, finally returning to the US in 1994 to serve with the Army National Guard. 68-17108 was therefore one of the last Cobras in Army service. Finally, in September 2001, the old warrior was placed in long term storage at Fort Drum.

That it is just starting another front-line assignment more than forty years after its combat debut says it all – 68-17108 continues to serve.

As noted elsewhere, de-militarised aircraft found their way to other government agencies and to various civilian operators. The US Forestry Service acquired twenty-five machines as 'FireWatch' Cobras for spotting and FAC duties. Fire services in Florida, Montana and Washington had aircraft actually designed to drop water/retardant under the 'FireSnake' designation.

Many Cobras now fly as 'Warbirds', the most well-known of these being the Army Aviation Heritage Foundation (AAHF) which 'owns' some fifteen airframes, operating five as the 'SkySoldiers' demonstration team. One now promotes a well-known energy drink in Europe and at least one is destined to fly in the UK airshow circuit.

Reverting to their 'Bell 209' designation yet more Snakes now haul logs and freight in Latin America.

There are few, if any, military aircraft that can claim to have given the taxpayer not only four decades of valuable service, but also a significant cash return on their initial investment. With this impressive programme the Cobra has achieved exactly that.

Just some of the Cobras gathered at Fort Drum in 1999-2000. All told, nearly 500 Cobras were to pass through the facility, many to fly again. (*Peyton DeHart*)

Many of the airframes had considerable history. 68-17108 was originally built as a G Model going directly to the USMC. Seen here around 1969 on LZ 'Baldy' in Vietnam as 'VT-25' whilst with HMA-367 'Scarface'. (*Buck Simmons*)

68-17108 was eventually returned to the US Army and rebuilt as an AH-1F. She became one of four refurbished aircraft delivered to the Royal Thai Army in 2012. Here the pre-delivery Maintenance Test Flight has just been completed. 'Mac' McMillan is in the cockpit. (*'Mac' McMillan*)

Other Fort Drum airframes were de-militarised and converted for various civilian uses, notably forestry departments where the Cobra's considerable lifting ability, speed and agility would be of value. (*Florida Department of Agriculture*)

The Forestry Service also uses converted Cobras, albeit in a 'spotter' role, hence the FLIR ball under the nose. (*US Forestry Service*)

This fabulously coloured and marked Snake flies in Chile as CC-CLF. Demonstrated here is the 'Bambi' bucket which can be stowed in the Cobras' capacious ammunition bay. (*Victor Cepeda Contreras*)

One of very few Cobras to make it out of the US is operated by the Red Bull organisation based in Austria. Reportedly rebuilt from two airframes N11FX was acquired from Chuck Erin in 2004 and arrived at Red Bull's Salzburg base in 2005. (*Red Bull*)

Currently N11FX wears this stunning livery for appearances at air shows around Europe. (*Jorg Adam / Red Bull*)

Probably the best-known Cobra demonstration team is flown by the Atlanta-based 'Sky Soldiers' of the Army Aviation Heritage Foundation. The Army Aviation Heritage Foundation holds some fourteen airframes, all ex-Fort Drum. Five are flown in this immaculate scheme whilst another retains 'Army Green'. (*Greg Davies*)

Chapter 12

Snakes Bite

Towards the sound of gunfire

As we have seen in earlier chapters, the Cobra earned its spurs almost from the moment it was deployed in Vietnam. The attack helicopter was capable of a surgical precision compared with the 'dumb' bombs of the day that were all that fixed-wing aircraft could deliver. Nearly half-a-century later, and despite the 'smart' weapons available to the 'fast-movers', that remains true. Today brave men continue to take it into harm's way and in so doing save countless lives. As these words were being written in late 2012, attack helicopters were delivering pin-point strike capability in Libya and Afghanistan.

Quite apart from the close-quarters combat that typified the Vietnam War, the Cobra was quickly found to be capable, in extremis, of combat rescue. Amongst the first to have cause to be glad that the 'Snake' has a big drop-down door for the ammunition bay was a wounded USAF security guard trapped by the VietCong during the ferocious Tet assault on Bien Hoa, Captain Ken Rubin winning a DSC for his courageous action in landing under fire and snatching him to safety. Another early rescue was one Captain R. Fogleman USAF. Having ejected from his F-100, his ride home was also made clinging to the Cobra's gun bay door. The Air Force should be grateful; Fogleman went on to be a Four Star General and Air Force Chief of Staff.

On 18 March 1971, Captain Terryl Morris of the 101st Airborne lifted three downed aircrew (the crew of an OH-6) from a cliff edge 3,000ft up a mountain. Only able to get the first three feet of the skids on the ground the rest of the aircraft hung over the sheer drop whilst the three men clambered gingerly aboard the ammo bay doors, two on one side. They were safely returned to Vandengriff, the brief and rather scary ride infinitely preferable to being trapped by the NVA advancing up the mountain towards them.

They were not to be the last, and a generation later USMC Cobra crews in Lebanon could be seen with a pair of snap-rings/Karabiners as standard part of their flight kit for just such an eventuality. Israeli Cobras extracted four infantrymen cut off in the Golan Heights in much the same way in the 1980s. It is not unknown for present day Special Forces and Recon types to ride the gun bay door in Afghanistan either (albeit highly unofficially). Marine Corps tactics are widely reflected in the British Attack helicopter community, (which has maintained an exchange programme for many years), and more recently in Afghanistan British soldiers clinging to the sides of two Apaches landed under intense fire to recover a badly injured comrade from the heavily defended fort at Jugram.

The Cobra was designed and built for the Vietnam war. In a far from permissive environment it gave the AirMobile soldier on the ground the close air support he needed. A modern version of Light Cavalry and Horse Artillery it fully lived up to expectation. (*US Army via Ray Wilhite*)

The Cobra was designed specifically to support and defend infantry. During the Vietnam War it did exactly that, escorting the troop carrying Hueys, 'Big Windies' (CH-47 Chinooks) CH-46 'Frogs' and the ever-oily CH-53 'Shitters' in to and out of hostile LZs. They scouted, took out bunkers and blunted attacks which were sometimes within yards of their own front line. Cobras even took part in 'black ops' in Laos escorting and protecting recce teams on 'Prairie Fire' missions. Stories of this conflict alone could, (indeed have), merited several books. Pilots of the time, however, recall getting their hands on the hottest of hot ships and flying it to its limits. This includes not always intentional aerobatics. The 'Snake' is not supposed to do loops and rolls, but this author has spoken to pilots who have done both and lived to tell the tale.

Perhaps surprisingly however it was an operation that the Cobra had not been designed for that helped to finally bring the war to an end.

MARHUK 1972

Towards the end of 1971, the Americans were trying to extract themselves from Vietnam. 'Peace' negotiations were stalled in Paris and looking precarious. Conducting the negotiations for the Americans was the redoubtable Henry Kissinger. Faced with a complete lack of progress he advised the White House of his frustration at the North's duplicity and intransigence in typically unequivocal terms. Recipient of this blunt assessment was President Richard Milhous Nixon, (who history would subsequently remember for entirely different reasons). He finally concluded that only direct action against the North would bring them back to the table. Accordingly (and as part of the much larger 'Linebacker II' operation) the mining of Hanoi and six other ports and harbours was ordered on 8 May 1972 to disrupt the flow of materiel reaching the North.

The Cobra was to play a crucial part in this effort. With the carriers heavily committed further south there remained a need for surveillance and interdiction of supplies at the Hon La deep water anchorage.

In June therefore, six AH-1J Cobras of HMA-369 deployed aboard the USS *Denver*, LPD-9, a 'flag configured' Austin-class amphibious transport. Effectively floating docks these vessels were designed to deploy landing craft. Whilst they had an aft landing deck capable of accepting CH-46 'Frogs' they were not 'aviation' ships *per se*. The Cobras were selected precisely because

The 'standard' loadout for the MARHUK birds was two seven-shot pods, and two Zuni pods (with only two missiles fitted) plus 750 rounds of 20mm ammunition for the turret gun. The scheme on this AH-1J is illustrated fully in the colour profiles section. (*Col David Corbett USMC*)

The MARHUK operation was a unique use of the Cobra to interdict seaborne supply lines. Faced with massive AAA defences, the aircraft had their markings hastily toned down. The huge Zuni pod, painted white because it normally hung under the wing of a fast-jet, rather compromised the scheme. (*Col David Corbett USMC*)

they could deploy from an austere platform but had sufficient offensive capability to deal with the anticipated threats.

The six month operation that ensued was known as MARHUK (MARine HUnterKiller). At the time highly secret, it was completely outside the USMC's normal operating doctrine and the small detachment had to work out new tactics as they went. Operating by day and night, the Cobras carried out surveillance, directed naval gunfire, and attacked supplies as they were brought ashore – the Chinese ships they were unloaded from could not of course be attacked. They were frequently subject to fire from the numerous AAA sights defending the anchorage; aggressive response from the Marines however limited their effectiveness. Despite 140 recorded instances of hostile fire on only seven occasions did the Cobras take hits. No crew members were injured and only one aircraft received damage that could not be repaired on the ship.

The MARHUK deployment also saw the first use of the massive 5 inch 'Zuni' FFAR (Folding-Fin Aircraft Rocket), by the Cobra, giving the 'Snakes' a useful stand-off from which to engage shore batteries. For much the same reason the 20mm M-197 proved to be the right choice for the 'J' Cobra. On two occasions a 'broadside' was considered necessary resulting in a 'Hog' configured (4x19-shot 2.75 pods) Cobra unleashing the entire load in one awesome pass.

The USMC was not anxious to repeat this type of operation as it felt that it was well outside its normal role. (There was also considerable opposition from the A-4 Skyhawk community who felt that their *raison d'etre* was in danger of being usurped) Nevertheless MARHUK served as an example of the flexibility and potential of the Cobra when properly deployed and supported that resonates to this day.

Whilst the next few years were to be relatively quiet for the Americans, it was not to be long before Cobras were in action elsewhere. The Israelis had taken delivery of a small number of G Models in the early 1970s. These were followed by TOW-capable AH-1Ss and by 1979 they had seen their first combat use, in South Lebanon. (see Chapter 11)

Iran-Iraq War 1980–1988

In 1972, with the MARHUK operation still in progress, the Shah of Iran had placed an order for J Model Cobras, albeit rather more capable versions than those the USMC were using. His demise in 1979 added to the political turmoil in the region and in 1980 hostility between Iran and neighbouring Iraq erupted into full scale war. Despite the complete cessation of American support for Iran's Cobras they remained a potent force and saw considerable combat during the eight year war. Used in their primary role as anti-armour/infantry support aircraft, they were reportedly very effective. Forced to improvise, the Iranians also managed to fire AGM-65 Mavericks from their 'J's as well as the TOWs they had been delivered with.

It was during this conflict that the Cobra came directly against the much vaunted Mi-24 Hind for the first time in anger. The Hind was (is) bigger and faster than the Cobra but lacked manoeuvrability. The possible outcome of such a duel was the subject of much Cold War speculation (especially by Cobra crews patrolling the East German border) none of which was resolved in the engagements that followed. At the end of the war, the Iranians had reportedly lost ten Cobras in air-to-air fighting, but in return had downed six Hinds. Two of these, it was claimed, using TOW missiles – presumably the Hinds hadn't seen the Cobras firing!

Today Cobra crews have real Mi-24s available for dissimilar combat training and the threat is a known quantity. They will tell you with some certainty that if you see him first, and can stay above his rotor disc, the Cobra has a more than even chance of winning the engagement.

Grenada 1983

As the 1980s dawned the US Marines found themselves trying to keep the peace in Lebanon. In 1982 at the other end of the world British forces had re-taken the Falklands marking a sea change in the west's attitude to getting involved in conflict. The following year, Marines en-route to a routine deployment in Lebanon were diverted to assist the legitimate Government of Grenada following a *coup* backed by Cuban troops. They were to extract a large number of students trapped by the fighting, a routine the Marines knew well.

Operation 'Urgent Fury' in October 1983 was to involve the Cobra in America's first real combat operations since the end of the Vietnam War. Due to the speed of the deployment, the four AH-1T Cobras aboard the USS *Guam* (LPH-9), an Iwo Jima-class amphibious assault ship, as part of HMM-261 'Raging Bulls' were the only attack helicopter support available to the

The rapid reaction to events in Grenada in 1983 meant that initially the 'Ragin' Bulls' four AH-1Ts were the only Cobras available for the initial assault. Tragically two of them were shot down. *El Tigre*, EM/33, 160747 shown here survived along with EM/31, *The Reaper*, below (*Peyton DeHart*)

Following the Grenada fighting, the USS Guam (LPH-9) resumed her course to take up station off Beirut. At some point in the deployment the aircraft, almost inevitably, acquired a 'sharkmouth'. 'EM/31', 160821, is illustrated fully in the colour profiles section. (*Peyton DeHart*)

Marines. The initial landings had been successful but the island was by no means secure and it became apparent that Sir Paul Scoon (Governor General, and the man recognised by the Reagan Administration as representing legitimate authority) would need to be rescued from the city of St Georges. A Special Forces mission was mounted to achieve this and the 'Bulls' found themselves covering the extraction. Sadly the intense fire they met resulted in the loss of two Cobras.

Cobra 160112 'EM 32' piloted by Captain Tim Howard was hit by 23mm fire, terribly wounding him, disabling the aircraft, and rendering the co-pilot, Captain Jeb Seagle USMCR, unconscious. Despite his injuries, (he had lost most of one arm and his leg was badly shot-up), Howard nevertheless managed to effect an upright crash landing in a football field. Recovering consciousness Seagle managed to drag his pilot out of and away from the burning aircraft and apply a tourniquet to his wounds. With hostile fire increasing and enemy soldiers approaching he knew that his colleagues' only chance would be if a medevac helicopter could reach him.

With no other support available, 1st Lieutenant Jeffrey Scharver and co-pilot Captain Pat Giguere in the remaining Cobra (160812 'EM 30') called for the extraction while continuing to suppress the AAA site, repeatedly making attack runs, even after their ammunition was exhausted. This enabled a CH-46 piloted by Major Mel Demars to get to the crash site.

On the ground Jeb Seagle continued to draw the enemy ground fire on himself and away from his pilot. When the medevac arrived he did not re-appear from the tree line where he had succumbed to his wounds. Tragically a minute after the CH-46 had lifted off, Scharver and Giguere were caught by another 23mm battery, crashing into the sea with the loss of both crew members.

For his selfless actions that day Jeb Seagle was awarded a posthumous Navy Cross, still the highest award ever given to a USMC Cobra pilot. Tim Howard received a Distinguished Flying Cross for his incredible airmanship in getting the aircraft safely down despite his horrific injuries. For the stubborn defence of their downed colleagues Jeff Scharver received a posthumous Silver Star as did Pat Giguere who was also posthumously promoted Major. Tim Howard also received a Silver Star and despite his injuries eventually returned to duty serving a full career in the Marines and retiring as a Colonel.

Two replacement 'T's from HMLA-269, plus crews, were hastily flown down to Salines airport in the back of Lockheed C-141 Starlifters. Led by then-Major Outlaw, some re-assembly was required when transported this way, so there was some delay from the landing time until they flew aboard USS *Guam* and joined the squadron for the closing days of the Grenada operation.

Starlifters from Pope also duly delivered the 82nd Airborne's AH-1S Cobras to Grenada. By then however, the fighting had largely finished. The sacrifices made had not been in vain, the return of the Island to legitimate rule was accomplished.

In a postscript to this action, twenty-five years later, the tail fin from Howard and Seagles' Cobra was discovered in a scrap yard on the island by former 'Bulls' who arranged for its recovery. The Marines never forget their fallen and thanks to the help of a C-130 Hercules from VMGR-252 at Cherry Point, this poignant artefact returned to Quantico on 27 April 2009. At the time of writing it is safely stored awaiting eventual display at Quantico's Museum.

On 23 October 1983, two days prior to the Grenada landings, a truck-bomb had been driven into the Marines' compound in Beirut. It was to result in the deaths of 241 US personnel, most of them Marines. Waiting only for the replacement aircraft and crews, the *Guam* quickly resumed its voyage eastwards.

Following the Beirut attack, Marine AH-1T Cobras were kept busy covering the extraction of civilians as well as artillery spotting and protecting their ships from mines and any fast-boat attacks that might develop.

When the *Guam* arrived on station from Grenada the 'Raging Bulls' immediately took up these duties. Towards the end of the 'Bulls' time on station it had become apparent that evacuation of vulnerable personnel would be necessary.

The squadron, especially the few Cobra pilots, had experienced a demanding cruise, the fighting in Grenada, the losses they had endured and now the high tension of operations off a less-than-friendly coastline. Amongst them was Lieutenant Colonel (then 1st Lieutenant) Peyton DeHart. The extracts below, from journals and letters written at the time, illustrate the dangers they faced on a daily basis. On the day in question they were covering the extraction of embassy personnel from a road near the Beirut seafront.

6 February 1984 'We briefed four 46's and four Cobras for an evacuation operation (the civilians from the embassy). The evacuation operation most likely won't go tonight, but it sure is an option that could be executed…'

7 February 1984 'I was a gunner that day; sitting in the front seat of my Cobra, peering through an optical sight that magnified and stabilized my view of the world from the moving platform. As we circled at two miles offshore, I looked at the landing zone where our Frogs were going to go. It was flat enough, but in the middle of a city of windows, buildings and side streets, any number of ambushes could develop. That was a given; our helicopters had already been hit on more than one occasion as they came in for landings around Beirut.'

'I relayed that the area was clear and the CH-46s proceeded inbound, landed and kept the rotors spinning for the two to three minutes that it took to load everyone aboard. As my Cobra wheeled inbound, I scanned in and around the landing zone, looking especially for vehicles that might be trying to drive up to, and through, the barricades. None appeared. The transport aircraft pulled up in the sky a few feet, as if lifted up by marionette strings, the noses dipped down and the Frogs flew forward. As the third helo cleared the zone and headed back for our ship, I saw the flash and mentally heard the 'krump' of artillery hitting the street where our aircraft had been.'

'It had taken some anonymous artillery position three minutes to get information on our landing, decide to do something about it, and lay in the gun data that would enable a round to hit near the zone. Someone had pulled the lanyard as the aircraft were lifting. The twenty seconds it took for the shells to arc through the air were all that stood between success and failure of that mission. As I watched the flashes on the empty street, I radioed that information in, but I couldn't find the source.'

'The offending artillery pieces could have been anywhere in that sprawling city or the populous mountains that surround it. That was no matter really, because the artillery was no longer a threat; it couldn't affect the accomplishment of our mission. The civilians were already safely on their way to our ship (and thence to Cyprus). The hot steel could explode in cold rage on the empty street; it didn't matter. We had been too quick.'

The Middle East continued to be a conflict zone throughout the 1980s, Israeli Cobras in particular seeing much action as detailed in Chapter 11. Meanwhile the Iran-Iraq war continued, threatening shipping in the Gulf. The mining of a US frigate, the USS *Samuel B Roberts* (FFG58), in 1988 finally provoked the Americans to retaliate. Iran was using oil platforms in the Gulf to control its attacks and as bases for fast attack boats that were harrying shipping. Operation 'Praying Mantis' was designed to neutralise them and became the US Navy's biggest naval engagement since the Second World War. Once again Marine AH-1Ts were involved. Operating from one of the ships that had been involved in MARHUK, the USS *Trenton* (LPD-14), another Austin-class amphibious transport, they destroyed the Sassan platform using TOW missiles. One Cobra and its crew was lost during the operation.

Panama 1989

The following year was to see Army Cobras in action during Operation 'Just Cause', the invasion of Panama in December 1989 to remove the dictator Manuel Noriega. This operation involved a text-book airfield take-down by the 82nd Airborne whose 'Snakes' quickly dominated the city. Significant amongst a number of firsts, this operation also saw the first combat deployment of the AH-64A Apache.

Operation 'Just Cause' in 1989 would see the first operational deployment of the AH-64 Apache. It was however small-scale and not without problems. The 82nd Airborne's AH-1F Cobras meanwhile just carried on. (*Bell via Mike Verier*)

The long and bitter Iran/Iraq war spilled over and affected ships of other nations using the Persian Gulf. Operation 'Praying Mantis' in 1988 became the USN's biggest engagement since World War Two and the AH-1Ts were heavily involved. (*US Navy*)

This AH-1W, 162571 'YP/42', is seen aboard the USS Tarawa in the Western Pacific, September 1989, and is featured in the colour profiles section. Embellishments such as the 'sharkmouth' are 'cruise only' and were removed once the aircraft return to the more regulated CONUS environment. (*Peyton DeHart*)

Above: The official captions just says, '09.00 Hrs Desert Storm'. This AH-1J is manoeuvred onto the '3 Spot'. Note that armed aircraft are parked pointing outboard so that any weapons accidentally fired will go into the sea. (*US Navy*)

Opposite: This rare shot illustrates the swansong of the J Model Cobra. On the eve of retirement, HMLA-775's AH-1Js were hastily camouflaged and sent to the Gulf to provide back-up for the fleet AH-1W squadrons involved in Operation 'Desert Storm'. (*Bell via Mike Verier*)

Then in late 1990, Saddam Hussein invaded Kuwait. The initial response, Operation 'Desert Shield' was to contain the situation whilst a coalition force was assembled to counter attack. When it came, Operation 'Desert Storm' was to provide perhaps the most powerful demonstration of the attack helicopter's capabilities ever seen. Historically it was also the only time that four different generations of Cobras ('F', 'J', 'T' and 'W') would be in a combat zone together.

The Cobras gave a remarkable account of themselves, the Marines in particular making full use of their aircraft. So aggressive was their approach that at one point an entire Iraqi tank battalion surrendered to three Cobras and a Huey.

Operation 'Provide Comfort' 1990-91

Following the Gulf War there was a Kurdish uprising against rule from Baghdad. Hundreds of thousands of Kurds, fleeing Iraqi depredations in the valleys below, escaped to the high mountain ranges that mark the Iraqi-Turkish border. In the early stages of this exodus Cobras were called upon to protect transport helicopters flying food and supplies to the hard pressed Kurds. This mission also marked the last operational deployment of AH-1Ts before they were reworked into 'W's.

Meanwhile in Europe the break up of Yugoslavia in 1991 was giving rise to terrible civil war that would eventually draw NATO forces into conflict. In Africa, Somalia was also descending into lawlessness. The original humanitarian mission, Operation 'Restore Hope', under the aegis of the UN, was seaborne with USMC Cobras providing the necessary cover. It was, however, Army aviators that were to discover how difficult combat in a dense urban environment could be. Operations in this benighted land were to last from December 1992 until May 1993. Whilst the Snake crews fought long and hard, they could not affect the inevitable outcome of the ill-fated mission.

Gulf II – Operation 'Iraqi Freedom' March 2003

By the time of the second Gulf conflict, much had changed in the 'Skid' community. The Army had retired its AH-1 fleet from both regular and reserve forces, with nearly 500 remaining airframes in various stages of repair being gathered at Fort Drum. Likewise, the USMC had retired its trusty J Models to the desert boneyard at Davis-Monthan and the final 'T's had been re-worked into 'Whiskys'.

Whilst the Army had transitioned to the AH-64 Apache, the USMC now had an all AH-1W fleet, albeit upgraded following the lessons of 'Desert Storm'.

These lessons had been well heeded and again the Marines gave good account of themselves. Unlike the previous war the Cobras had also acquired extra Forward Air Control (FAC/A) duties due to the withdrawal of the OV-10 from service. This meant that as well as their primary mission of supporting ground units with reconnaissance and firepower, they were talking to and directing the fast jets, artillery units and the troops on the ground. Many of the missions, especially in the early phase of the war, were flown at night in conditions of almost nil visibility where the dust in the air rendered even the NVGs near useless.

Deployed from ships initially, the HMLAs often found themselves living in the desert alongside their aircraft as the ground forces pushed forward. The 'Gunrunners' of HMLA-269 flew some 3,000 combat hours with twenty-seven aircraft during the two-month campaign. Remarkably they suffered no casualties or accidents during this time. A quote from Major Jamie Cox, Operations Officer at the time, illustrates the complexity of such operations:-

'On another day mission, we're working the highway that connects Al Kut to Baghdad. To the north of that highway, a Marine unit is screening into the countryside. Iraqi tanks are located in that vicinity. Talking to the FAC, he cannot observe the Iraqis from his position, so he delegates the clearance to fire to me. Checking in on station at the same time is a section of Air Force A-10s with the callsign 'Eager 31' and '32'. Giving them my coordinates, I directed the A-10s to my position. Simultaneously, I cleared Wally, who was my wingman, to start engaging the Iraqi tanks. With the A-10s overhead, I began to talk their eyes onto the various

A 7th Cavalry AH-1F with chalked 'shark' additions in January 1991. (*Floyd Werner*)

tank targets. Clearing them to use their 30mm cannon, they roll in from above and begin to strafe the tanks. Their cannon is so loud that I can hear it from two miles away in my aircraft. It was quite an awesome sight. That day, we destroyed eight T-72 tanks.'

IFOR/Bosnia December 1995 to December 1996

In stark contrast the last combat deployment for the Army's F Models was in the wintry depths of Europe.

Floyd Werner:-

'The ONLY Cobra unit in Bosnia was the 1st Squadron, 1st Cavalry Regiment, 1st Armoured Division. It was the last operational deployment of an Army Cobra unit. We flew out of Germany around 21 December 1995. We had to perform some maintenance on two aircraft at Grafenwohr, which is where I did the test flights. I eventually got to Hungary, Tasar to be exact. We lived in some old SCUD bays on the airfield for a while. From there we deployed into Croatia, outside of Gradacheck (sic). We stayed there for quite some time. While there I had the opportunity to land in a minefield to recover a Cobra that landed there on a precautionary landing. Very memorable. Then we moved into Bosnia itself, just up the road from the minefield. Our mission, which lasted from 21 Dec until June '96, was to provide separation of the warring factions. We were to look intimidating and imposing which is the only thing they understood. We eventually turned in the aircraft in June '96.'

Certainly one of the brightest set of teeth to emerge from the desert war this is 79-23245 which was later lost in a crash following engine-failure over Germany. By then all that remained of the magnificent teeth was an Olive Drab shape where they had been painted out. (*Floyd Werner*)

The 'Skids' had very little time to prepare for deployment to Iraq and a number of the camouflage jobs utilised whatever paint was available, including some from local DiY stores. HMLA-169 chose to overpaint the green and black areas of the standard scheme with sand. Seen here back at Camp Pendleton after the hostilities, the temporary paint is beginning to peel. (*USMC*)

Turkey

Since the mid-late 1990s, Turkish Cobras have seen considerable action against rebels in their mountainous border regions. Turkey has a fleet of mostly F Model 'Snakes', but also purchased a small number of 'Whiskys'. These latter aircraft have all received the NTS upgrade and continue to demonstrate the Cobra's ability to operate in the most adverse conditions.

Working in high mountain passes, frequently from the most austere locations with no shelter from the snow and weather, the rugged 'marinised' 'Whisky' just gets on with its job. Despite a political decision to cancel an order for the 'Zulu' upgrade, Turkey's 'Whisky' Cobras remain seemingly indispensable. Although they are due to be replaced by the new (*Mangusta* derived) aircraft on order, the Turks have nevertheless recently taken delivery of some Cobra attrition replacements.

AH-1F 79-23445 serving with IFOR (implementation Force) in spring 1996, by which time the snow had turned to mud. Shortly afterwards this aircraft became the last Cobra to leave Europe when flown to retirement in England by Floyd Werner and Jud McCrary. (*Fernando 'Fred' Zayas via Floyd Werner*)

An AH-1W in Iraq. The advantage helicopters have is that you can land and talk to the troops on the ground – a tactical conference 'somewhere in the desert'. (*USMC*)

Afghanistan 2001 to date

At the time of writing, fighting in Afghanistan continues. The Cobras, with their exceptional 'hot 'n high' capability, are much in demand to support the ground troops. Talking to recently returned crews in 2011, this author was struck by the confidence they have in the Snake. The 20mm gun, its earlier reliability issues now a distant memory, is regarded as 'the best weapon on the aircraft'. Technology has given the gun a laser pointer and great accuracy. Consequently the now rather 'clunky' mechanical-linkage HSS is seldom used.

Marine aircrews fly the aircraft aggressively and never 'stop, aim, fire'. Despite the stand-off advanced weaponry now makes possible, engagements in Afghanistan are typically below 1,000 metres range, and very close to friendly forces (TIC – 'Troops in Contact' in the jargon).

These two very interesting photos show an AH-1W picking up a Special Forces soldier in Afghanistan. Highly unofficial, this technique is not in the Training Manuals. It does however allow 'Recon' types to be dropped at remote locations without arousing the attention that a Chinook or Blackhawk would. (*Via Mike Verier*)

Like their predecessors in Vietnam, the Marines quickly found that the bad guys learnt to keep out of sight until the Cobras had passed overhead before emerging to shoot at their blind spot. Unlike earlier generations however they were able to mix an armed Huey (which sounds the same as a Cobra) into the flight to cover their 'six'. The insurgents in turn discovered to their cost that taking pot-shots at a Marine with a MiniGun is a bad plan. The flexibility provided by the Huey/Cobra mix will of course continue with the deployment of the 'Yankee' and 'Zulu' variants.

When the discussion turned to comparison with newer attack types the phrase, 'it's the Marine in the machine that makes the difference' was heard more than once. This is no mere bravado, throughout the history of air combat attitude, doctrine and training have been deciding factors. A fact clearly not lost on the current generation of pilots.

Given the intensity of fighting in Afghanistan, and that the HMLAs have been continuously deployed since entering the inventory, it is now reckoned that 'Whisky' Cobras have flown more combat hours than any other Cobra variant.

Who you gonna call?

This brief overview of Cobra combat operations provides but a snapshot of some of the engagements it has been, and continues to be, involved in. Apart from major counter insurgency operations, the most likely scenario for more action is the rapid evacuation of US and other personnel from imminent danger.

From the embassy roof in Saigon, through Grenada and Lebanon, the Snakes were there to cover the evacuation, tenaciously protecting their charges until the last Marine had embarked. Many times in the decades since the versatility and rapid responsiveness of the deployed MEU (Marine Expeditionary Unit) has been called upon to evacuate civilians threatened by anarchy and civil strife in their country. From Somalia (1990), Liberia (1990, 1996), Rwanda (1994), Sierra Leone (1997), to the Congo and Albania (both 1997), Marines have responded to the State Department's requests to evacuate embassies and US citizens. If the objective was within the Cobra's reach they went with the transports, if it wasn't they prowled around the parent ship daring anyone to hinder the mission.

Elsewhere in a troubled world, Cobras continue to see combat. There may already be Cobras in museums, but the ever-adaptive 'interim' Snake refuses to recognise obsolescence. This author for one has no intention of predicting its retirement from combat any time soon...

AH-1W 160815 of the 'Gunrunners' at a Desert FARRP during Operation 'Enduring Freedom'. The aircraft are being 'hot' refuelled and armed with the engines running to minimise the time away from the troops on the ground, something the Marines are very good at. (*Capt R Weingart USMC*)

A Pendleton-based HMLA-267 Snake uploads Hellfire missiles whilst the pilot gets a SITREP. The well-rehearsed evolution minimises time on the ground and again emphasises the flexibility of the Cobra on the battlefield. (*Capt R Weingart USMC*)

Chapter 13

Life Beyond

Civil Snakes

The military origins the Cobra have endowed it with some specific qualities that make it ideal for a number of roles that do not involve guns and rockets. It has found a remarkable, and growing, range of employment in civilian hands.

The quest for knowledge – NASA's scientific Snakes

The first civilian user, (albeit a Government agency), of the Cobra was NASA. Over nearly four decades NASA's Cobras have contributed to numerous research programmes, serving both as research platforms in their own right, and as a chase aircraft for other projects.

The first of three Cobras assigned to NASA was AH-1G 66-15248, actually the third true production Cobra. Following Army service it was delivered from the US Army depot maintenance at Corpus Christi, Texas, to NASA's Langley Research Centre on 18 December 1972.

Initially retaining its military Olive Drab scheme save for orange elevators and the designation 'NASA 541' applied to the tail boom over the 'United States Army' titling, (both in white), the aircraft eventually acquired a striking white paint scheme with red and blue trim.

When received, the aircraft had 515.1 total airframe hours, and an engine (serial number LE 17603) with only 446.1 hours on it. During its time at Langley it participated in a number of programmes concerning rotor aerodynamics and performance as well as being involved in acoustic phenomena investigation. During this work, in the mid-1970s, a novel method of measuring rotorcraft impulsive noise had been developed by Fred Schmitz and his Army/NASA team, initially using an OV-1 as the recording aircraft.

The Cobra, as one of the Army's noisiest aircraft could subsequently be seen in formation with Lockheed's limited production YO-3A (their quietest) – the latter type serving as a mount for the microphones. The YO-3 was instrumented with both wing and tail mounted microphones and flown in formation with the test helicopter at selected airspeeds and rates of sink at which the helicopter was known to radiate large amounts of impulsive noise. The distance between the aircraft and the helicopter was held within 1 metre accuracy using a visual range finder.

Helicopter directional control/stability problems were still a concern at the time and wind tunnel testing led staff at Langley to propose a 'butterfly' or 'V' tail as a possible solution. Bell had in fact received a contract to carry out preliminary design when a 1976 decision by NASA headquarters to move all research helicopters to the Ames Research Centre at Moffett Field, California, cut short further work on the project.

NASA's first Cobra 66-15248 as she arrived at Langley with a fresh coat of Olive Drab and the NASA designation '541'. 66-15248 was the third true production Cobra (ie the sixth one built). Note the cover plate on the fin where the tail rotor has been moved to the more effective starboard location – early production Cobras had the rotor on the port side and this mod was applied retrospectively. (*NASA via Mike Verier*)

Bell modified a NASA picture of '541' to depict the proposed 'Butterfly' or 'Vee' tail. The ending of rotorcraft research at Langley meant that this interesting proposal went no further. (*Bell via Mike Verier*)

'NASA 541' after repaint in the scheme of the day. The badge just forward of the wing is the US Army Airmobility R&D Laboratory. (*NASA via Mike Verier*)

On arrival at Langley 66-15248 was re-designated 'NASA 736' and the scheme changed to the then current 'Red Wurm' NASA logo. Note that the tops of the rotor blades are now Orange with white calibration striping. (*NASA via Mike Verier*)

Eventually, on 1 March 1978, the aircraft departed cross-country for assignment to Ames, accompanied by Langley's UH-1H which had VOR (VHF Omnidirectional Radio range) for navigation. The Cobra was far more comfortable to fly than the Huey so NASA pilots Dan Dugan and John Henderson alternated the two. At the time of departure the Cobra had accumulated 661.4 hours, still with the same engine.

The Cobra's *raison d'etre* was emphasised during the long ferry flight by the difference between its 140-150kt cruise, and the plodding 100-110kt cruise Huey. As the Huey droned steadily along, Dan Dugan remembers being easily able to make forays away from the flight path in the Cobra, '... we checked out interesting rock formations and historic sites such as Columbus, New Mexico where Pancho Villa 'invaded' the United States'. Later, the temptation to make a few gun runs on a lumbering Navy SH-3 Sea King encountered over Arizona proved impossible to resist too. Save for a hairy moment as they landed to refuel at Dryden, (the Cobras' NiCad battery committed suicide and fried itself), the transfer was otherwise uneventful.

At Ames, the aircraft tail number was changed to 'NASA 736', and following further work as a chase aircraft it was returned to Army control in 1983, serving with the California National Guard at Livermore, California, before returning to the Bell plant at Amarillo, Texas for re-building as an S Model. Remarkably 66-15248 still survives, preserved at Fort Rucker's Museum of Army Aviation.

The second NASA Cobra was JAH-1S 77-22768. This aircraft was distinguished by the Apache PNVS turret mounted on its upturned nose. Arriving at Ames on 8 May 1985, 77-22768 was assigned the NASA identity '730' and set to work as the FLITE (Flying Laboratory for Integrated Test and Evaluation) Cobra. This aircraft was actually assigned to the US Army Aeroflightdynamics Directorate, but operated by NASA (being co-located since 1966, these two organizations conducted joint research at Moffett Field).

The JAH-1 was the first Cobra on which the prototype AH-64 visually coupled night vision system helmet mounted display (HMD) was installed, and was a fundamental player in the development of the Apache's night vision system. The aircraft took part in the Army's first use of visually coupled HMD systems and was later involved in a study of a modified communication

'NASA 736' was extensively fitted with test equipment, much of it in the old ammunition bay. Also visible here is the instrumented test boom and various specialised antennae. (*NASA via Mike Verier*)

66-15248 'NASA 736' in flight. The top of the main rotor appears to be International Orange. (*NASA via Mike Verier*)

'NASA 730' as received from the Army. The development aircraft for the Apache PNVS and prototype for Rucker's small fleet of Surrogates, it has the blackout screens in the rear cockpit. (*NASA via Mike Verier*)

'Mother, the JAH-1 (nearest the camera), in formation with NAH-1S. Note the difference bet ween the rather angular nose of 'Mother's nasal modification and the rather more elegant curves of the 'production' Surrogate. (*NASA via Mike Verier*)

77–22768, alias 'NASA 730', now marked with the red NASA 'wurm' and a discreet sharkmouth. (*NASA via Mike Verier*)

Lockheed's YO–3 in formation with an anonymous Cobra. Although it has an instrumentation boom the Cobra is not '730' (NASA's 'flat plate' bird) as evidenced by the M-28 turret, M-65 nose and lack of the alternator bulge ahead of the intake. Its identity remains a mystery. (*NASA via Mike Verier*)

system. It allowed pilots to switch between three radios and internal communications with the co-pilot, without removing either hand from the flight control sticks. This system was the beginning of today's HOCAS (Hands On Collective and Stick) technology.

NASA '730' retained her Army Green paint job whilst at NASA, save for the '730' designator and the red NASA 'Wurm' logo on the fin, although at various times 'sharkmouth' embellishments were also sported. As the prototype development aircraft for the Apache PNVS (Pilot Night Vision System) she was known locally as 'Mother'. NASA '730' also became the prototype for ten similar Cobra conversions from ICAP/ICAM (Improved Cobra Armament Program/Improved Cobra Agility & Maneuverability) S Models. These aircraft were developed to train future AH-64 Apache pilots in the difficult art of landing using only the PNVS. Known at Rucker as 'surrogates' they avoided risking an expensive new Apache in the process. The aircraft was returned to the Army on 5 July 1988. It served for some time as a test aircraft at Rucker but the ultimate fate of the airframe is not known.

'730' was joined by a second Cobra on 10 November 1987. One of the 'surrogate' airframes, 70-15979, was known as the NAH-1S. Confusingly for historians NASA number '736' was re-assigned to it (making it the second NASA-operated Cobra with the same tail number). Continuing the FLITE programme, '736' was used simultaneously with a fixed-base crew station simulator to conduct simulation sickness and other human factors studies. Unlike its sister-ship the 'new' '736' eventually received the full (and it has to be said very attractive) NASA 'Blue 'n White' scheme.

The FLITE Cobra was also used to validate military rotorcraft flying qualities specification manoeuvres, visual cues, and test methods in a degraded visual environment, such as the limited fields of view and depth perception encountered with NVG equipment.

In these studies, before the GPS satellites were available, the aircraft's flight path was precisely tracked using a laser which tracked reflective tape wrapped around the main rotor shaft. These flight tests were conducted at Crows Landing (at the time a Naval Auxiliary Landing Field), California. At Moffett Field the aircraft was used to test prototype panoramic night vision goggles, providing the pilot with an amazing 100 degrees field-of-view. Throughout the testing, Loran Haworth was the primary test pilot on the aircraft, and Zoltan Szoboszlay was the principle engineer.

In support of the Boeing-Sikorsky RAH-66 Comanche attack helicopter programme, the aircraft acted as a radar target and flew prototype fibre-optic connectors to gather long-term fibre-optic attenuation data. In another test, a colour video camera was installed and bore-sighted to the PNVS. Several hours of infrared and colour video imagery were collected over various types of terrain for use in a collaborative programme with the Israeli Ministry of Defence which eventually led to the CNITE and NTS upgrades for 'F' and 'W' Model Cobras.

The aircraft was also modified to test an early computer voice input and output system for the pilot using what was then a state-of-the-art 'ruggedized' IBM-XT computer with magnetic bubble memory. The aircraft also flew early versions of active noise reduction headsets, and earplugs with speakers. Dr Carol Simpson demonstrated improved radio communications with the devices (which have since become the Army standard). Before leaving Ames in 2000, the aircraft was flying a programmable helmet-mounted display system, and an automated gearbox health-monitoring system.

70-15979 was returned to the Army at Ft Eustis to continue with development work. Now repainted in a smart black and gold scheme she still proudly serves with the AATD (Applied Aviation Technology Directorate) who believe it to be the very last Cobra in the Army's active inventory.

Already confusingly marked as 'NASA 736' – the designation of the original Cobra was re-used – the NAH-1S was originally one of the 'Surrogate' conversions used at Rucker for Apache crew training. It went on to be the last Cobra in the US Army's active inventory. (*NASA via Mike Verier*)

The 'new' 'NASA 736' received a smart blue and white scheme which it retained for the duration of its life with NASA. (*NASA via Mike Verier*)

Apart from the PNVS nose, 'NASA 736' also retained the upturned 'sugar scoop' exhaust it was delivered with. Interestingly there is very little evidence of discolouration of the white paint which would indicate that the reduction of heat was quite effective. (*NASA via Mike Verier*)

Night shot of 'NASA 736' during research into wide angle night vision goggles. Dr Carol Simpson is in the front seat. Note the immaculate condition of the aircraft. (*NASA via Mike Verier*)

Far from retiring 70–15979 continues to serve the US Army at Fort Eustis. Repainted in 'Army' black and gold it is the very last Cobra in the active inventory, more than 40 years after it left it's birthplace at Fort Worth. (*NASA via Mike Verier*)

Snakebitten – Customs Cobras

The second Government agency to use the Cobra was the US Customs Service. Ever since taxation was invented, there have been Revenue Men and smugglers trying to outsmart each other. By the early 1980s drug smugglers had taken to using aircraft flown at low-level to try and evade detection.

Intercepting them was one thing, but to actually arrest the smugglers once they had landed, a helicopter has clear advantages over fixed-wing. Unfortunately many modern GA types were faster and had longer range than the Jet Rangers and Hueys the Service then had available.

Roger Woolard ferries a Cobra for conversion. Other than replacing the turret with a searchlight and some work on the radios very few changes were made. The aircraft were not even repainted. The first aircraft was 68–15023 later registered N1177B. It returned to the Army eventually becoming an AH-1S. (*Roger Woolard*)

In response to a paper written in 1981 by Roger Woolard, a former military pilot serving with the Miami Air Branch, it was agreed that the possibility of using Cobras in the role should be investigated. A brief test flight was undertaken at Hunter Army Airfield. This was sufficient to conclude that the proposition was viable and in July 1981 Roger and fellow pilot George Thurman reported to Fort Rucker for training on the AH-1G. They duly completed the standard Army course, with the exception of the gunnery phase (technically civilians, the Customs Service could not fly armed aircraft).

With two qualified pilots available to conduct an operational evaluation, Roger collected AH-1G 68-15023 from Rucker on 26 August 1981 and ferried it back to Homestead AFB where the Miami Air Branch was resident. The Army had removed the guns and the empty turret was duly fitted with a 30 million candlepower 'NiteSun' searchlight. Losing no time the first 'bust' was recorded on 3 September. Over the next two months ten further arrests were made, two in one night.

The work was certainly dangerous, but exciting. A Cobra could be 'scrambled' very quickly when a suspect was detected. One aircraft would be kept on what the British would call QRA (Quick Reaction Alert) duty – pre-flight checks done and the aircraft 'cocked'. Roger recollects that he could be '... ten feet from the Cobra to a three foot hover in one minute and thirteen seconds.'

The incoming smugglers, usually running 'lights out', no transponder and below (they thought) radar coverage, would be picked up as they approached the US coastline. The Air Branch used a variety of ground and airborne assets to do this, one being a Cessna 550 fitted with an F-16 radar (ie with a 'look-down' capability). In order not to alert the smugglers both Customs' aircraft would also be flying lights out. The Cobra would be vectored on to the shadowing Cessna, which could show only its tail light so that the Cobra could locate it and fly to the smuggler.

It should be kept in mind that the G Model Cobra was not designed for night operation. Whilst NVG goggles were in use at that time they were not suitable for, or compatible with, the Cobra's cockpit. All interceptions were carried out using the Mk 1 Eyeball.

The Cobras were fast enough to catch most GA types then in use. Once the suspect aircraft had landed the Cobra put down to make the arrest. The Air Officer in the front seat was first out, closely followed by the pilot, who had to first make sure that the idling aircraft was properly secured. (Not fully frictioning-down the collective could lead to the aircraft trying to take off on its own, beating itself to death in the process).

This was the primary limitation of the Cobra as the two-man crew only had their personal weapons and often found themselves outnumbered by the smugglers until back-up arrived.

Roger Woolard:

'The technique I used on a bust was to follow the smuggler aircraft (my lights out) until he landed. Then when he turned onto a taxiway or did not have runway enough to take off I would swing around in front of him nose to nose and turn on the 30 million candlepower search light, shining it directly into the cockpit. The idea was to blind him so he would not attempt a takeoff.

If he landed on a dike or open field I would start the manoeuvre as soon as he slowed to taxi speed. If I did it right, the first time he knew we were there was when the light came on. I would have the rotor blades overlap his cockpit. (One smuggler actually wet his pants at this point.) We would then land about half a rotor blade diameter in front of the smuggler and bail out for the arrest.

Detail of a Customs AH-1G Cobra showing the NiteSun searchlight fitted to the turret mount, the very discreet civil registration, and the 'clip on' Customs badge. (*Brian Wilburn*)

We always turned the searchlight off before we landed because it was so hot it would start a fire if there was any grass or brush around. I never had a smuggler takeoff after he had landed when I was flying the Cobra.'

Roger also devised a 'Snake Bitten' sticker to 'zap' every aircraft they captured, the device also appearing on golf-shirts presented to the Air Officers concerned when a bust included the aircraft, pilot and dope.

The point having been made, on 25 March 1982, Roger and Oscar Vera undertook a major cross-country, going to Fort Orde, California, to collect two more Cobras and ferry them to Rucker, in Alabama, where the Army removed the guns and carried out other modifications. The Customs aircraft were also allocated Civil Registrations at this time.

The Cobra's time with the Customs Service was brief and by 1986 the more capable Black Hawks had taken over the role. During the five years they were in use however the six Cobras used by the Air Branch successfully interdicted millions of dollars worth of drugs and other contraband, not to mention increasing the smugglers' laundry bill when a mean-looking black attack helicopter suddenly came at them out of the night!

As well as any drugs seized (which of course only had a theoretical 'value') the aircraft involved in smuggling were also impounded. These were frequently impressed into Air Branch service. That of course gave a real dollar-return to the taxpayer. Just as decades later, when retired Cobra airframes were generating income at Fort Drum, the 'temporary' acquisition of Cobras was proving a sound investment.

Firebirds – the phoenix Snakes

Potentially, a larger user is the US Forest Service who have twenty-five airframes against a requirement for spotting and control of airborne fire fighting. Three prototype 'FireWatch' conversions are flying (at the time of writing) and if successful more will be converted. The aircraft feature advanced FLIR and sensors which can provide other aircraft and ground-based fire fighters with real-time imagery showing the location and movement of forest fires. As they can 'see through' smoke that would obscure purely visual systems 'hot spots' can be targeted accurately. Their purpose is to direct operations rather than actually fight fires. The aircraft are characterised by enlarged bubble transparencies that give the pilot unprecedented view below the aircraft.

The Florida Department of Agriculture has also used Cobras, albeit theirs are used to directly fight fires using an under slung bucket. Converted by Garlick Helicopters the 'FireSnake' is intended as a first response aircraft. The conversion is quite extensive – the aircraft are effectively gutted with some 500lb of surplus wiring and military equipment being removed. New cockpit panels and avionics are fitted, along with the bulged canopy panels to improve downward view. A 6,000lb capable cargo hook is provided so that the aircraft can lift a 320 gallon Bambi Bucket, which is stowed in an enlarged area where the old ammunition bay was.

Alternatively the 'FireSnake' can mount 360 gallon tanks with foam injection pumps and a drop-down tube to draw water directly from any suitable source. Total cost of each conversion is reckoned at about $300,000.

Fire Cobras come in a number of forms. Stripped of military equipment they have a formidable lifting capacity. This example from Washington State is notable in that all four cockpit transparencies have been bulged. (*Washington State Department of Natural Resources*)

Florida uses its Snakes for direct 'first response' fire attack. This aircraft has had the stub–wings removed altogether in order to accommodate the massive 360 gallon tank and its associated drop–down tube used to pick up water. (*Florida Department of Agriculture*)

Known as 'FireWatch' the Forestry Service Cobras are equipped with a FLIR ball and intended for spotting and direction duties. The FLIR gives them the ability to see through smoke and pinpoint the seat of a fire. A comprehensive communications fit then allows co–ordination of ground and air resources attacking the fire. (*US Forestry Service*)

This ex-TAH-1P, 76-27707, has migrated to Chile where it too has been used for fire-fighting as well as more general lifting work. Now registered CC-CLF it is described as a '209 Cobra Lifter'. (*Victor Cepeda Contreras*)

CC-CLF has also worn this stunning scheme. Interesting in this view is the pilot making use of the bulged canopy – a prudent move judging by the plethora of wires in the vicinity. (*Victor Cepeda Contreras*)

CC-CLF about to lift a 'Bambi Bucket'. One of these holds 320 gallons of water, well within the aircrafts' hook limit of 6000lb. (*Victor Cepeda Contreras*)

The Army Aviation Heritage Foundation

Almost qualifying as a small air force, the Army Aviation Heritage Foundation (AAHF) is one beneficiary of the Cobra retirement programme. Based at Tara Field in Atlanta, the AAHF actually 'owns' (the inventory has to be confirmed annually to the Army) some fifteen airframes, mostly TAH-1Fs but including two S Models that were built as 'G's. Their mission is to preserve and honour Army aviation history, and initially they used a Cobra in their 'Vietnam' demonstration which of course also includes the Huey (UH-1) and Loach (OH-6) amongst several other rotary and fixed wing types. More recently they have provided, under contract to the Army, a flight demonstration team (the Sky Soldiers) to promote Army Aviation. Five of their Cobras operating in a dramatic black and gold 'ARMY' scheme, whilst a sixth is kept in 'combat' green as part of their regular presentation. The other airframes are at present in storage to provide back–up.

The Army sees the team as a recruitment tool, which brings a neat symmetry to the use of the Cobra as the chosen vehicle. Part of the Cobra's design brief was exactly that. The sleek lines of the bird, (now somewhat blurred by functionality but still evident), owing more than a little to an instruction to 'make it look like it's doing 200mph even when it's parked.' AAHF associates also flew a rare and superbly restored G Model – possibly the last remaining airworthy one. In 2012 this aircraft was sold to a new owner in Texas.

The Celebrate Freedom Foundation (CFF) also received five AH-1F Cobra helicopters from the United States Army. Media had the first opportunity to see a restored Cobra at a press conference on 9 November 2006 at the Curtiss Wright Hangar at the Columbia Owens Downtown Airport. The public's first glimpse of the Cobra was during the Veterans' Day Parade the following day.

A stripped 'Snake' has a fairly impressive lifting capacity (around 6000lb) and at least one Cobra has been tried for logging operations in South America. Former TAH-1P 76-27707 has shed its military identity and become a '209S CobraLifter'. Now registered in Chile as CC-CLF she certainly qualifies as one of the most colourful 'Snakes' anywhere in the world.

Warbird 'Snakes'

Other Cobras have been rescued to become Warbirds – privately owned ex-military aircraft – often to be seen at air shows as a way to defray the massive costs of such a possession. In the world of Warbirds, machines are recovered, sometimes as derelict hulks, restored and brought back to life to fly again. Never an easy path, this is more so with Cobras.

The United States Army may have retired its Cobras but the aircraft is still current in many armed forces overseas, including at least one that might be hostile to the US. The possibility that aircraft or spares may fall into the wrong hands gives rise to some tortuous paperwork and legal costs if you fancy spending your weekends in the Classic Sports Car of the helicopter world.

Nevertheless a number are now on the civil register, and have already begun to change hands, one such is N2734D. One of a hundred 'Production S' (AH-1P) Models manufactured, 77-22734 was modified to become a TAH-1S in April 1984. The 'T' prefix meant that it was a 'Training' airframe, this subtle distinction allows it to be sold legally onto the civil market.

Its new owner decided to display it as an Israeli machine and it accordingly received a replica paint job as '734' of the IDAF. Negotiations are underway at the time of writing with a potential British buyer who plans to operate it in a 'Vietnam' scheme alongside their existing Huey and an OH-6 'Loach'. Interestingly the new owner plans to revert to the 540 metal blades as it is felt that these will be more durable and easy to maintain in the UK environment than the K747 composite blades the aircraft is currently fitted with.

One other civil Cobra operates outside the US. The impressive collection of aircraft at Red Bull includes a Cobra, which is displayed in a stunning black scheme with the eponymous bovine in dramatic red and silver on its side. N74FX was reportedly originally restored from two airframes, carrying out some film work before it was acquired by the Austrian-based organisation as part of their growing collection. Given the legal and political difficulties noted above, the paperwork (and consequent cost) of getting it exported were reportedly 'lengthy and interesting'. It now regularly demonstrates at airshows and other events in the capable hands of display pilot 'Blackie' Schwartz.

As well as 'living' Cobras, a considerable number of static airframes have been preserved, some in superb condition in museums, albeit in some cases in spurious colour schemes, with others suffering the ravages of weather as gate guards or stuck 'on a stick' at various locations. Over fifty single engine variants and around ten J Models and two 'T's are on display in the United States alone. There are two in Australia, at least two in the UK and one in Spain. The South Koreans have one of their rare 'J Internationals' preserved and the Israelis have preserved Cobras too.

Very recently an ex-ANG S Model discovered in NASA's hanger at Ames, (68-15155 probably originally acquired as a 'spare' for the NAH-1S), has gone on display at the Moffet Museum situated, appropriately, next to their historic dirigible hanger.

Finally of course there are a number of historic Cobras – including N209J – preserved (or at least stored) at the Army's Museum at Fort Rucker – many of these are noted in the text and if you find yourself in Alabama, it's well worth a visit, if only to see the very first 'Snake'.

The only Cobra flying in private hands in Europe at the time of writing. The Austrian-based Red Bull Company operates this superbly marked example. (*Jorg Adam Courtesy Red Bull picture library*)

This warbird is painted in the 'Arctic' scheme worn by G Models at Fort Richardson in the 1970s. Built as a AH-1G, 70-15945 has been updated to S Model standard as evidenced by the large tail-rotor gearbox and K-747 blades. (*Via Army Aviation Heritage Foundation*)

Until recently flown under the auspices of the Army Aviation Heritage Foundation, 67-15737 is a genuine Vietnam AH-1G. Backdated from an 'S' airframe the restoration is very detailed including an original pantograph sight and correct G Model wing pylons. Only the tail rotor gearbox and K-747 blades betray that it is more than a G under the skin. (*Mike Verier*)

Army Aviation Heritage Foundation pilots also operate the unique 'SkySoldiers' demonstration team which continues to thrill crowds throughout the United States. (*Greg Davies*)

As Peyton DeHart brings 67-15589 in to pick up the author it can be seen that the Cobra has lost little in appearance over the years. Now appropriately registered N589HF this aircraft too was originally a Vietnam AH-1G. (*Mike Verier*)

Mike Brady has now sold 67-15737 to a new owner, reportedly close to its birthplace in Texas. This superb Greg Davies study amply demonstrates the Cobras sleek lines. (*Greg Davies*)

Chapter 14

The Long Search

US Army helicopter procurement programmes

The Cobra was originally seen as an 'interim' type because the US Army wanted something much more ambitious. They believed (correctly as it turned out) that the Air Force, concerned as it was in the late 1950s with big bombers and fast jets, could not provide true close support for their troops in contact.

Funding to study armed helicopters was first formally made available following the Howze report in 1962 and in 1964 RFPs went out for Advanced Aerial Fire Support System (AAFSS, usually pronounced 'AyFuss'). It envisaged a fast, deep penetration type, heavily armed and day / night capable. It was to be the first of several abortive programmes spanning four decades and resulting in only one operational type.

Some highly original entries were offered, including the rather bizarre Convair Model 49. Bell were eliminated at an early stage and in November 1965 the Lockheed AH-56 Cheyenne

The Sikorsky S-65 AAFSS contender was similar in concept to the winning Lockheed design. (*Sikorsky via Ray Wilhite*)

The Convair Model 49 featured a tubular wing and was arguably the most bizarre of the AAFSS entrants. (Convair via *Mike Verier*)

was selected. Seven years, ten prototypes and millions of dollars later the programme was cancelled. The AH-56 was not a bad aircraft and may eventually have been developed into an effective operational type, but cost and complexity proved too much and the plug was pulled in August 1972. At a cost reportedly greater than the entire Cobra fleet the Army had not a single operational aircraft to show.

As AAFSS had dragged on, other manufacturers had sought to offer alternatives. Not least amongst these was Bell who built two private venture Model 309 KingCobras in 1971 in order to

Lockheed's winning AH-56 Cheyenne was potentially an excellent aircraft but the technology of the day couldn't overcome the problems created by such an ambitious specification before the money and political support ran out. (*US Army via Ray Wilhite*)

demonstrate that an updated Cobra could more than meet the requirement. Sikorsky also built a PV type the S-67 Blackhawk.

Following a competitive evaluation of all three types in 1972 however, the Army still thought that something better was required and almost immediately issued an RFP for the **AAH** (Advanced Attack Helicopter).

This time Bell, Boeing, Lockheed and Hughes were amongst the finalists in a contest that seemed to include extreme ugliness in the specification. Eventually Bell's Model 409 and the Hughes Model 77 were awarded contracts for prototypes. They were allocated the designations YAH-63 and YAH-64 respectively.

In December 1976 the Hughes aircraft was declared the winner. The AH-64 eventually matured into an extremely effective aircraft but it was to be the mid-1980s before Apaches were available in any numbers, and the 1990s before it truly began to supplant the Cobra in the front line. Only now, in its third generation has it finally achieved (some of) the capabilities aspired to by the AAFSS programme more than three decades earlier.

With the arrival of the AH-64, Army doctrine was refined towards the European scenario integrating Air Force A-10s, Army helicopters and ground-based anti-tank troops into Joint Air Attack Teams. The Cobras, now seen as armed scouts, were to be upgraded to a common standard incorporating a number of planned improvements. Bell were not unaware of the approaching obsolescence of the Cobra and during the late 1970s and early 1980s offered the Army a number of Cobra upgrades featuring their proven four-blade rotor.

In the event, the Army decided to divert the money into development of a completely new armed scout to replace the Cobras. AH-1 development was effectively ended and in 1982 a new programme, LHX was born.

LHX – Light Helicopter eXperimental – was very much of the 1980s. The aircraft had to be 'Stealthy' and have only a single pilot, technology replacing the second crewman. Advanced composites would also be needed to keep the weight down to the planned 8,000lb (3,636kg) – an ambitious target given that an Apache weighs 18,352lb (8,324kg). Weight growth eventually saw the LHX around the same as a (single engine) Cobra at about 9,500lb (4,309kg).

At one point Bell had proposed its D329 BAT – Bell Advanced Tiltrotor – for LHX. This was a very neat and potentially viable aircraft based on the extremely successful XV-15 demonstrator. It was however ruled out on weight grounds.

LHX would have been a major prize. The driver was the Scout/Attack (SCAT) configuration, from which a utility type would be derived using the same engine, dynamics and major systems. At one time it was thought that the buy might reach 6,000 airframes as it was intended that LHX would replace all existing AH-1, UH-1, OH-58A/C and OH-6 aircraft in the Army inventory. Eventually the numbers settled at 2,000 SCAT airframes and 2,500 utility versions.

This sparked a number of related programmes. Advanced Composite Airframe Program (ACAP) which resulted in two demonstrators, built by Bell, based on their Model 222, and Sikorsky based on the S-75.

Sikorsky, teamed with Boeing, also built a single pilot technology demonstrator with a new pilot station grafted onto the nose of an S-76 and called 'SHADOW' (a rather contrived acronym standing for Sikorsky Helicopter Advanced Demonstrator of Operator Workload).

Demonstrators also flew under the ARTI, Advanced Rotorcraft Technology Integration, programme. Bell using the now redundant 249 to show that the aircraft could be flown 'hands-off'. An AH-64 was also flown in support of ARTI (with the profile of the proposed new aircraft prominently marked on the side to show how much smaller it would be).

The Bell KingCobra and the Sikorsky S-67 BlackHawk were both Private Venture types proposed as an alternative to the ailing AAFSS. In the event neither was selected. Seen here at Farnborough on 1 September 1974, the Blackhawk prototype was tragically lost during a demonstration shortly after this photo was taken. (*Dick Ward*)

The AAH contest spawned some strange concepts. Boeing's contender never got beyond this mock-up. In a reflection of the Cobra story it is clearly based on the YUH-61 UTTAS (Utility Tactical Transport Aircraft System) proposal. Sadly for Boeing that contest went to the Sikorsky UH-60, also destined to be named Black Hawk. (Boeing)

The Lockheed proposal was clearly based on the AH-56 design and again did not proceed beyond mock-up. (*Mike Verier*)

Bell's Model 409 was awarded a development contract as the YAH-63. Two flying prototypes competing against the Hughes AAH. (*Bell*)

The Hughes Model 77, designated YAH-64, was declared the winner, maturing to become the highly successful Apache which is still in production. The Hughes Aircraft Company has long gone and the aircraft now belongs to Boeing so it could be argued that they won the contest in the long run. (*US Army via Ray Wilhite*)

The search for a new generation scout continued. Having decided that it wanted an all-new-technology aircraft the US Army instigated the LHX (Light Helicopter Experimental) programme and Bell were quick to suggest their tilt-rotor technology in the initial shape of the BAT (Bell Advanced Tiltrotor). (*Bell via Mike Verier*)

The definitive LHX proposal is depicted here in a somewhat prophetic 'mountain and desert' scenario. Ultimately the aircraft proved to be too heavy to meet the specification. (*Bell via Mike Verier*)

As LHX became the more concrete LH proposal two industry teams were formed. This artist impression of the Bell/McDonnell Douglas contender clearly still envisages war in Europe. (*Bell via Mike Verier*)

The Boeing/Sikorsky team won the competition in 1991, their aircraft becoming the RAH-66 Comanche. After a long and protracted development during which the number to be procured dropped and the unit cost rose the programme was cancelled in 2004. (*US Army*)

By the late 1980s the technology was within sight, but the requirement had changed with the political landscape. The success of the S-60 Blackhawk led to the dropping of the utility variant and in 1988 the Army issued an RFP for a SCAT type that was to be procured under complex 'teaming' arrangements within industry. Two groups, the Bell/McDonnell Douglas 'SuperTeam' and the Boeing/Sikorsky 'FirstTeam' were formed.

The Bell/McDD proposal was a sleek machine using NOTAR (No Tail Rotor) technology, whilst the 'FirstTeam' aircraft featured a shrouded tail rotor and prominent T-tail. Both (in their initial form at least) carried all weapons internally to preserve 'stealth' characteristics, and both had two crew members.

In April 1991 the Boeing/Sikorsky proposal was declared the winner and LH became the RAH-66 Comanche, (RA standing for Reconnaissance/Attack).

In February 1992 however the programme was restructured extending the R&D phase and again in 1994/5. The first prototype was not to fly until 1995, the second following three years later.

With the numbers to be procured falling as the budget reduced so the unit cost rose. Testing with so few airframes available was long and protracted with the tail surfaces in particular going through a number of iterations. Inevitably the attempt to increase the capabilities of the aircraft led to various 'bolt-on' excrescences which compromised the Stealth characteristics.

On 3 April 2004, the Comanche was finally cancelled on the grounds of cost escalation. The Army, as of this writing, has yet to resolve what to do as an increasingly ageing fleet of 'legacy' helicopters reaches the end of their lives, a process accelerated by constant combat in recent years which is rapidly burning airframe hours.

Chapter 15

Pilot's Quotes
Comments from the Snakepit

Great though the Cobra undeniably is, it remains simply a piece of precision engineering without the men (and increasingly women) who fly it. It is they who breathe life into the machine, flex its muscles and give it wing. The following quotes are from a range of pilots and eras from Vietnam to the present day.

Gathered over many years I am struck by the similarity of experience between different generations of pilot – almost universally however I have found that the descriptions are positive, interviewing Cobra pilots is like interviewing Spitfire pilots – they recognise its foibles and limitations, and that like all aircraft it will bite the unwary; but they all love flying it.

When the Cobra entered service there was simply nothing like it, helicopters were unglamorous haulers of people and cargo with a 'Utility' prefix; they were regarded as dangerous, noisy, collections of components that were constantly trying to tear each other apart. Like the Bumble Bee they shouldn't be able to fly but just didn't know it.

The Snake changed all that. It was a hot ship, the Ferrari of the helicopter world, and it had guns 'n rockets – next to fast jets it was what young pilots aspired to. Given the new machine and a need to explore new tactics pilots of the Vietnam era took the Cobra to, and sometimes beyond, the edges of the envelope.

One of the earliest independent evaluations of the Cobra was carried out, oddly enough, by the British. During a European tour that included the Paris Air Show, Cobra prototype N209J spent a day at the home of the Army Air Corps, Middle Wallop in rural Hampshire.

The great and the good came to see it. Bell's Clem Baily flew many of them in the Cobra during a busy afternoon that followed a presentation by Joe Mashman and his team. A detailed evaluation of the aircraft was carried out, including its systems and armament, and even what additional trades (mostly armourers) would be required if it were to enter AAC service.

The UK trip had been arranged by former Fleet Air Arm pilot John Sproule, who was Agusta's London representative at the time. Apart from the military, one or two journalists were able to fly the Cobra. One such was an ex-Squadron Leader and former Fairey Aviation Chief Test Pilot, Basil Arkell. Then editor of 'Helicopter World' magazine he was invited at short notice to fly '209'. He remembers being '... off like a shot within an hour of putting the phone down.'

He dutifully covered the technical aspects of the aircraft in some detail, the excitement it could generate is however palpable in his report:

'The HueyCobra is the thirty-seventh helicopter type I have flown. At this stage, one begins to wonder whether there is anything really new and different in the field from the pilot's point of view. Having flown it, I can now positively assert that there is – the HueyCobra. Although the machine is designed around the dynamic systems of the Bell UH-1 series, its handling characteristics are as different from the UH-1 as chalk from cheese… the HueyCobra is in a new class of it's own.'

His own evaluation of the aircraft's handling qualities was expanded by some very impressive flying demonstrated by Clem Bailey including a near vertical dive from a high hover which had the aircraft some 20kts over the theoretical 'red line' 200kts in less than 15 seconds.

The same day Major J.A. Pike, AAC, flew the aircraft and also found it 'impressive' whilst noting that the prototype lacked power (production aircraft had the T53-L-13 engine rated at 1400shp, whilst the prototype only had the 1100shp rated –11 engine) which 'limited manoeuvrability'. (In view of Basil Arkell's experience one can only speculate what the Major thought the production machines would be capable of!)

Major Pike also noted the Cobra's distinctive and directional noise:

'The noise made by the Huey Cobra at full speed is similar to the (Westland) Scout with a very pronounced main rotor beat superimposed. Like the Scout, it gives ample warning of its approach. In the first hour of flying on 13 July, five complaints were made about the disturbance by local residents. This is obviously a point to be watched in a battlefield aircraft. Especially as the noise is most pronounced when the aircraft is pointing towards the observer.'

[Author's note: these were complaints from locals who live next to a very busy helicopter base so the noise must have been impressive!]

This is of course true, but in the Vietnam context the Snake also sounded exactly like a Huey which meant the bad guys kept their heads down as they wouldn't know which it was.

The blade characteristics were also turned to unexpected advantage at times. Buck Simmons was amongst the first USMC pilots to fly the Cobra in Vietnam:

'One of the neat features of the G Model was that, when you turned sharply to the right, the blades smacked the air turbulence from the preceding blade with a truly loud pop. The

Buck Simmons – 'Scarface 48'.

noise was close to the sound and frequency of the 40mm grenade launcher in the chin turret. Several times, including while out in Laos, when we ran out of ordnance, we could 'pop' our blades and get out of a sticky situation by keeping their heads down with this trick.'

The rotor system is the key to any helicopter. Bells' two-blade teetering rotor was highly effective but it had limitations if mishandled. In the early days these were not fully understood and the phenomena of 'mast-bumping' claimed a number of lives. Dan Dugan:

'All teetering rotor helicopters are subject to it and it is just about always fatal to the occupants. Hiller ran into this issue early on in their development of the H–23 aka UH–12. They had a circular cut out in the mast which, as it turned out, did not allow enough blade flapping and they had a couple of fatal mast bumps early in their test program. The solution was pretty simple – an elongated cut out to allow significantly more blade flapping.

'It was initially encountered in the Cobra not long after it was introduced. When I went to the Cobra course at Hunter AAF, Savannah, GA back in January 1968, we all noticed a big burned out grass area not to far from the helicopter ramp. It was from a Cobra crash the week before – a mast bump. The problem in the Cobra was that if you sustained an engine failure, especially at high speed, the SCAS pitched the nose down thereby unloading the rotor. The instinctive reaction of a Huey pilot in the event of engine failure was then to dump the collective down immediately to avoid bleeding off too much rotor rpm. That would prove fatal in the Cobra because the hub would shear the mast, so it was ingrained in us to pull back on the cyclic to load the rotor then lower the collective and enter autorotation.

'In RVN, we would typically fly Hueys at least 1500' AGL to stay out of the effective range of small arms fire. When the Russian Strella shoulder-fired, heat-seeking missile was introduced into the Theatre of Operations, everyone flew down on the deck. When following the terrain, you would push over to go back on the deck after clearing the terrain or obstacle.

Dan Dugan at Pax River with 159227, probably the last J model in USMC service it has the distinction of flying chase to the V–22.

The rotor was then at less than one 'g' and if you had an aft CG and some sideslip – mast bump! It really became a problem and the Army took steps to avoid this unnecessary loss of life and helicopters. They quickly had Bell produce a 'thick walled' mast to prevent a light tap from severing the mast. There were a few dents sustained in the 'lucky' cases where the mast was not hit too hard. Then hub springs were designed and installed to retard blade flapping. These measures, especially the training, seemed to resolve the issue.'

The Army put a great deal of effort into the training, including some less than riveting films. Nevertheless they got through and mast bumping is not considered an issue nowadays. Fast forward to a pilot of the 1990s, Floyd Werner:

'I flew AH-1Ps and AH-1Fs. I liked the F Model the best. The HUD and the armament systems were easy to use. Sure the helicopter was a little heavy but God it was fun. I can tell you that I've had a Cobra to about 110 degrees wingover before I lost my nerve. I've got a picture somewhere with an AH-1F in a vertical dive and he entered that by coming over the top in a wingover. Never had mast bumping.'

Floyd touches on the subject of 'aerobatics' – downright dangerous in helicopters of the Cobras' era. The Cobra is supposed to be flown within tight 'G' limitations which specify a maximum of 0.5 negative G. The US Army still refuses to countenance such things (even with the entirely capable AH-64). For many years the doctrine was that the attack helicopter's airspace was 'from the top of the grass to the top of the trees' so it didn't apply anyway.

There have always been unsubstantiated stories about pilots who had 'looped and rolled' Cobras. As every pilot knows however, '… there are old pilots and there are bold pilots….' And many of the stories remain just that because there were no survivors.

However it was quickly found that regulation did not actually preclude pushing the boundaries of the envelope to see what the aircraft was capable of in the event of a 'combat' situation. When Cobras first met Marines in Vietnam the experience formed a bond between man and machine that remains unbroken to this day. Buck Simmons:

'We took up our normal orbit at about 1,000 feet and slightly outside the perimeter of the island. While the Marines were still deploying, VC started squirting out the sides of the island. It looked like ants leaving the cake. My pilot yelled for me to begin shooting, so I opened up with mini gun fire on a concentration on the south side of the island. We were flying east to west and passing the concentration, when Capt Bell rolled us upside down and calmly told me to keep shooting as he did an aileron roll into a steep turn to keep us on target. The strobe took over, and I only have snapshots. Most of my stomach and all

Floyd S Werner Jr – 'Bounty Hunter 27'.

of my nervous system is still somewhere above Go Noi Island. The gunner's controls looked like two black pistol grips attached to the illuminated sight in the middle. I was hanging on to them so hard, I'm sure I squeezed the black juice out of those plastic grips, but Captain Bell kept us at 1G all the way through.'

The Cobra's unique design certainly contributed to this confidence. Flying the Cobra, especially from the front seat with its unprecedented view, remains an experience helicopter pilots never forget. Major Pike's report commented at some length on the visibility from, and comfort of, the cockpit:

'One of the most impressive things about this aircraft was the very comfortable cockpits. It was appreciated that on a demonstration aircraft there would be a little more carpeting than on production machines; however the seats were extremely well shaped, layout of instruments and controls was logical and the sidearm controls in the front cockpit were surprisingly easy to use and gave a most comfortable seating position.'

His report also noted that the high seat and downswept nose made attitude difficult to judge from the front seat and that tactical flying at 160kts would require 'some experience'. Once gained however, the Cobra became a joy. Buck Simmons again:

'Up to 120 knots, the Cobra handled like a helicopter. At airspeeds over 120 knots, the Cobra handled like a fixed-wing. It would zoom climb, roll, do steep turns and do all the other fun stuff a fixed-wing would do. Flying at 10 to 20 feet that low to the ground is every pilot and hot rodders' dream. The pilot sat in the rear cockpit and had to look though a gun sight, his co-pilot's head, 9 feet of air space and a speckled Perspex windscreen to see what was coming at 145 knots or so. The real give away for obstacle clearance was the co-pilot's screaming, which rose in pitch with the increasing proximity of an obstacle.'

Twenty-odd years later, the Army had tried to spoil the pilots' view even more with the less-than-aesthetic 'flat-plate' canopy, but the experience was remarkably similar. Floyd Werner:

'Flying the front seat of a AH-1F Cobra was like sitting in an easy chair. You had the cyclic in the right hand which felt like having the remote control and the collective was like holding a beer. It was great to sit there as you felt like you were suspended on a pinnacle. Very easy to fly and loads of fun.

'Flying the back seat was like strapping the helicopter to you. The aircraft was only 36 inches wide at the pilot's compartment. When you looked down to the side it was like you could see everything. The view forward was not the greatest as you had the HUD, GPS on the left side and if the front seater was tall you had to look around him too. The power was intoxicating and if the Army still had Cobras I would still be in flying them. They were the best helicopter I've ever flown. Sure one tried to kill me but sometimes you have to be a snake wrangler and do pilot sh*t.'

G Model Cobras were neither intended nor equipped for night flying. During the Vietnam era they operated in darkness nonetheless. It was dangerous and difficult trying to find an LZ marked only by the light of a cigarette stub shielded by an empty mortar round canister, or knowing where the side of a mountain was only when you saw the strobe light reflecting off rocks and trees. Despite many attempts at a true night capability such as CONFICS and SMASH, the Snake community had to wait a generation for it, when the NVGs finally arrived they proved very effective, but only to a point. This comment from an unidentified Desert Storm pilot in 2003 proves that even the most modern technology has it's limitations:

'Around dinnertime, the word to launch finally comes, and of course, it's GO RIGHT NOW! My flight of four is supposed to be the lead flight out of the airfield, but our timing is all screwed up. The winds have picked back up, and visibility is less than a mile. In the confusion, another flight of Cobras departs the airfield ahead of us. Oops. Lots of talking on the radios to sort it out. For those of you who haven't looked through a pair of NVGs (Night Vision Goggles), they are built for use in darkness. If there is too much light, then they don't work correctly. The worst time to fly on the goggles is right after sunset. And of course, that's when we had launched. The sand in the air is something that we hadn't dealt with too much in training. In accordance with our peacetime training rules, if visibility is poor, you don't fly. Common sense – safety. But in war, when American lives are at stake, sometimes you have to push the edge of the envelope and deal with conditions that you're not normally accustomed to. With the reduced visibility and lack of moon that night, I can say that that was the darkest night I've ever flown in my life. Now mind you, I've been a Marine for almost 15 years. I've been flying Cobras since 1990. I've got a fair amount of experience. But this was dark. Seat-cushion-clenched-in-your-butt dark. Not only did the sand hang in the air to minimize horizontal visibility, but also the desert that we were flying over was completely smooth and lacked any detail. You couldn't tell, from 200 feet above ground level (AGL), how high you were. No depth perception. You couldn't see obstacles until you were right on top of them. That's a bit nerve-wracking.'

As an aside other echoes of past warriors' experience travel through time too. Three decades earlier Buck Simmons had noted:

'Fear of that magnitude was known as sucking the rivets out of the armor plated seat. The seat rivet replacement shop was our busiest maintenance effort... .'

The G Model in Vietnam was operating at the limits of its performance with regard to the available power. Frequently encountered 'hot'n high' conditions meant it sometimes struggled to get into the air. Buck Simmons:

'To tank up for the extreme range mission the co-pilot would get out of the Cobra in the fuel pits and lift the tail 'stinger' on his shoulder. Tilting the Cobra forward allowed another 50lb to be pumped into the tank. During the heat and with a full bag of fuel and ordnance, the Cobra did not have enough power to fly. We would normally pull in power and tilt the Cobra up on its skid 'toes'. When we got enough tilt in, she would begin dragging forward, ever faster. The stick had to be held absolutely still as 'stirring the pot' would transmit inputs to the rotor system that would disrupt what little aerodynamic lift we were generating. If all went well, translational lift would occur about halfway down the 3,200 foot runway and the usually graceful Cobra would wallow off into the air, developing about 100 feet per minute of climb.'

As the Cobra developed more power and better systems things improved. First the J Model, which was the same weight as the 'G' but with much more power, the 'Tango' which put the weight back on, and then the mighty 'Whisky' with approaching twice the power and weight of the G Model. Peyton DeHart:

'There was a brief period during the Marine Corps' AH-1W introduction phase, when I was rated to fly both the AH-1J and the AH-1W. My logbook shows May – September 1988 as transition months for HMLA-367 that saw me regularly fly one, and then the other, on successive days and occasionally on the same day; usually in the post–maintenance Functional Check Pilot role.

Peyton DeHart –' X Man'.

'I was supremely impressed by the power and stability of the 'W' but felt that the 'J' had a better instantaneous ability to change direction (to 'jink').

'Although I never had occasion to stage, or take part in, a head-to-head race, my repeated experience in the traffic pattern at Camp Pendleton brought me one insight. From a 3 foot hover starting position, shoving the cyclic forward for a maximum performance level acceleration, while pulling collective for 100% transmission torque, would get the AH-1J to a point 1,500 feet down the runway faster than the AH-1W could do it. At the 1,500 foot mark though, the AH-1J had essentially reached max level speed. The AH-1W blew past the 1,500 foot mark still smoothly accelerating toward 150-155 knots."

'I attributed this to the significantly greater gyroscopic effect of the AH-1W's main rotor system (at roughly twice the weight of the 'J', it took an extra second or two to greatly change the rotor disc's orientation), and to a lesser extent the 'W's higher gross weight. This difference could not detract from the experience of flying the AH-1W; a better machine in every other measurable way.'

Whilst the USMC was following the 'more power allows more weight, which needs more power which allows more kit to be carried' spiral, the Army was also upgrading the single-engine Cobras with more power, better weapons and greater stand-off capabilities.

Post Vietnam, the Army saw its Cobras as helping to stop Eastern Bloc hordes in frontline Europe. The Snake therefore had to change from a visual-range/anti-infantry weapon, to a fast scout capable of taking out a Main Battle Tank. Much discussion in crew rooms centred on how to deal with opposing Hind gunships, which it was assumed would attempt to sweep the skies ahead of the armour.

Until actual combat between the types occurred some years later, a number of interesting encounters took place as East and West prowled the East German border. Floyd Werner:

'While I was in Germany in 1985-88 there was an incident where a 2nd ACR Cobra and Hind were shadowing each other. The Cobra progressively slowed down with the Hind matching the manoeuvre until finally they came to a hover. The Hind must have had a tail wind or insufficient power and settled with power, crashing and exploded. The Communists quickly came out to the site, did virtually nothing as far as accident investigation goes, picked up the

'Mac' McMillan –
'Blue Max 27'.

trash. Then overnight they painted the grass green where the post crash fire burned the grass. You couldn't tell where there had even been a fire.'

Ultimately of course the Cold War came to an end and the Superpowers stepped back from the nuclear brink. This did not mean however that peace had come to Europe. As earlier described Floyd Werner found himself attempting to keep warring factions apart in Bosnia. With that mission complete there remained a final job to do:

'One aircraft, 79-23445, was flown out of Bosnia to Germany. Once there myself and Captain Jud McCrary flew the aircraft to the Royal Military Academy of Science in Schrivenham, England. This was my last flight in a Cobra. Very memorable flight across the Channel. Then buzzing the White Cliffs. We actually flew the Cobra around the south of England. It was great. Low, fast and lots of fun.'

Cobras such as '445' now rest in museums around the world, a now-silent but still impressive testimony to the world's first attack helicopter. Others, however, simply go on. The Sky Soldiers, their line-up including at least one airframe originally built as a 'G', continue to delight air show crowds as do a number of others. Some original G Models are still warriors.

As earlier noted 'Mac' McMillan, currently an Instructor and Maintenance Test Pilot, has recently delivered refurbished Cobras to Thailand. Going through Cobra Transition in May 1970 en route to Vietnam he has flown the Snake on and off for all of his career with the Army and Bell.

Rated in the G, S, E, P, F and W Models he has also flown the AH-1Q, AH-1R, JAH-1S and the AH-1J. Few people are as well qualified to compare the Snake's many variants.

'While I enjoyed all my AH-1 flying, the "G" is my baby. It's the aircraft I went to war in and it's probably where I got my foundation as an aviator. The G Model was my primary aircraft from May 1970 until January 1980 when I went to the fixed-wing transition and my tour as a King Air pilot in Saudi Arabia. The G was a pilots aircraft. Not too electric, a basic point and shoot for the back-seater. It was an art to shoot curve balls and knucklers. At the top of my game, I could shoot within 25 meters of an American unit. And I wasn't special. We had some guys really provide close support!

I enjoyed F's and W's, but the G was the bird. Hell, a Blue-tinted canopy, air conditioned, 76 trombones, mini-gun and a chunker...and almost enough engine to lift it all. She wasn't perfect but I was proud to be a Cobra Pilot.'

The Snake's influence has remained powerful down the years too. Way back in the summer of 1967 John Sproule managed to wangle his two young children a brief sit in '209. The then 7-year-old Sandy Sproule went on to become a helicopter engineer and pilot. Finding himself once again in the rear seat of a Snake as part of his work over forty years later he still rates it as the coolest helicopter in the world – there can be few who would disagree.

Every Cobra pilot that has ever sat in the aircraft for the first time… Sandy Sproule in N209J in 1967.

Appendix 1

Out Takes

During its long life the Cobra has trialled many different weapon systems, night vision devices, aerodynamic and other mods. Indeed the very last Cobra in the Army inventory is still serving as a test platform as these words are written.

Many of these made it to hardware, others fell by the wayside. Some concepts were products only of the fervid imagination of the marketing department (who apparently didn't always talk to the engineers).

Other projects survived the sketch phase to become models. Many of those illustrated clearly owe their existence to the accuracy with which the Revell company reproduced the Cobra in 1/32nd scale. Modellers will recognise the classic (and still available) 1967 plastic model kit which obviously served Bell engineers well in the days before CAD computers.

One of the more obscure possibilities investigated was an aircrew ejection system for the Cobra. The Stanley Aviation Corporation fitted one of its 'Yankee' seats to a Cobra and apparently tested it on a sled rig.

The Yankee system was developed for (and successful on) the Douglas A-1 Skyraider by founder Robert Stanley, former Naval aviator and one-time Bell test pilot. Strictly speaking it is not an ejector seat but a rocket-extraction system designed to haul the pilot out of the aircraft at low speed and altitude. The problem with a helicopter, as the Russians found out some years later, is that you have to shed the rotor blades first.

Sadly, no photos of the test or detail information has ever come to light save the cryptic comment 'the seat survived, the Cobra didn't...'

Presented here are a few fascinating 'what ifs' from Bell's archives, some Army 'one offs' and just a little marketing hype.

This 1968 photo is captioned 'Night Stalker' and seems to feature a 'radar' (MTI?) nose and what appears to be a turret mounted (infra-red?) searchlight alongside the gun. More interestingly the main and tail rotor blades feature swept tips as later trialled on the King Cobra. (*Bell via Mike Verier*)

Possibly this photo from the DARCOM archives is the living incarnation of a radar nose Cobra. Nothing is known about this project. (*US Army via Ray Willhyte*)

The 'Flip Tip' was an ingenious attempt to provide a wheeled undercarriage for the Snake without compromising weapon carriage. (*Bell via Mike Verier*)

Flip–tip landing configuration (*Bell via Mike Verier*)

RESCUE CONFIGURATION

The rescue version of the HueyCobra would utilize the same airframe, engine and dynamic components as the Army AH-1G helicopter. The versatility, high performance and reduced vulnerability which were designed into the Cobra would be retained for this critical mission. Minor modifications would include:

- Pilot's station forward with full controls
- Helmet mounted sight providing fire control for the pilot
- Seating for four in the aft compartment
- Variable speed hydraulic hoist

Taken from the original Cobra sales brochure, this artist's impression of the Cobra with a rescue winch doesn't exactly match the description claiming that only 'minor modifications' would enable the Cobra to accommodate four passengers in the back! (*Bell via Mike Verier*)

It is likely that the penny dropped when they realised that starting from a J Model Cobra they had actually designed an aircraft remarkably like… er … a Huey! (*Bell via Mike Verier*)

This may have been an anti-spin device or some sort of airbrake to facilitate steep diving attacks. No detailed information has ever surfaced. (*Bell via Mike Verier*)

The folding rotor was too complex to be of use on a twin-blade Cobra. Decades later it became a necessity for the 4-blade Zulu. (*Bell via Mike Verier*)

This hulk photographed at White Sands was evidently to be a remotely piloted drone dressed up to look like a Kamov Hokum. Despite the considerable work clearly involved, it was obviously just too ugly to proceed with! (*via Ray Willhyte*)

Extensive cosmetic changes included a fake fuselage and 'Kamov' wing tip pylons. New exhausts were also created. (*via Ray Willhyte*)

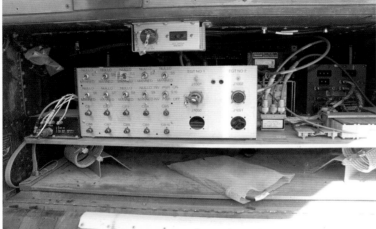

The drone electronics have been installed in the former ammunition bay, the switches offering 'MANNED' or 'NULLO' operation – NULLO stands for 'Not Under Live Local Operation' but is also Latin for 'zero'. (*via Ray Willhyte*)

Optional Wheel Landing Gear

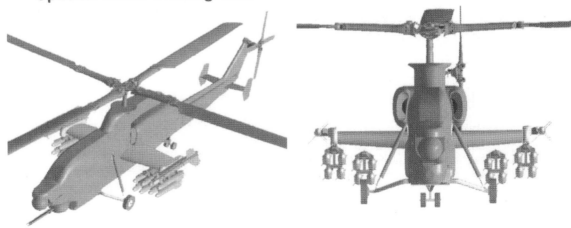

A fixed-wheel undercarriage has been offered to potential customers, notably Turkey. It has not as yet been taken up. (*Bell via Mike Verier*)

Before the Zulu design was finalised, the art department visualised another attempt at a retractable wheeled undercarriage layout. This one clearly designed to appeal to the historically minded Marines with its similarity to the legendary F4U Corsair. (*Bell via Mike Verier*)

Snakeskins
Cobra Colours

The colour schemes used on military aircraft are a fascinating study in themselves. Indeed the word 'camouflage' implies a chameleon-like ability to blend with the background. 'Paint' is in fact an important passive defence system and its importance should not be underrated. Popular perception would assume all such machines are either 'green' or 'grey' depending on the fashion of the time – a misconception that this book should by now have thoroughly dispelled.

Detailed in this appendix are the basic schemes worn by the Cobras of various nations. Even these represent only starting points for a vast range of temporary and expedient variations that operational service throws up. The personal (and often highly unofficial) embellishments beloved of service crews, the effects of weather and heavy use, local interpretation or even the whim of a commander, all play their part in individualising machines that leave the factory in anonymous and identical colours. The colour profiles below have been selected to illustrate some of the more interesting service variations. Many of which are transient 'operation only' schemes that have to be removed once the aircraft return to a more regulated 'peacetime' environment. Some of the 'unofficial' schemes are illustrated for the first time having been painstakingly researched from original partial images and personal notes.

The notation used for colours is keyed to a US Government publication known as Federal Standard 595A. This document gives colour chips of hundreds of standard shades used by all government agencies, including the military. Each colour is identified by a four-digit code number, prefixed by 1 (for gloss finish), 2 (semi-gloss) or 3 (lustreless, or matt). FS595A is available for purchase by the public, and is therefore a readily accessible reference. More to the point, manufacturers quote FS595A numbers, so the colour given is the actual colour used, and not a visual approximation using another system. I am indebted to the Paint Shop at Bell for the very detailed assistance provided.

US Army

All the early AH-1G Models were delivered in an overall finish of Olive drab FS34087 (now renumbered FS54088). Some had matt black anti-glare panels forward of the windscreen, and all carried the title UNITED STATES ARMY on the tail boom, and the aircraft serial on the fin. The lettering in both cases was 6 inches high, again in matt black. Cockpit interiors were Dark Gull Gray FS36231, and the interiors of cowlings and access panels were a chromate colour approximating to FS23793. This situation continued throughout the Vietnam period, although the New Equipment Training Team did experiment briefly with multi-colour schemes. US Air Force 'South East Asia' colours were applied over the Olive Drab (primarily FS30219 Tan and FS36622 Gray) paint being traded for Army C-rations. Officialdom however frowned on both the trading and the colour schemes, and they were short lived as a result.

Operational experience soon showed that the low-flying helicopters needed to be more, not less, visible from above. This led to the adoption of International Orange FS12197 for the top surfaces of the elevators, and one or two white bands on the top surfaces of the main rotor.

During the early 1970s, the Army carried out a great deal of experimental work on possible camouflage schemes for both aircraft and ground vehicles. As well as the actual design of various schemes, research was conducted into the ability of a surface finish to absorb, rather than reflect, radar energy. An officer at Fort Hood is also reputed to have had his car painted in 'anti-radar' colours. It looked horrible, but at least it enabled him to confuse police speed traps! The result of all this work was a scheme called 'Pattern Painting', in which the Army boffins worked out an exact pattern for every vehicle and aircraft in service. These consisted of four-colour designs, applied on a sort of 'painting-by-numbers' basis. The idea behind it all was that changing one or two colours, rather than the whole scheme, would enable climatic and terrain variations to be incorporated more readily. These paints were an early attempt at stealth technology, and are said to have worked so well that pilots occasionally baited Austin Approach by switching off their transponders and disappearing from radar screens.

Figure 1

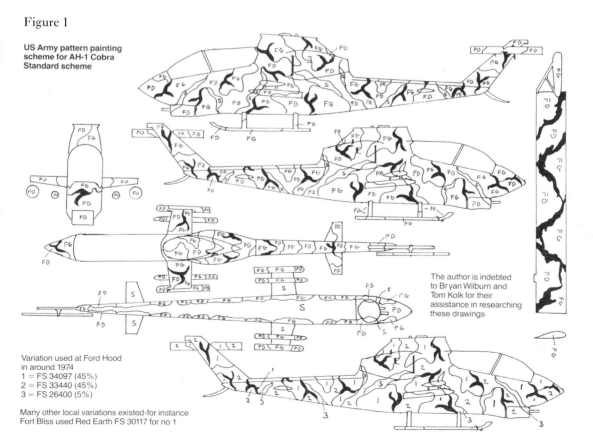

US Army pattern painting
scheme for AH-1 Cobra
Standard scheme

The author is indebted
to Bryan Wilburn and
Tom Kolk for their
assistance in researching
these drawings

Variation used at Ford Hood
in around 1974
1 = FS 34097 (45%)
2 = FS 33440 (45%)
3 = FS 26400 (5%)

Many other local variations existed-for instance
Fort Bliss used Red Earth FS 30117 for no 1

COLOUR DISTRIBUTION – CONDITION COLOUR NUMBER	45%	45%	5%	5%
Winter US and Europe – Verdant[1]	FG	FD	S[3]	BL
Snow – temperate w/trees and shrubs[2]	FG	W	S[3]	BL
Snow – temperate w/open terrain[2]	W	FD	S[3]	BL
Summer US and Europe – verdant[1]	FG	LG	S[3]	BL
Tropics – verdant	FG	DG	LG[3]	BL
Gray desert	S	FD	EY[3]	BL
Red desert	ER	EY	S[3]	BL
Winter arctic	W	W	W	W

NOTES
1. Verdant means generally green – in summer due to trees, shrubs and grass; in winter due to evergreens.
2. This colour combination is for use only in areas that occasionally have snow which does not completely cover the terrain.
3. This 5 per cent colour should be the camouflage shade that matches most closely the colour of the soil in the local area. A typical colour for such use is Sand, but Earth Red, Earth Yellow, or one of the others may be closer to the predominant soil colour and, in that case, should be used.

COLOUR	ABBREVIATION	FS595 Ref
White	W	37875
Desert Sand	DS	30277q
Earth Yellow	EY	30257
Earth Red	ER	30117
Earth Brown	EB	30099
Field Drab	FD	30118
Olive Drab	OD	34087
Light Green	LG	34151
Dark Green	DG	34102
Forest Green	FG	34079
Black	BL	37038

An early camouflage trial using what appears to be Field Green applied over the standard Olive Drab (*Bryan Wilburn*)

As can be seen from Fig 1 (which is taken straight from the manual), the drawings provided to field units were rudimentary, and the expected variation in the finished articles certainly appeared. Essentially, the two main colours each covered forty-five percent of the subject, and the other two, one of which was generally black, covered the other ten percent between them. The accompanying tables are from the same manual and give the colours, their approximate FS595A equivalents, and their intended use.

Although widely used on ground equipment (where it could be accomplished by soldiers with paint brushes) pattern-painting on aircraft was a rather more specialised job, and it eventually proved impractical. For the remainder of their careers, all US Army Cobras were painted in a very

Pattern Painting was trialled extensively. The big shiny canopy even being provided with a custom camo-cover. (*U.S. Army via Ray Wilhite*)

'By the book' rendition of the Pattern Scheme. 67-15666 of D Troop, 2-1 Cav /2AD, pictured up from Fort Hood Circa 1973. (*John Repcik*)

matt (the finish is almost like fine sandpaper) dark grey/green, known as Mil-C-46168 'Aircraft Green'. The nearest FS595A equivalent is FS34031, although the colour can be perceived as anything from a dark brownish olive to nearly black, depending on light conditions (which is of course the point). In keeping with the low visibility doctrine, cockpit interiors and all external markings are black. Army aircraft on field service do not carry national insignia.

During the 'Desert Storm' deployment a number of cobras received 'sand' paint jobs using FS33717 (or possibly a mixed similar shade – some of the schemes were applied in great haste).

US Marine Corps

'Stateside' J Models (and latterly some 'G's) for the USMC were painted overall in their distinctive gloss, Field Green FS14097. Full national insignia, with white MARINES and serial presentation were standard, as was a yellow (FS13538) tail rotor warning band. The tail skid was often striped red and yellow, and the cockpit interiors were all Dark Gull Gray FS36231.

G Models deployed to Vietnam were diverted from Army orders and delivered in Army Olive Drab, J Models came matt Field Green (34095) and devoid of national markings save (of course) for MARINES in black on the tail boom. Initially at any rate they retained the yellow safety markings.

It became common practice to paint the tail fin and part of the boom black, usually with a sweeping demarcation aft of the stabilisers. Whilst this added a rather rakish touch to the scheme it was primarily in recognition of the Cobras exhaust plume which inevitably blackened these areas anyway.

After the Vietnam War, all USMC Cobras gradually went into drab colours and all markings, including a now rather skeletal national insignia, were rendered in matt black. Due to the salt-laden atmosphere of a marine environment, the finish invariably weathered badly, and the overall effect was often patchy and characterised by much retouching.

Like the Army, the Marines experimented with temporary 'field' camouflage, In around 1980, at least two AH-1Ts were delivered from Bell in what appears to have been Israeli Tan. At Camp Pendleton they were finished in a scheme reminiscent of the Army's pattern painting ideas using green and black areas over the Tan base. The idea didn't take hold (probably for similar reasons

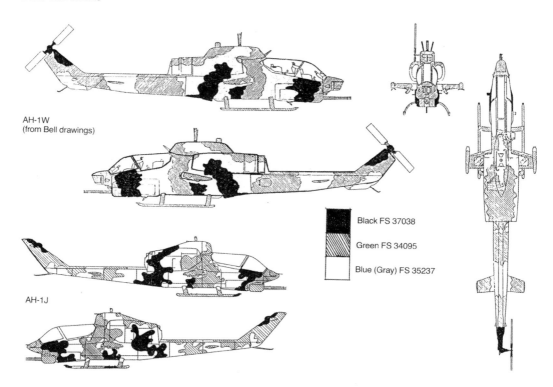

USMC 1978 scheme

AH-1W
(from Bell drawings)

AH-1J

Black FS 37038

Green FS 34095

Blue (Gray) FS 35237

to the Army) and the AH-1Ts served most of their life in matt Field Green FS34095. In the late 1980s/early 1990s a number were given an overall grey (reportedly FS36320 Dark Ghost Gray) scheme.

From about 1987, the USMC standardised on a three-colour 'wraparound' scheme, consisting of green FS34095, gray FS35237 and black FS37038. The first batch of AH-1W aircraft left the factory finished in this way, and surviving AH-1J and T Models were progressively repainted in the same scheme at unit or depot level. Markings and insignia were black, reversed where they crossed a black camouflage field. By this time cockpit interiors, like those of other Cobra operators, had become black.

Whilst complex 'tactical' schemes did not enter general use, they were still tried from time to time for specific exercises or deployments. Both 'J' and 'W' Models received temporary schemes, most notably for 'Desert Storm' where everything was repainted before embarkation, the squadrons devising their own solutions ranging from a thin grey overspray of the three-tone scheme, to a complete respray using whatever 'desert' colours came to hand (including some sourced from local DIY retailers)

Post 'Desert Storm' all of these schemes gave way to the ubiquitous grey movement, becoming overall FS36375 except for the plan view in the slightly darker FS35237. Markings and insignia are generally rendered in the darker shade, reversing where necessary.

Foreign Military Sales operators

The US Army finish was also standard on most AH-1S/F Models supplied under FMS. Pakistan, Japan, Thailand, Turkey and South Korea all received aircraft in this scheme. Some have been repainted locally as detailed below

Bahrain

Delivered in an overall tan FS33531

Iran

Originally the Iranian scheme, which uses standard 'Asia Minor' colours, consisted of Brown FS30140 and Tan FS30400 topsides, with Gray FS36622 on the underside. On some aircraft the grey was omitted, and the brown and tan extended underneath the fuselage. Recent rebuilt/refurbished J Models seem to use local colour mixes, the tan in particular having a rather more pink tone. This author has not been given access to any further information. At least one of the *Shabaviz* reverse-engineered hybrids has appeared in a dark green overall scheme.

Israel

Cobras for this most secretive of nations were initially delivered in standard US Army Olive Drab FS34087. Later production machines left the factory in an overall finish which was supplied to Bell by the Israeli Government and known in the paint shop simply as 'Israeli Tan'. More recently it has emerged that this shade was FS30029. Currently Israel's Snakes are FS30145. (See the export section for more detail)

Japan

Japanese Cobras were initially delivered in the US Army's Aircraft Green FS 34031, albeit this camouflage was originally compromised by bold white markings and full colour national insignia, but these soon gave way to a 'low-vis' presentation with black markings. Currently the aircraft have a three-tone scheme using brown FS30219, and greens FS34096 and FS34097, accented with black 'highlights' in a style very reminiscent of the US Army's 1970s pattern painting ideas.

Jordan

This very attractive scheme again features the 'Asia Minor' colours of FS30140 and FS20400, but this time in combination with Green 34097. The wingtips and extreme nose look black, but they are actually painted in the US Army's Aircraft Green.

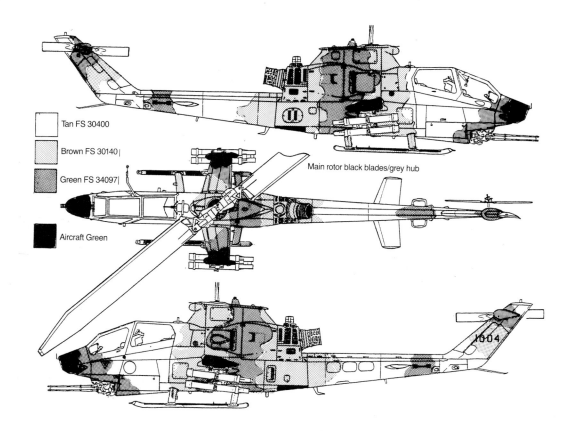

Tan FS 30400

Brown FS 30140

Green FS 34097

Aircraft Green

Main rotor black blades/grey hub

Korea

The eight AH-1Js supplied to South Korea were finished overall in Olive Drab FS34087. Subsequent F Models used the standard dark green as described above.

Spain

The AH-1Gs supplied to Spain were painted overall in two coats of Sea Blue Gloss FS15042.

Taiwan

The 'W' Models supplied to Taiwan are overall FS34031

Thailand

The F Models supplied to Thailand are overall FS34031

Turkey

The 'W's supplied used the standard USMC pattern except that the grey was replaced by a tan, believed to be FS20400. Their F Models were originally delivered in standard US Army FS34031. Some at least have been repainted in a scheme that appears to use the same colours as the 'Whiskies'.

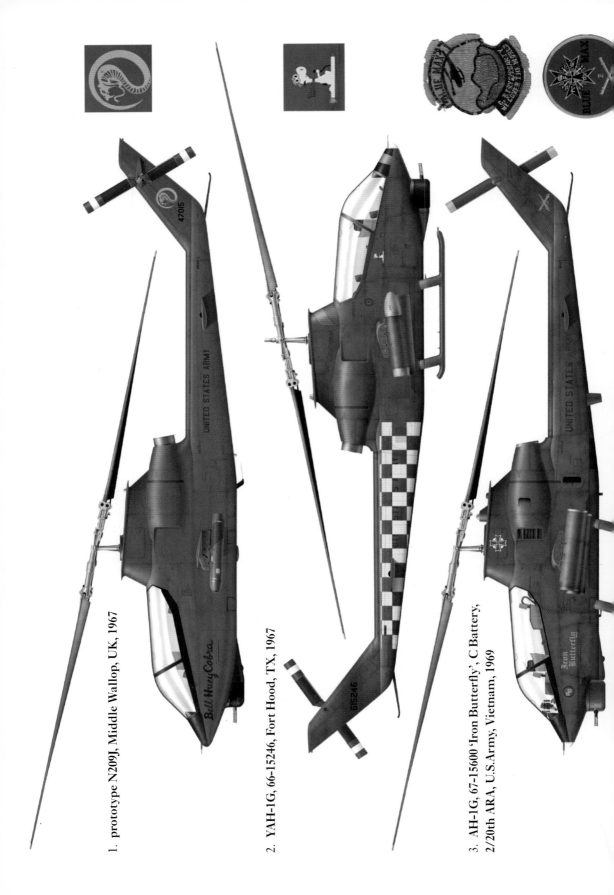

1. prototype N209J, Middle Wallop, UK, 1967

2. YAH-1G, 66-15246, Fort Hood, TX, 1967

3. AH-1G, 67-15600 'Iron Butterfly', C Battery,
2/20th ARA, U.S.Army, Vietnam, 1969

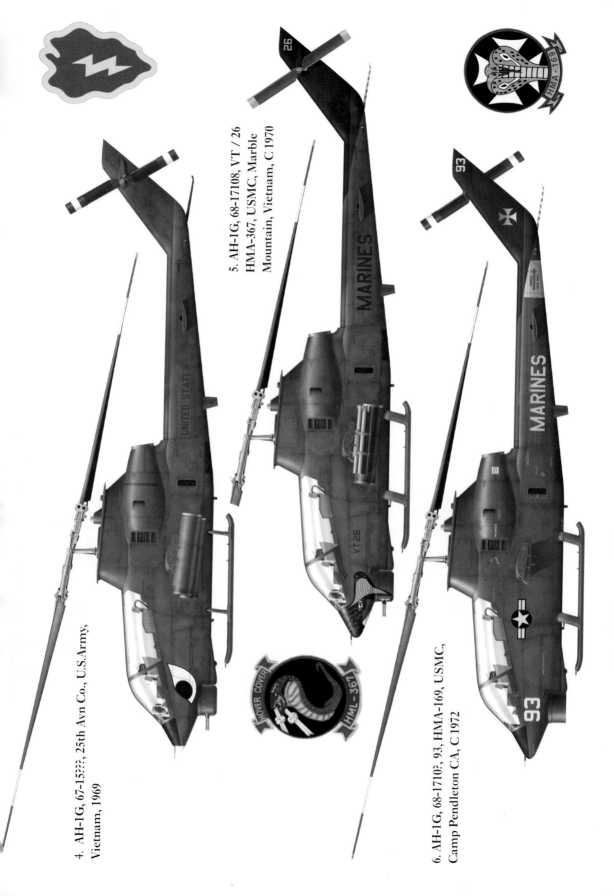

4. AH-1G, 67-15???, 25th Avn Co, U.S.Army, Vietnam, 1969

5. AH-1G, 68-17108, VT / 26 HMA-367, USMC, Marble Mountain, Vietnam, C 1970

6. AH-1G, 68-1710?, 93, HMA-169, USMC, Camp Pendleton CA, C 1972

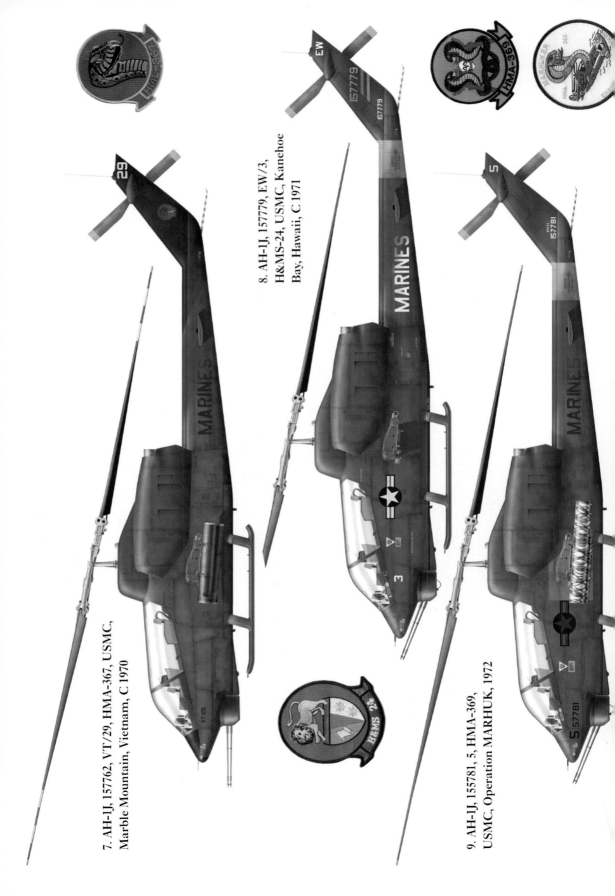

7. AH-1J, 157762, VT/29, HMA-367, USMC, Marble Mountain, Vietnam, C 1970

8. AH-1J, 157779, EW/3, H&MS-24, USMC, Kanehoe Bay, Hawaii, C 1971

9. AH-1J, 155781, 5, HMA-369, USMC, Operation MARHUK, 1972

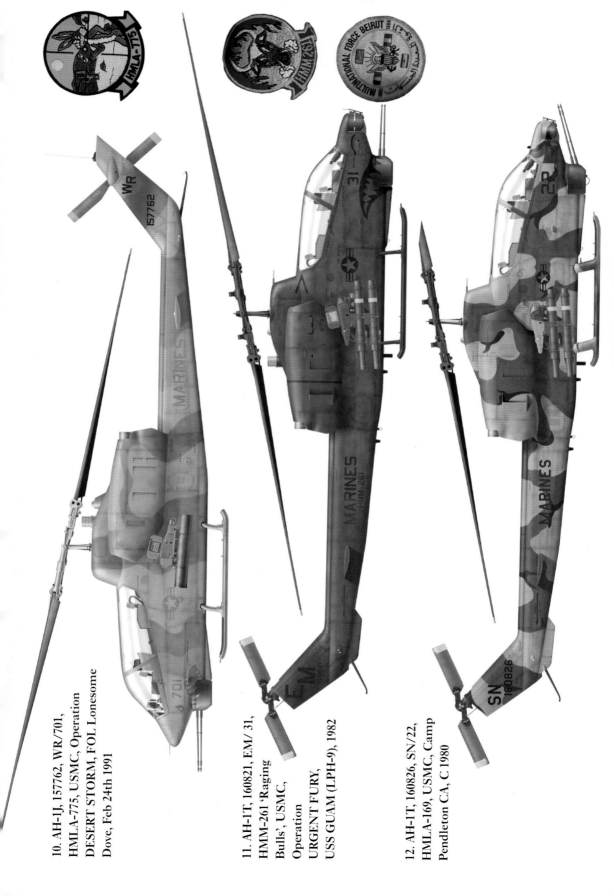

10. AH-1J, 157762, WR/701,
HMLA-775, USMC, Operation
DESERT STORM, FOL Lonesome
Dove, Feb 24th 1991

11. AH-1T, 160821, EM/ 31,
HMM-261 'Raging
Bulls', USMC,
Operation
URGENT FURY,
USS GUAM (LPH-9), 1982

12. AH-1T, 160826, SN/22,
HMLA-169, USMC, Camp
Pendleton CA, C 1980

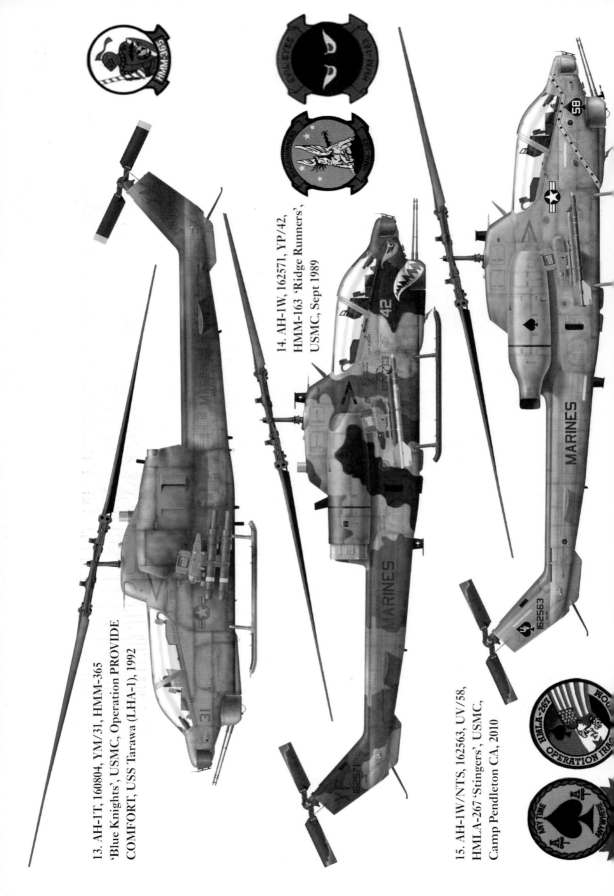

13. AH-1T, 160804, YM/31, HMM-365
'Blue Knights', USMC, Operation PROVIDE
COMFORT, USS Tarawa (LHA-1), 1992

14. AH-1W, 162571, YP/42,
HMM-163 'Ridge Runners',
USMC, Sept 1989

15. AH-1W/NTS, 162563, UV/58,
HMLA-267 'Stingers', USMC,
Camp Pendleton CA, 2010

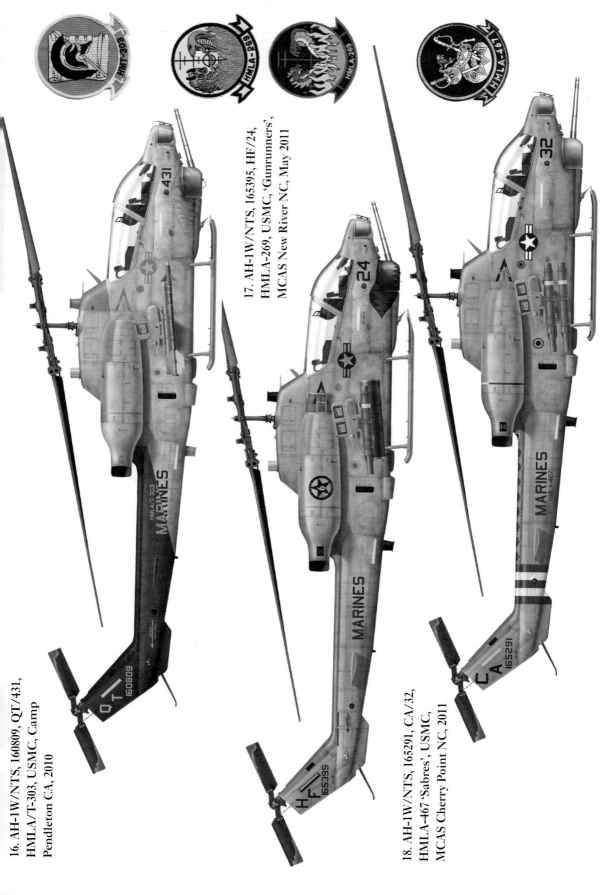

16. AH-1W/NTS, 160809, QT/431,
HMLA/T-303, USMC, Camp
Pendleton CA, 2010

17. AH-1W/NTS, 165395, HF/24,
HMLA-269, USMC, 'Gunrunners',
MCAS New River NC, May 2011

18. AH-1W/NTS, 165291, CA/32,
HMLA-467 'Sabres', USMC,
MCAS Cherry Point NC, 2011

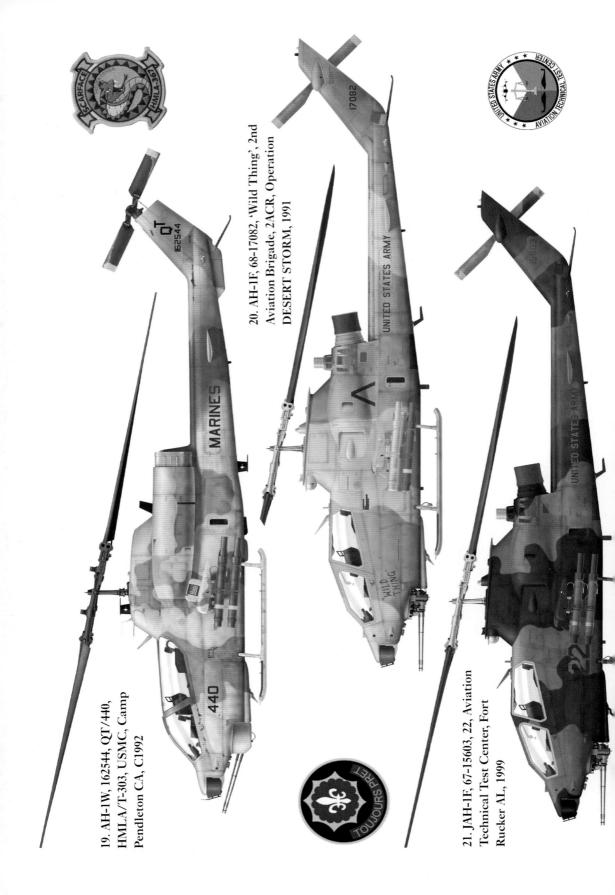

19. AH-1W, 162544, QT/440, HMLA/T-303, USMC, Camp Pendleton CA, C1992

20. AH-1F, 68-17082, 'Wild Thing', 2nd Aviation Brigade, 2ACR, Operation DESERT STORM, 1991

21. JAH-1F, 67-15603, 22, Aviation Technical Test Center, Fort Rucker AL, 1999

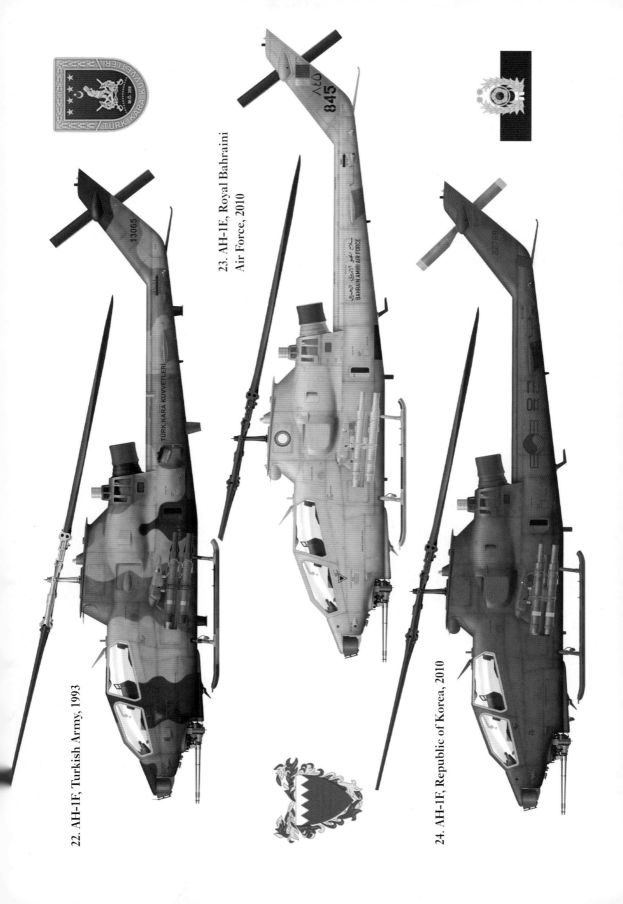

22. AH-1F, Turkish Army, 1993

23. AH-1E, Royal Bahraini Air Force, 2010

24. AH-1F, Republic of Korea, 2010

Colour Profile Notes

1. The prototype Cobra toured Europe during 1967 making its debut at the Paris Air Show. A brief but thorough British evaluation was made by the Army Air Corps at Middle Wallop. Aircraft is overall FS 24087 with black lettering. The 'serial' was applied for the tour duration, The prototype was technically a civil registered aircraft, and the only Cobra with a retractable undercarriage.

2. The 1st YAH-1 was used for weapon trials, hence the temporary chequers which were for photographic reference. Aircraft was FS 34087 overall. Orange 'dayglo' areas denote 'TEST' status. Note the unofficial Snoopy cartoon below the cockpit.

3. This early G was flown by W/O 'Mac' McMillan. It's 'artillery' heritage shown by the crossed cannon on the tail. The red circle denoted 'C' Company, within which is the 'last two' of the aircraft serial. Aircraft is overall Olive Drab FS 34087, with FS 12197 International Orange top surfaces on the elevators.

4. This aircraft from the 25th Aviation Co. 'DiamondHeads' sported this massive eye motif. This was eventually reduced in size when the unit adopted an equally impressive sharkmouth for its aircraft. This early G Model is 'Hog' configured with four 19 shot pods. Aircraft is FS 34087 overall, Main rotor (top) o/d with yellow tips and one white stripe, black underneath with yellow tips.

5. This USMC G was flown by Buck Simmons and sports the spectacular Snakehead adopted by HMA-367 'Scarface'. Colour scheme should be matt Field green FS34095, photographic evidence however suggests that the aircraft may have been delivered in 'Army' Olive Drab, VT is the squadron code. 17108 survived to be returned to the Army and upgraded to AH-1F. Fully refurbished in 2012 it flies today with the Royal Thai Army

6. This G from HMA-169 home-based at Camp Pendleton shows the black tail adopted at various times for many USMC Cobra variants. Whilst its rakish sweep looks well it is primarily there to mask the exhaust staining typical of Cobras. Surviving Gs were returned to the Army as the Js became available. Aircraft is Overall gloss FS14097

7. Freshly delivered to the USMC the first Js in Vietnam were overall F34095, with the black tail and a 'toned down' squadron patch added in-theatre. This marked the start of the 'lo-viz' movement with very few markings. The main rotor is O/D with two one-foot white bands on the top surface in addition to the yellow tip – this was to identify the aircraft from above

8. This aircraft sports the 'stateside' full national insignia and markings. The yellow stripes on the tail reflect the aircrafts' attachment to a 'composite' unit that included OV-10s. Hueys, and even A-4 Skyhawks. Aircraft is overall FS34095

9. The MARHUK Js had their markings 'toned down' en-route to Hon La. The white stars and bars of the national insignia were over-painted and large markings other than 'safety' legends were mostly rendered in black rather than white. The grey areas on the fuselage and wings are protective paint needed to reduce the damage caused by the powerful exhaust of the Zuni rockets deployed for the first time during MARHUK. 'Pistol Pete 5' was Flown by Lieutenant David C Corbett. Aircraft is overall FS34095.

10. The same aircraft as (7) above. The Js were deployed to Iraq for Desert Shield / Storm. The existing Grey /green/black scheme was oversprayed with grey to achieve a 'three tone grey' effect. Markings were either black or FS-36118 grey. The Sharkmouths were applied by the crew chiefs in-theatre and showed considerable variation. Remarkably, this aircraft also served in MARHUK.

11. Flown by Peyton DeHart, this aircraft was one of four that saw combat in the Grenada operation in 1982 (note the ZSU kills tally). The Sharkmouth was added when the aircraft reached Lebanon. Such embellishments are 'cruise only' and removed when the aircraft return to their home base. Overall FS34097 Field green.

12. The USMC also experimented with multi-colour camouflage schemes and at least two T Models were given an extensive make-over featuring very similar patterns to those adopted by the U.S. Army. The idea was not carried forward. In this instance the colours are believed to be FS30029 Tan, FS34095 green and FS37038 Black.

13. Late in their career remaining Ts received an overall FS36375 Grey scheme. As is the case with the Whisky fleet this quickly became very weathered and re-touched in service. This was the last operational deployment of the T Model Cobras.

14. The three-colour black / grey / green scheme was adopted for the W Model when it first entered service. The aircraft flown by Peyton DeHart in 1989 briefly featured a spectacular sharkmouth during its deployment aboard USS Tarawa (LHA-1) with 'Evil eye' callsigns

15. With a sense of history this aircraft has been decorated with markings last worn by the OV-10 Broncos of VMO-2, the unit which gave birth to the first Cobra squadrons in the USMC.

16. This specially marked aircraft again reflected the black tail first seen in Vietnam. The basic 'Grays' scheme (FS36375 and FS35237) is apparent, the darker shade being used for the subtle 'Shark-mouth', This airframe was originally built as an AH-1T.

17. The 'boss bird' from HMLA-269 'Gun Runners'. The star insignia on the nose and cowling reflects the 'US Marshall' badge. The legend translates as 'No better friend, no worse enemy'

18. The newest Cobra unit in the USMC was formed when Atlanta-based HMLA-775 was stood down, the 'diamond back' markings, stripes and national markings are in black and white

19. When HMLA-367 deployed for Operation DESERT SHIELD / STORM they took an enlarged Cobra element (18 rather than 12) Aircraft were drawn from any that were available / serviceable at Camp Pendleton. The 'desert' scheme achieved by painting over the green and black parts of the standard scheme (including all markings) with sand FS33711 (or a near equivalent from whatever source was available). On return the original unit markings were applied directly over the temporary scheme until the maintenance cycle permitted a full re-paint.

20. Unlike the Marines, the Army repainted very few of its aircraft for DESERT STORM. This aircraft however managed to receive not only the basic FS 33711 sand overpaint but a camouflage pattern in FS30117 Brown as well. The 'stripes' below and to the rear of the cockpit are where the serial stencil was simply taped over during the re-spray. The inverted chevron was a recognition feature much used on Coalition armour and helicopters.

21. Fort Rucker's resident test unit operated a number of Cobras for trials and weapon testing. These have been finished in a number of schemes over the years. This one appears to use the same colours applied to vehicles, the colours are FS37030, FS30051, and FS34094

22. Turkish F Models were originally delivered in the standard US Army green finish. Subsequently a number of them have acquired the same scheme as the Whisky Models FS30400 Tan / FS34095 green and FS37038 black.

23. The Royal Bahraini Air Force operates two squadrons (the 8th and 9th Helicopter Squadrons) of AH-1Es and some TAH-1Ps. All are finished in overall Tan FS33531

24. South Korean Cobras remain on the front line. All are to AH-1F configuration and painted FS34031 Aircraft Green with black markings.

Snake Fangs

Cobra weapons

The Cobra is first and foremost an armed helicopter. As the first of its kind it has carried and fired virtually everything in the inventory that it could actually lift. The development of weapons and their associated targeting systems to the precision state of the art we see today owes everything to the development work carried out over the years by the Cobra.

Bell picture from the Paris Air Show in 1967 shows the basic rockets and guns armament envisaged at the time. Shown here are nineteen shot rocket pods (with and without aerodynamic covers), a seven shot pod is on the wing. An M-18 gun pod (in white). On and forward of the packing case larger calibre guns indicate growth potential. In front of the turret is 7.62 ammunition and an M-129 40mm grenade launcher and ammunition already planned for the production turret. (*Bell via Mike Verier*)

Armament

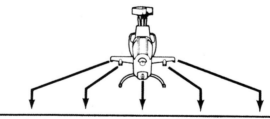

LEGEND:

M197	— 20MM CANNON
M18	— 7.62M MINIGUN POD
M118	— SMOKE GRENADE DISPENSER
CBU-55	— FUEL AIR EXPLOSIVE
LAU-68	— 7 ROCKETS
LAU-69	— 19 ROCKETS
LAU-61	— 19 ROCKETS
MK45	— PARACHUTE FLARE
MK115	— BOMB
HMMS	— HELLFIRE MODULAR MISSILE SYSTEM
SUU-44	— FLARE DISPENSER

XM118	M18	M197	M18	XM118
CBU-55/B	CBU-55/B	M197	CUB-55/B	CBU-55/B
SUU-44	SUU-44	M197	SUU-44	SUU-44
MK115	LAU-68/A	M197	LAU-68/A	MK115
MK45	LAU-68B/A	M197	LAU-68B/A	MK45
LAU-69/A	LAU-69/A	M197	LAU-69/A	LAU-69/A
LAU-61/A	LAU-61/A	M197	LAU-61/A	LAU-61/A
LAU-68/A	LAU-68/A	M197	LAU-68/A	LAU-68/A
4 HMMS		M197		4 HMMS

This Bell picture has often been mis-captioned as a 'T'. It is in fact a J and intended to demonstrate all the things it might carry depending on variant. On the aircraft and immediately in front are covered 19-shot rocket pods. Forward of those are seven-shot pods flanked by rockets. The two massive stores on the ends of the row are CBU-55 fuel-air explosives. Between them, interestingly, are TOW rounds which only the Iranian Js were equipped for. TwoXM-8 dispensers are flanked by grenades, parachute flares and practice bombs. To the front is a pair of M-18 gun pods flanked by 20mm and 7.62 mm ammunition.(*Bell via Mike Verier*)

The TAT-102 turret fitted to early production Cobras pending the arrival of the dual–weapon M–28. (*U.S.Army*)

The definitive M28 turret could house two miniguns. (*U.S.Army*)

More usually the turret would house one gun and one grenade launcher – the weapons were completely interchangeable. (*U.S.Army*)

The one-off Emmerson turret fitted to the prototype N209J. (*Bell via Mike Verier*)

It was to be some years after the USMC that the Army finally got the 20mm M-197 20mm turret. This one is on an AH-1S. The Army always kept its gun uncowled for ease of maintenance. (*Mike Verier*)

The Marines always cowl their guns however. The M-197 has served for many years and is now considered extremely reliable. Recently the addition of a laser spot pointer, seen here below the barrels. Has greatly enhanced accuracy. (*Mike Verier*)

A re-barrelled 30mm version of the M-197 was also trialled. (*USMC via Mike Verier*)

Nothing is known of this apparent development of the M-197 which has appeared on some Japanese Cobras. (*Via Floyd Werner*)

This development aircraft features yet another potential gun turret option, possibly the Hughes 'Chain Gun'. It also totes the early 'podded' TOW rig and an early version of the associated M-65 sighting system. (*Bell via Mike Verier*)

Fixed Guns

The earliest fixed gun used was the M-18A1, again the M-134 7.62 minigun, (GAU-2B in Air Force nomenclature) this time in the standard Air Force pod. It could be mounted on any of the four wing stations, and saw extensive service in Vietnam. The Army also quickly realised that 20mm was a good idea, and hastily developed the XM-35, which was simply a standard six-barrel Vulcan on a special adaptor to allow it to hang from (usually) the port inboard (No 2) station. Ammunition for this monster weapon was carried in panniers mounted above the skids on both sides of the aircraft. M-35 capable Cobras were easily identified by the additional 'appliqué' panels on the port side of the forward fuselage that the blast from the gun necessitated. A self-contained 20mm pod also existed (the GPU-2A) which was occasionally used by the USMC during the AH-1T era.

Turrets

The most innovative feature amongst the many the Snake pioneered was the turreted gun. This gave a trainable weapon that could sweep either side of the flight path and deal with off-axis threats as well as adding to the fixed, forward-firing weapons.

N209J had a one-off Emmerson turret housing a single M-134 7.62 'minigun', a 'Gatling' type weapon with a phenomenal rate of fire. The YAH-1Gs and all early production aircraft had a larger turret, the TAT-102A, still with the same gun. This was however an interim solution pending development of the definitive M-28 turret which could house two weapons side-by-side.

The M-28 could accept any combination of the M-134 or the M129 40mm grenade launcher, the usual configuration being one of each. Range of both weapons was around 1500 metres.

Pending a 20mm turret gun the Army fielded the XM-35 – almost unchanged from the fast jet 'Vulcan' it carried its ammunition in sponsons linked by a cross-feed. (*Bell via Mike Verier*)

Shown here is the starboard XM-35 sponson. Unusually the loadout includes an XM-18 gun-pod and a M-159 nineteen-shot pod (The Cobra would struggle to carry that much weight for any distance). (*U.S. Army via Floyd Werner*)

Blast (overpressure) damage from the gun necessitated additional reinforcement of the fuselage on the port side. (*U.S. Army via Floyd Werner*)

Whilst this combination was adequate for anti-personnel use at close range it was already recognised that a larger calibre weapon would have more hitting power and greater stand-off. The J Model introduced the M-197 20mm gun (a three-barrel modification of the M-61 'Vulcan' gun used on fast-jets) in a new 'universal' turret that was intended to be able to house interchangeable weapons of up to 30mm. Whilst both a re-barrelled 30mm M-197 and the Hughes 'chain gun' (as used on the AH-64 Apache) were tested they were never adopted for the Cobra.

Unlike the Marines, the Army did not immediately adopt the larger weapon, the M-28A3 remaining in use until the ECAS ('UpGun S') model finally saw the introduction of the 20mm gun. The weapon is the same for both Army and Marine Cobras, the only difference being that the Army do not see the need for an aerodynamic cowling, whilst the Marines keep their gun covered to protect from salt-spray and the like. The M-197 has been continuously developed and improved, better stabilisation, recoil compensation and laser spot sighting making it highly viable even today. A variation has appeared recently on Japanese AH-1S ('F' equivalent) aircraft which features a louvered cowling with what appears to be a shell case collector 'tray'. No details are available.

Rockets

The primary 'heavy' armament for the early Cobras was the Folding Fin Aerial Rocket (FFAR). These 2.75" rockets come with various fuses and warheads, and are carried in either seven or nineteen-shot re-loadable pods. The pods originally came with 'frangible' aerodynamic covers which were designed to disintegrate when the rockets were fired. They proved to be more trouble than they were worth however and were almost never seen operationally.

The pods themselves have ranged through a number of 'mods' which results in a variety of different designations for what appear visually to be almost identical equipment. Thus seven-shot pods could be XM157A or B, or (in USMC nomenclature) LAU-68. Widely used was a 'stripped-down' variation M-158A1, which did away with the outer casing leaving a 'bundle of tubes'.

Similarly nineteen-shot pods could be XM-159, XM-200 (Army) or LAU-69/61 (Marines) variants.

'Frangible' aerodynamic covers were available for both sizes of rocket pod. They were simply blown apart when the rockets were fired. Very little used in the field they were nevertheless occasionally seen on deployed Marine Cobras where there was a requirement to keep salt spray etc off the rockets. (*U.S. Army via Ray Wilhite*)

AH-1G with M-18 gun pod inboard and M-158 7-shot. (*U.S. Army Via Ray Wilhite*)

In the early days these unguided rockets were seen as aerial artillery, with a full 76 rocket salvo from a 'hog' configured Cobra being likened to a broadside from a cruiser. In truth they were something of a 'shotgun' weapon, albeit their accuracy increased with better sighting and the British-developed Air Data Sensor that improved ballistic calculation. Still a primary weapon for the Cobra they are much more capable now as the PKWS (Precision Kill Weapon System) has endowed individual rockets with precision guidance.

The Marines, ever-anxious to expand the Snake's capabilities, also used the LAU-10 launcher which can carry four 'Zuni' 4.5" rockets (but was often weight-restricted to two). A ballistic weapon like the 2.75 it has much greater range and therefore stand-off.

Droppable stores

The USMC also cleared their Snakes for a wide range of free-fall weapons. This even included Mk 82 series 250 lb 'iron' bombs (officially at least, these have never been used on operations). The CBU-55 FAE (Fuel / Air Explosive) on the other hand was deployed operationally, principally as a blast weapon to clear landing grounds.

The Marines also developed 100gal fuel tanks to increase the range / loiter time of their aircraft. All four wing stations on the Whisky and Zulu Cobras are 'plumbed' for fuel tanks and stressed for 'indiscriminate' (asymmetric) loading of stores making the Snake one of the most flexible weapon platforms they possess.

The requirement for 'droppable' (as opposed to merely 'jettisonable') stores led to the development of the outboard-cranked inner pylons distinctive to 'J', 'T' and W Cobras, the offset allowing stores to clear the skids. (the wider wings of the Zulu accomplish this with conventional pylons)

One of only two pictures known to exist of the locally-dubbed 'AH-1B' with what appears to be a live 250lb Mk 82 bomb. Whilst carrying any store is perfectly feasible, aiming was bound to be somewhat vague! (*Mike Sloniker*)

AH-1J at what appears to be Camp Pendleton carrying a pair of CBU-55 FAEs. This blast weapon was used primarily to clear landing areas. (*USMC*)

The 100 Gal. fuel tank is widely used by the USMC. Despite the fact that this one is mounted on an AH-1F it is clearly a trial. Army aircraft were not 'plumbed' for drop tanks. (*U.S.Army via Ray Wilhite*)

This early S Model sports the standard 'four TOW' rig adopted by the U.S. Army, loaded in this case with inert rounds (denoted by the blue band) (*Bell via Ray Wilhite*)

Below: This Israeli Snake carries the standard TOW rack and two live rounds of BGM-71 TOW. The Cobra can accommodate two of these (i.e. four missiles) on each side but weight limitations often restrict the aircraft to just two. The racks remain on the aircraft, whilst TOW re-loads come pre-packed in a canister and simply clip into the assembly. TOW remains the primary armament of F model Cobras still in service. A copy at least also serves on Iranian J models. (*Ray Ball*)

Above: Again not adopted for the Cobra fleet by the Army, AGM-114 Hellfire was qualified using Cobras, note the seeker head mounted in the nose of this aircraft (*Bell via Ray Wilhite*)

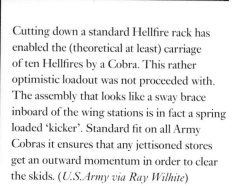

Cutting down a standard Hellfire rack has enabled the (theoretical at least) carriage of ten Hellfires by a Cobra. This rather optimistic loadout was not proceeded with. The assembly that looks like a sway brace inboard of the wing stations is in fact a spring loaded 'kicker'. Standard fit on all Army Cobras it ensures that any jettisoned stores get an outward momentum in order to clear the skids. (*U.S. Army via Ray Wilhite*)

Guided Missiles

The advent of guided rather than ballistic weapons was to hugely enhance the Cobra's potency. First deployed towards the end of the Vietnam conflict the BGM-71 TOW wire-guided AGM and its associated M-65 sighting system gave the Cobra a reach of well over 3000 metres. It was also relatively cheap, rugged, unjammable, and being pre-packed in its launch tube, handled as a round of ammunition. Designed as an anti-armour missile TOW has also proved very effective against bunkers, tunnels, shipping and even other helicopters.

Even after the introduction of the 'fire and forget' AGM-114 Hellfire, TOW retained an edge. The newer weapons attack profile hits a tank from above – so simply hiding under a bridge would defeat it. Not so TOW which could be steered directly into whatever confined space the tank commander thought he was safe in.

Not without controversy therefore has the faithful TOW finally been cited for retirement in favour of Hellfire on the 'Zulu' fleet. The newer missile however has almost doubled the range at which targets can be engaged and is extremely effective.

Other AGMs cleared for, and fired from the Cobra include AGM-65 Maverick (used operationally by the Iranians) the British developed Brimstone and the Norwegian Penguin. Newer missiles are currently being developed by the Israelis too.

Air-to-air engagements are also possible with the Cobra. The 20mm remains highly effective in extremis but the weapon of choice is the AIM-9 Sidewinder. Although not adopted, Cobras have also test-fired AIM-92A Stinger and the earlier MIM-43 Red Eye IR homing missiles, both of which have their origins as shoulder-launched MANPADS.

Using the same body as the AIM-9C the AGM-122A SideArm Anti-radar missile even gave the J model Cobra a limited 'Wild Weasel' capability to add to its repertoire. AIM-9s require an adaptor shoe for their LAU-7 launch rail and would normally be carried on the outboard or wingtip station.

The AGM-65 Maverick has been successfully fired from Whisky Cobras and, it is claimed, Iranian J models. (*Bell Via Mike Verier*)

Red Eye, originally a shoulder-launched infantry anti-aircraft weapon was trialled on a modified AH-1J. At one point it was offered as an option on the still-born 'Cobra ASH' Model 249 derivative. (*Bell Via Mike Verier*)

This 'Evil Eye' Whisky is operating from the USS Tarawa (LHA-1) in 1989. Carriage of the AIM-9 Sidewinder on one of the wing stations gave the aircraft a meaningful air to air capability and serves to illustrate the flexibility of the Cobras armament. (*Peyton DeHart*)

Smoke and Flame

Bearing in mind it's origins as an armed scout, 'G' model Snakes came equipped with a belly-mounted XM-20 smoke grenade dispenser which had two six-round chambers and was used for target marking. Smoke grenades could also be carried by the XM-8 dispenser, which could hold 12 canisters and appeared as a long beam, usually strapped under the outer rocket pod.

2.75-inch rounds were also available with flare (illumination) or White Phosphorus 'WP' (target marking) warheads.

Not all stores are offensive or defensive. This custom-built smoke tank is used by the 'Sky Soldiers' demonstration team on their immaculate TAH-1F aircraft. (*Mike Verier*)

Heat and Light

With the increase in effectiveness of the weapons fired at the Cobra came a need for active defensive measures to counter them. These took two forms, the fixed AN/ALE-144 'Disco-Lights' IRCM, and various chaff / flare dispensers. In 'J' and early 'W' Models the USMC utilised the AN/ALE-39 dispensers housed in suitcase-like containers mounted above the wings.

Seen here mounted on an AH-1T the ALE-39 chaff / flare dispenser has been standard fit in these overwing boxes for USMC Cobras since the AH-1T came into service. Retro-fitted to the J fleet it also carried over onto the Whiskys. The rough grey material applied to the leading edge of the wing and pylons is known as 'Flexfram' and is designed as a 'sacrificial' layer to protect the aircraft skin from rocket exhaust damage. (*Mike Verier*)

More recently a 'double box' has been developed to give a wider 'spread' and greater capacity in high-threat environments. In Zulu Cobras the housings are built into the fuselage as the overwing arrangement would compromise the new wingtip stations. (*Mike Verier*)

More recently these have morphed into 'double' housings faced slightly fore and aft to give a greater spread. In the 'Zulu' the housings have been built into the fuselage.

Late in the Cobra's Army career a single M-130 chaff dispenser was mounted on the port side of the tail. The Israelis adopted a very similar system, but operating in a much more threatening environment festooned their Cobras with these and other defensive measures, many of which remain classified.

Close study of this photo will reveal that both crewmen have stowed their rifles and combat gear in the cockpit. The USMC doctrine is that everyone is a Marine first. Your specialisation comes after that. If forced down for any reason these two will simply climb out of the wreckage and become heavily armed infantrymen. (*Capt R Weingart USMC*)

There is also a need for realistic training without the risks (and expense !) 'live fire' brings. The MILES (Multiple Integrated Laser Engagement System) equipment uses strobes and lasers to simulate firing. Receivers on the aircraft, vehicles and even individual soldiers, accurately record 'hits' and the system can be interrogated to determine how dead you are (with typical black humour the exercise referee's scanners are known as 'God Guns'). The electronic equipment is housed in a pod mounted on the inboard pylon. Receivers (the small black circular 'buttons') are mounted on the aircraft or vehicle. In this case the beam holding them fits into the TOW rack. (*Mike Verier*)

Small Arms

The other weapons carried by the Cobra are inside the cockpit. Operational crews have to consider the possibility that they might find themselves on the ground in a hostile environment. It would be a foolish enemy that overlooked the fact that a Cobra also contains two heavily armed (and dangerous) Marines (not for nothing was Buck Simmons known as 'Fire Base' in Vietnam)

In Afghanistan Cobras in forward areas had every spare inch of cockpit jammed with survival gear and the crews' personal weapons of choice.

Over its lifetime the Cobras' armament has constantly evolved. From visual range / daytime only, rifle-calibre guns and unguided rockets – manually sighted and reliant on 'Kentucky Windage' – to precision guided weapons that can take out a Main Battle Tank six or seven kilometres away in total darkness.

The evolution continues and serves to underline the flexibility of the Snake as a weapon platform. The great Cold War tank battles once envisaged are unlikely to emerge but in the meantime the Cobras continue to confront whatever threat the 'grunts' on the ground encounter.

Engagements are frequently back to within a thousand metres nowadays, but the firepower and precision now available make the 'surgical' strike routine and very, very, effective.

Appendix 4

Plans and Tables

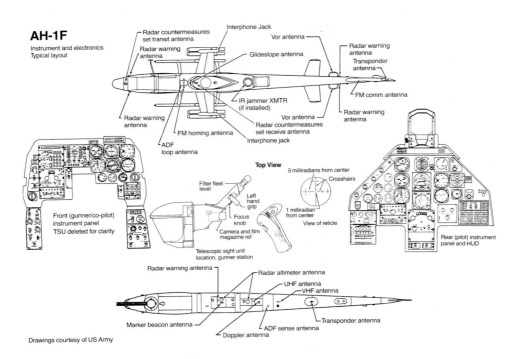

AH-1F

Instrument and electronics
Typical layout

Radar countermeasures set transit antenna
Interphone Jack
Vor antenna
Radar warning antenna
Radar warning antenna
Transponder antenna
Glideslope antenna
IR jammer XMTR (if installed)
FM comm antenna
Radar warning antenna
Vor antenna
Radar countermeasures set receive antenna
Radar warning antenna
FM homing antenna
Interphone jack
ADF loop antenna

Top View

Front (gunner/co-pilot) instrument panel TSU deleted for clarity

Filter fleet level
Left hand grip
Focus knob
Camera and film magazine ref
Telescopic sight unit location, gunner station

5 milliradians from center
Crosshairs
1 milliradian from center
View of reticle

Rear (pilot) instrument panel and HUD

Radar warning antenna
Radar altimeter antenna
UHF antenna
VHF antenna
Marker beacon antenna
Doppler antenna
ADF sense antenna
Transponder antenna

Drawings courtesy of US Army

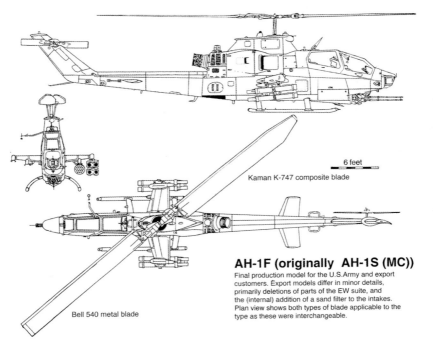

6 feet

Kaman K-747 composite blade

Bell 540 metal blade

AH-1F (originally AH-1S (MC))

Final production model for the U.S.Army and export
customers. Export models differ in minor details,
primarily deletions of parts of the EW suite, and
the (internal) addition of a sand filter to the intakes.
Plan view shows both types of blade applicable to the
type as these were interchangeable.

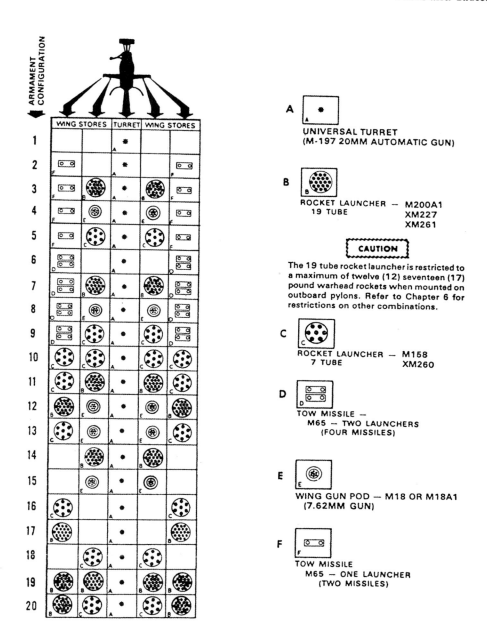

Authorized Armament Configuration

Taken from the AH-1F flight manual, this is a typical armoured configuration for a late model Army Cobra.

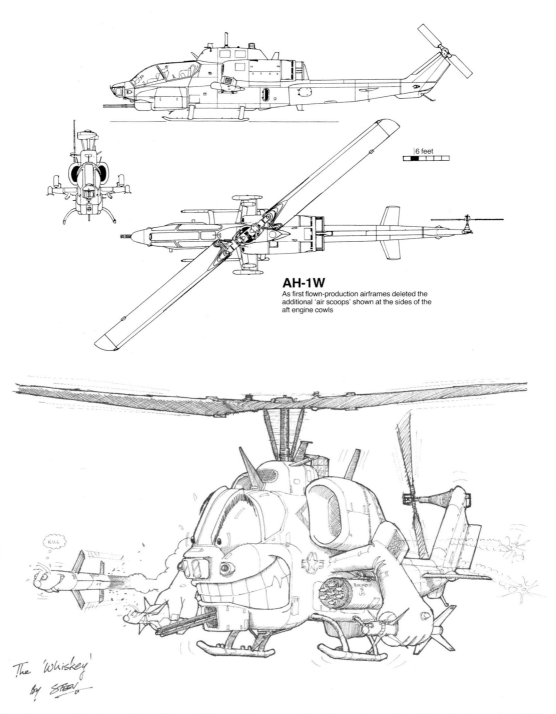

AH-1W

As first flown-production airframes deleted the
additional 'air scoops' shown at the sides of the
aft engine cowls

6 feet

The 'Whiskey'
by STEEV

Aircraft recognition is a vital military skill requiring more than just a three view. Like the immortal Chris Wren before him renowned artist Steev has a gift for capturing the character of an aircraft perfectly. In real life Commander Steve George RN served with the Fleet Air Arm, his long service including active duty in the Falklands and a spell as a Defence Attache. Now technically 'retired' he continues to work in aviation and, of course, contribute his wonderful drawings to the world.

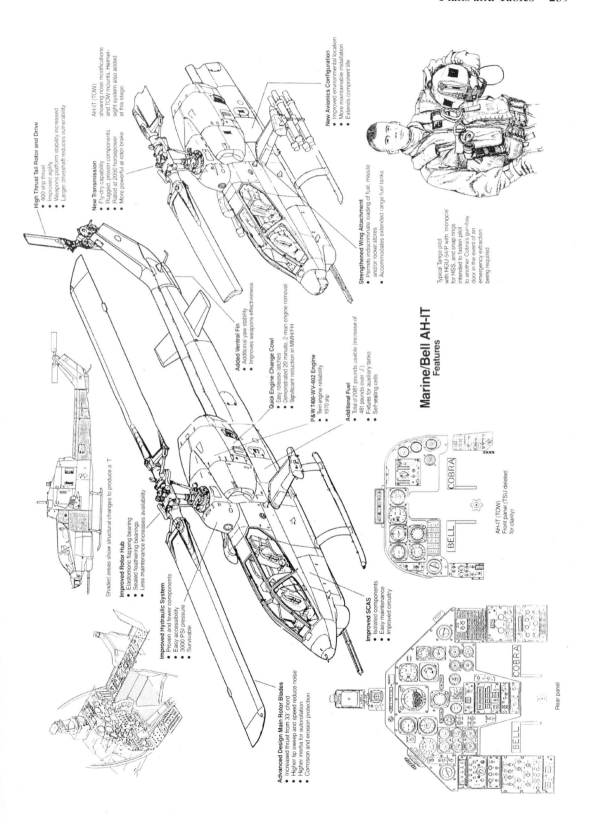

High Thrust Tail Rotor and Drive
- 400 strip thrust
- Improved agility
- Weapons platform stability increased
- Larger driveshaft reduces vulnerability

New Transmission
- Fly-dry capability
- Rugged, proven components
- Rated at 2050 horsepower
- More powerful at rotor brake

New Avionics Configuration
- Improved environmental location
- More maintainable installation
- Extends component life

AH-IT (TOW)
showing nose modifications
and TOW mounts. Helmet-
sight system also added
at this stage.

Strengthened Wing Attachment
- Permits indiscriminate loading of fuel, missile and/or rocket stores
- Accommodates extended range fuel tanks

Typical Tango pilot
with HGU-54-P with monocle
for HSS, and snap rings
intended to fasten pilot
to another Cobra's gun-bay
door in the event of an
emergency extraction
being required

Shaded areas show structural changes to produce a T

Added Ventral Fin
- Additional yaw stability
- Improves weapons effectiveness

Quick Engine Change Cowl
- Easy release latches
- Demonstrated 20 minute, 2-man engine removal
- Significant reduction in MMH/FH

P&W T400-WV-402 Engine
- Twin engine reliability
- 1970 shp

Additional Fuel
- Total of 2081 pounds usable (increase of 481 pounds over 'J')
- Fixtures for auxiliary tanks
- Self-sealing cells

Marine/Bell AH-IT
Features

Improved Rotor Hub
- Elastomeric flapping bearing
- Sealed feathering bearings
- Less maintenance increases availability

Improved Hydraulic System
- Proven and fewer components
- Easy accessibility
- 3000 PSI pressure
- Survivable

Improved SCAS
- Isolated components
- Easy maintenance
- Improved circuitry

AH-IT (TOW)
Front panel (TSU deleted
for clarity)

Advanced Design Main Rotor Blades
- Increased thrust from 33' chord
- Higher tip sweep and speed reduce noise
- Higher inertia for autorotation
- Corrosion and erosion protection

Rear panel

Cobra Designations

Bell Model	Service Designation	U.s.army Redesignation 1988	Notes	First Flight
209	N209J		First PV prototype	1965
	UH-1H (YAH-1G)		2 pre-production a/c (66-15246 & 15247) UH-1H re-designated AH-1G before delivery	1966
	AH-1G		1127 produced including 38 for USMC and 8 for Spain. Basic production version.	1966
	Z-14		AH-1G in Spanish service	–
	TH-1G		Early Army designation for training airframes	–
	JAH-1G		1 a/c (71-20985) used for Hellfire trials	1972
	AH-1J		69 produced. Twin engine version for USMC also known as 'Sea Cobra'	1969
	AH-1J (IRAN)		202 produced for Iran and 8 for South Korea. Also known as 'J International'	1974
	AH-1Q		(ICAP) 92 Gs modified for TOW	1974
	YAH-1R		(ICAM) 1 a/c (70-15936) modified G	1975
	YAH-1S		(ICAM) 1 a/c (70-16019) modified Q see also Model 249	1976
	AH-1S (IMPROVED)	AH-1S	378 modified Gs including all Qs	1976
	AH-1S (PRODUCTION)	AH-1P	100 produced. Flat-plate canopy	1977
	AH-1S (UPGUN)	AH-1E	(ECAS) 98 produced	1978
	AH-1S(MC)	AH-1F	Common standard with all ICAM / ECAS /UPGUN and other mods.	1979
	TAH-1S	TAH-1F	Aircraft modified with front cyclic booster for training	–
	JAH-1S		NASA designation for AH-1S (77-22768) used to trial PNVS	–
	TH-1S		10 'surrogate' modified S airframes with Apache PNVS nose	1985
	NAH-1S		NASA designation for AH-1S	–
	AH-1T/T (TOW)		57 produced for USMC.' Also 'Improved SeaCobra.' (TOW)' suffix dropped once all a/c TOW equipped.	1976
	AH-1T+		1 a/c (161022) converted to qualify T-700 engines. Designation also used for proposed Iranian production version. See also 4BW	1979
	AH-1W		288 new-build and T conversions produced including 63 for Taiwan	1986
	4BW		161022 with 4 blade rotor. Demonstrator	1988
	AH-1Z		Current production version. 152 new-builds (ZBN) and 37 re-manufactured Ws planned.	2001
249			1 a/c (formerly YAH-1S 70-16019) fitted with 4 blade rotor. Also 'Cobra II' 'PAH II' 'Cobra ASH' and ARTI demonstrator	1979
309	N309J / N309K		KingCobra. Two PV prototypes	1971
409	YAH-63		AAH competition. Two prototypes 74-22246 & 22247	1975

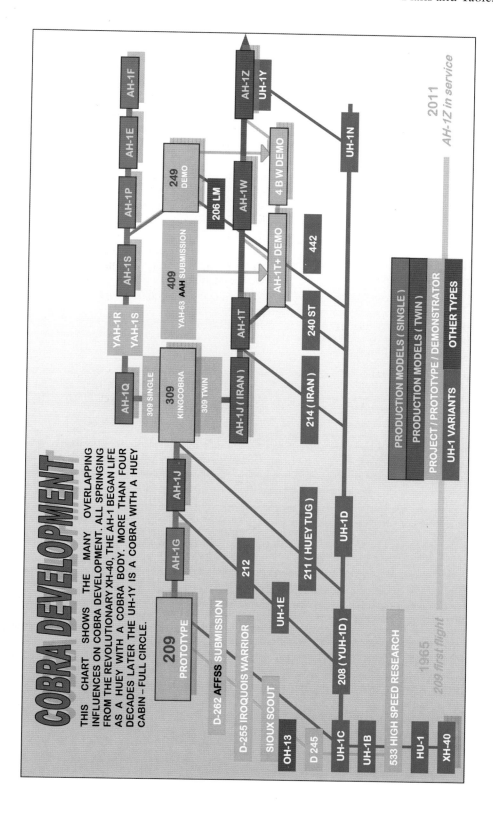

COBRA DEVELOPMENT

THIS CHART SHOWS THE MANY OVERLAPPING INFLUENCES ON COBRA DEVELOPMENT. ALL SPRINGING FROM THE REVOLUTIONARY XH-40. THE AH-1 BEGAN LIFE AS A HUEY WITH A COBRA BODY. MORE THAN FOUR DECADES LATER THE UH-1Y IS A COBRA WITH A HUEY CABIN – FULL CIRCLE.

AH-1F
AH-1E
AH-1P
AH-1S
249 DEMO
206 LM
AH-1W
4 B W DEMO
AH-1Z
UH-1Y
UH-1N
YAH-1R
YAH-1S
409 YAH-63 AAH SUBMISSION
AH-1T+ DEMO
442
AH-1Q
309 SINGLE
309 KINGCOBRA
309 TWIN
AH-1T
AH-1J (IRAN)
240 ST
AH-1J (IRAN)
214 (IRAN)
AH-1J
AH-1G
212
211 (HUEY TUG)
UH-1D
209 PROTOTYPE
D-262 AFFSS SUBMISSION
D-255 IROQUOIS WARRIOR
SIOUX SCOUT
OH-13
D 245
UH-1C
UH-1B
533 HIGH SPEED RESEARCH
HU-1
XH-40
UH-1E
208 (YUH-1D)

1965
209 first flight

2011
AH-1Z in service

PRODUCTION MODELS (SINGLE)
PRODUCTION MODELS (TWIN)
PROJECT / PROTOTYPE / DEMONSTRATOR
OTHER TYPES
UH-1 VARIANTS

Cobra Weights and Dimensions

Comparative Data (Bell figures for Cobra variants)		AH-1G	AH-1Q	AH-1J (USMC)	AH-1J (International or Iran) with TOW	AH-1F (K-747 rotor)	AH-1T with TOW
Length overall (rotors turning)		53' (16.14 m)		53' 5" (16.29m)		53' (16.14 m)	58' (17.68 m)
Fuselage length		44' 5" (13.53 m)	44' 7" (13.58 m)	44' 5" (13.53 m)	44' 9" (13.61 m)	44' 7" (13.58 m)	45' 7" (13.90 m)*
Wingspan		10' 4" (3.15 m)			10' 9" (3.28 m)††		10' 7" (3.25 m)
Elevator span		6' 11" (2.12 m)					
Rotor (main)	Diameter	44' (13.41 m)					48' (14.63 m)
	Chord	2' 3" (0.69 m)				2' 6" (0.76m)	2' 9" (0.84 m)
Rotor (tail)	Diameter	8' 6" (2.6 m)					9' 9" (2.95 m)
	Chord	8½" (0.21 m)		11½" (0.27m)			1' (0.30m)
Weights	Empty	5809 lb (2634 kg)	6249 lb (2895 Kg)	6610 lb (2998 kg)	6899 lb (3129 kg)	6598 lb (2992 kg)†	8553 lb (3879 kg)
	Gross	9500 lb (4309 kg)		10,000 lb (4536 kg)			14,000 lb (6350 kg)
Speed	Max (VNE)	230 mph (370 km/h)‡		207 mph (333 km/h)		195 mph (315 km/h)	
	Cruise max	190 mph (305 km/h)‡				141 mph (227 km/h)	154 mph (247 km/h)
Engine	Manufacturer	Lycoming		United Aircraft of Canada	United Aircraft of Canada	Lycoming	United Aircraft of Canada
	Designation	T-53-L-13		TwinPac T400-CP-400	TwinPac T400-WV-402	T53-L-703	TwinPac T400-WV-402
	Horse power	1400 shp		1800 shp	1970 shp	1800 shp	1970 shp

†   Basic aircraft. Added equipment places current aircraft around 7000Ib.
††   Including TOW launchers
*   Fuselage lengthened by 3'7" insert (total) but cut down of fin reduces total by 2'5"
**   Gunship configuration
‡   Prototype clean – see J or S for representative figures

AH-1W	AH-1Z	KingCobra	YAH-63	AH-64 Apache	AH-56 Cheyenne	S-67 Blackhawk
58' (17.68 m)	58' 0" (17.68 m)	59' 3" (18.06 m)	69' 8'/2" (21.20 m)	58' 2" (17.73 m)	60' 3" (18.31 m)	74' (22.58 m)
45' 7" (13.90 m)*	45' 6" (13.87m)	48' 9" (14.86 m)	60'9" (18.52 m)	49 '6" (15.23 m)	51' 9" (15.92 m)	64' 2" (19.56 m)
	14' 4" (4.39 m)	13' (3.96 m)•	17' 11" (5.47 m)	17' 2" (5.23 m)	26' 81/2" (8.14 m)	27' 4" (8.33 m)
48' (14.63 m)	48' (14.63 m) Four blade	48' (14.63 m)	N/A	11' 2" (3.41 m)	11' (3.39 m)	15' 10" (4.82 m)
			51' 6" (15.70 m)	48' (14.63 m)	50' 4" (15.36 m)	62' (18.9 m)
9' 9" (2.95 m) Four blade	9' 9" (2.97 m)	9' 9" (2.95 m) or 13' (3.96 m)	3' 6" (1.06 m)	1' 9" (0.525 m)	2' 3" (0.69 m)	
		10' 2" (3.10 m)	9' 6" (2.89 m)	9' 9½" (2.97 m)	9' (2.74 m)	10' 7" (3.26 m)
			1' 5" (0.42 m)	9" (0.225 m)	1' (0.30 m)	
10,920 lb (4953 kg)	12,300 lb (5,591 kg)	8926 lb (4048 kg)		10,759 lb (4880 kg)	11,725 lb (5323 kg)	12,514 lb (5681 kg)
14,750 lb (6690 kg)	18,500 lb (8,409 Kg)	15,000 lb (6804 kg)	19,224 lb (8734 kg)	18,352 lb (8324 kg)	22,000 lb (9988 kg)	14,000 lb (6356 kg)
218 mph (312 km/h)	222 kts (410km/h)	230 mph (370 km/h)	197 mph (317 km/h)	235 mph (378 km/h)	253 mph	193 mph (311 km/h)
183 mph (294 km/h)	155 kts (265 km/h)			182 mph (293 km/h)	242 mph (389 km/h)	187 mph (301 km/h)
General Electric	United Aircraft of Canada/ Lycoming		General Electric	General Electric	General Electric	General Electric
T700-GE-401 (x2)	T700-GE-401C (x2)	T400-CP-400 or T55- L-7C	T700-GE-700 (x2)	T700-GE-700 (x2)	T64-GE-16	T58-GE-5 (x2)
1625 shp each	1800 shp each	1970 shp 2850 shp	1596 shp each	1536 shp each	3435 shp	1500 shp each

Similar and connected types

Reference points for fuselage length

Reference points for overall length

Significant Airframes

Spain

Spanish Cobras C'No	Airframe Tail No.	Type	Spanish Designation	Status	Notes
21050	68–15090	AH–1G	Z14–1	Returned to US	Preserved Ft Rucker
21051	68–15091	AH–1G	Z14–2	Returned to US	Converted to AH–1F. Preserved at Sackets Harbor NY
21052	68–15092	AH–1G	Z14–3	W/O 23rd July 78	
21053	68–15093	AH–1G	Z14–4	Returned to US	Converted to AH–1F. At Fort Drum 2001
21124	72–21461	AH–1G	Z14–5	W/O 22nd Feb 74	
21125	72–21462	AH–1G	Z14–6	W/O 12th Jan 78	
21126	72–21463	AH–1G	Z14–7	W/O 7th May 80	
21127	72–21464	AH–1G	Z14–8	Preserved Spain	

Marhuk

Marhuk Cobras C'No	Airframe Bu No.	Type	Marhuk HMA-369 Nose No.	Desert Storm HMLA-775 Tail Code/Nose No	Notes
26006	157762	AH–1J		WR/701	AMARK 23rd July 91.WFU 1991
26007	157763	AH–1J			WFU 1991
26008	157764	AH–1J			Preserved Camp Pendleton
26016	157772	AH–1J			WFU March 8th 1990
26025	157781	AH–1J	5	WR/705	WFU 1991
26028	157784	AH–1J		WR/706	Preserved El Toro
26033	157789	AH–1J	7		AMARK 1st Feb 1989. W/O China Lake 6th Dec 1997
26031	157792	AH–1J	0		Lost during Operation Frequent Wind 29th April 1975
26037	157793	AH–1J			W/O Desert Storm 1991

Grenada

Grenada Cobras C'no	Airframe Bu No.	Type	Urgent Fury HMM-261 Tail Code/Nose No/Name	1983 Status	Notes
26077	160112	AH–1T	EM/32	shot down 23 10 83	
26911	160747	AH–1T	EM/33/EL TIGRE		Converted to W. w/o 20th Feb 1996
26934 (?)	160812	AH–1T	EM/30	shot down 23 10 83	
26931	160816	AH–1T	EM/3?/LEVIATHAN	replacement	Converted to W 2000. TV /34 with HMLA 167
26922	160817	AH–1T	EM/3?	replacement	Preserved Mid America Air Museum Liberal KS
26905	160821	AH–1T	EM/31/THE REAPER		Converted to W/NTS. Stricken 13th April 2009

AAHF

AAHF Cobras C'no	Airframe Tail No.	Type	Cobras At Tara Field Civil Reg	2012 Status	Notes
20039	66-15283	TAH-1F	N830HF	Sky Soldiers black	built as G. 35th Cobra built
20051	66-15295	AH-1S	N950LE	storage	built as G
20145	67-15481		N481HF	storage	built as G
20253	67-15589		N589HF		built as G
20401	67-15737	AH-1G	N209AH now N737HF	restored G	Built as G – actually an S back-dated to G configuration
20430	67-15766	TAH-1F	N766HF	Sky Soldiers black	ex Rucker test bird ?
20490	67-15826	TAH-1F	N826HF	Sky Soldiers black	built as G
20518	67-15854	AH-1S	N854HF	storage	built as G/round canopy/ sugar scoop exhaust
20810	68-17082	AH-1F	N820HF	storage	has inlet diverter
20886	70-15942	AH-1S	N942HF	storage	
21069	71-20998	TAH-1F	N998HF	Sky Soldiers black	
22240	79-23195	AH-1F	N195LE	storage	
22278	79-23233	TAH-1F	N233LE	Sky Soldiers black	
22345	83-24197	AH-1F	N197LE	green' paint	

Glossary

AAA	'Triple-A', Anti-aircraft artillery
AAFSS	Advanced Aerial Fire Support System
AAH	Advanced Attack Helicopter
AGI	Soviet intelligence-gathering ship
AGM	Air-to-Ground Missile
AHIP	Army Helicopter Improvement Program
ALLD	Airborne Laser Locator/Designator
ARTI	Advanced Rotorcraft Technology Integration Program
ASH	Advanced Scout Helicopter
ATAFCS	Airborne Target Acquisition Fire Control System
BITE	Built-in Test Equipment
CAS	Combat Air Strike
CASEVAC	Casualty Evacuation
CDEC	US Army's Combat Development Experimental Command
CEP	Circular Error Probable is a measure of the expected accuracy of ballistic weapons. Expressed as a distance, it describes the radius of a circle, into which 50 per cent of the rounds fired at the centre of the circle will consistently fall. Obviously the better the aiming system, the smaller the circle will be.
CONFICS	Cobra Night Fire Control System
ECAS	Enhanced Cobra Armament System
ECM	Electronic Countermeasures
ENSURE	Expedite Non-Standard Urgent Requirement for Equipment
FAC(A)	Forward Air Control (Airborne)
FAC	Forward Air Control
FARRP	Forward Aircraft Rearm & Refuel Point
FARP	Forward Arming and Refueling Point
FEBA	Forward Edge of Battle Area
FFAR	Folding-Fin Aerial Rocket
FLIR	Forward-looking-Infra-red
FOB	Forward Operating Base
HARM	High-speed, Anti-radiation Missile
HE	High Explosive
HEAT	High Explosive Anti-Tank warhead for FFARs
HEI	High Explosive Incendiary
HML	Helicopter, Marine, Light (Early squadron designator)
HMLA	Helicopter, Marine, Light Attack (Current squadron designator – also HML/A)

MMLAT	Helicopter, Marine, Light Attack, Training (training squadron also HMLA/T)
HMM	Helicopter, Marine, Maintenance
HMT	Helicopter, Marine, Transport (Note: HMMs & HMTs also become 'parent' units for HMLAs when deployed)
HSS	Helmet Sighting System
HUD	Head-up Display
ICAM	Improved Cobra Agility and Maneuverability programme
ICAP	Improved Cobra Armament Program
IHADSS	Integrated Helmet and Display Sighting Sub-system
IR	Imaging Infra-red
INS	Inertial Navigation System
JAAT	Joint Air Attack Team
JCS	Joint Chiefs of Staff
KIA	Killed in Action
LHX	Light Helicopter Experimental
LLTV	Low-light Television
LPH	Amphibious transport dock—assault ship
LZ	Landing Zone
MAAG	Military Assistance Advisory Group
MAG	Marine Air Group
MARHUK	MARine HUnter Killer operation during Vietnam War
MAW	Marine Aircraft Wing
MRAM	Medium Range Attack Missile
NETT	New Equipment Training Team
NOE	Nap of Earth flying
NPE	Navy Preliminary Evaluation
NVG	Night Vision Goggles
RADHAZ	RADiation HAZard
RFP	Request for Proposals
RWR	Radar Warning Receiver
SAM	Surface-to-Air Missile
SAR	Search and Rescue
SCAS	Stability Control Augmentation System
SCAT	Scout/Attack Helicopter
SMASH	SE Asia Multi-sensor Armament Sub-system for HueyCobra
SMS	Stabilized Multi-sensor
SSPI	Sighting Station Passive Infra-Red
TADS/PNVS	Target Acquisition Data System / Pilot's Night Vision System
TOW	Tube-Launched, Optically tracked, Wire guided missile
TSU	Telescopic Sighting Unit
VNE	Velocity never: exceed
WIA	Wounded in Action
WP	White Phosphorous
WSPS	Wire Strike Protection System